AN ECONOMICAL HISTORY OF THE HEBRIDES AND HIGHLANDS OF SCOTLAND • JOHN WALKER

Publisher's Note

The book descriptions we ask book-sellers to display prominently warn that this is an historic book with numerous typos, missing text or index and is not illustrated.

We scanned this book using character recognition software that includes an automated spell check. Our software is 99 percent accurate if the book is in good condition. However, we do understand that even one percent can be a very annoying number of typos! And sometimes all or part of a page is missing from our copy of a book. Or the paper may be so discolored from age that you can no longer read the type. Please accept our sincere apologies.

After we re-typeset and design a book, the page numbers change so the old index and table of contents no longer work. Therefore, we usually remove them.

Our books sell so few copies that you would have to pay hundreds of dollars to cover the cost of proof reading and fixing the typos, missing text and index. Therefore, whenever possible, we let our customers download a free copy of the original typo-free scanned book. Simply enter the barcode number from the back cover of the paperback in the Free Book form at www.general-books. net. You may also qualify for a free trial membership in our book club to download up to four books for free. Simply enter the barcode number from the back cover onto the membership form on the same page. The book club entitles you to select from more than a million books at no additional charge. Simply enter the title or subject onto the search form to find the books.

If you have any questions, could you please be so kind as to consult our Frequently Asked Questions page at www. general-books.net/faqs.cfm? You are also welcome to contact us there.

General Books LLC™, Memphis, USA, 2012. ISBN: 9781458810380.

◆◆ ◆◆ ◆◆ ◆◆ ◆◆ ◆◆ ◆◆ ◆◆

ECONOMICAL HISTORY OF THE HEBRIDES AND HIGHLANDS F SCOTLAND.

INTRODUCTION.

The following Work was the result of six journies made into the Highlands and Hebrides, from the year 1760, to the year 1786, during which, a greater extent of these distant parts of the kingdom was surveyed, than what had probably ever been traversed by any former traveller. Two of these journies were particularly extensive; each of them having been Vol. I. A continued from the month of May till late in De.r cember. In the year 17o'4, the Author received a commission from the General Assembly of the Church of Scotland, to enquire into the state of religion in the Highland countries; into the distribution of his Majesty's bounty, granted for the religious instruction of the inhabitants; and to point out the districts where the erection of new parishes might be judged most necessary and expedient. He at the same time received a commission from his Majesty's Commissioners on the Annexed Estates, to examine the natural history of these countries, their population, and the state of their agriculture, manufactures, and fisheries. In the year 1771, he received a similar commission from those two respectable bodies, in order to extend his survey over those parts of the country which he had not formerly visited. One report on the business of the General Assembly was. communicated in the year 1765, and another in the year 1772; when both were inserted in the Records of the Assembly. His report to the Annexed Board formed a large folio volume, which remained for some time in possession of the Board, but was afterwards sent to London, and of which no exact copy was retained. This volume has since disappeared, and, even after much enquiry to recover it, has been given up as lost.

The present performance contains all that was observed on the above jqurnies, and whatever has since occurred concerning the agricultural and economical history of the Hebrides and Highlands. This part of the national territory, considerable as it is, has been in all times past, comparatively, but of small advantage to the public. And when we reflect that it affords many hundreds of miles of sea coast, the most spacious and secure harbours, extensive fisheries, much land capable of cultivation, and is inhabited by a virtuous and hardy race of people, it must be admitted to be a source of national prosperity that has hitherto been inexcusably neglected.

The agriculture of these countries appears to have undergone but little improvement since the a?ra that domestic cattle and the cultivation of grain were first introduced; which happened probably in the third or fourth century. Any alterations for the better have taken place only within the last fifty years; and among these, the introduction of potatoes and of white oats seems to be the most valuable. The inhabitants, by their remote and insular situation, remained long almost a separate people from the rest of their countrymen. Their difficult access to the more cultivated parts of Scotland, rendered communication infrequent, and has kept them strangers to the improvements that have been made in the southern parts of the kingdom. They have, from this cause, been left far behind the rest of their fellowsubjects with respect to the arts, and especially in the art of agriculture.

Any account to be delivered of the agriculture and agrestic economy of the Highlands and Islands, must, in one respect, be widely different from such a history of any other district or county in Britain. It was natural to suppose, what now appears by the agricultural surveys, that there are few counties in the kingdom from which others may not learn something useful in husbandry. Beneficial practices in agriculture were formerly more confined than at present; but they are still slow in their progress. They are often limited, and for a long time, to a spot, oi a particular district, by want of communication. To render them universally known, is a happy consequence of these surveys. Each county in Britain has now access to know the practice of all the others. Every individual farmer may have the opportunity of reaping benefit from the experience and prudent management of his brethren through the whole kingdom. But while he and his county thus receive instruction, they are likewise capable of making a return in kind to others.

The case, however, is quite different with the inhabitants of the Highlands and Islands. They stand much in need of instruction in the cultivation of their country, and have little to communicate, that can be useful to the more cultivated parts of the kingdom. The practice of farmers in England or Scotland, three or four hundred years ago, would but little edify their successors in the present times. The skillful cultivators in Scotland and England, have therefore nothing to expect from this quarter. On the contrary, it is to them that the inhabitants of these remote countries must be indebted for their skill and proficiency in agriculture.

It is not, therefore, to be expected, that the practice in these unimproved countries can afford much that is useful, or that requires to be adopted in places where cultivation has made considerable progress. Yet the improvements suggested in this treatise for the melioration of the Highlands and Islands, may deserve attention in all places where there is a similarity of soil and of climate. Some of these improvements may deserve notice in almost every part of the three kingdoms. But most of them are peculiarly applicable to the north of Ireland, and to all the districts in Scotland and England that are elevated more than 500 or $00 feet above the level of the sea.

The subject proposed in this treatise is indeed extensive, and consists of many different branches. But before entering on a particular consideration of the state of agriculture in the Highland countries, it may be proper to take a general view of their soil, their climate, and the nature of their inhabitants; as on these the operations and success of husbandly must everywhere intirely depend.

SOIL.

All the soil hitherto cultivated in the Highlands is of two sorts, and which, in some degree, are to be found on every farm. The first, commonly called Infield, is always situated near the farm house, and is a piece of land that has been immemorially in tillage, and cropped either with bear or oats. Its soil is generally a light loam, of a deep black colour, and stretched over either rock or gravel. In most places this spot of black soil is easily worked, very free of weeds, and is exceedingly fertile. The other sort of cultivated land, which is termed Outfield, is only ploughed at intervals. It is generally situated on declivities, is of a brown hard mould and very stoney. It never received any manure, and after lying five, six, or more years in grass, it is ploughed two or three years for oats, which seldom form a crop worth the cultivation. These two sorts of soil are on every farm very inconsiderable in extent, and totally inadequate for the support of the cattle which it contains.

All this cultivated land forms not one hundredth part of the country, and the vast extent which is uncultivated, may be arranged under the following kinds. The first consists of extensive tracts of a moorish soil, covered with heather, or grasses of the coarsest nature. The second contains all the tracts in which peat earth is predominant, and which vary exceedingly, according to the situation, the depth, and nature of the peat. The third consists of extensive sandy downs, many of which afford exceeding good pasture, but are so light as to be apt to blow when they are broken up.

The fourth contains large tracts where the soil is good, but so encumbered with fixed stones as to be unserviceable for cultivation till they are removed.

The fifth is composed of fields of blowing sand, unprofitable in themselves, and destructive by their invasions, but which by skill and industry may be so fixed, as to be rendered not only harmless, but useful.

These different sorts of wild land may, to a great extent, be reclaimed, and reduced to cultivation, wherever they are not too far elevated above the sea.

Rut there is a sixth kind still more extensive than any of the former, that must be given up, as totally irreclaimable. This consists of the mountainous tracts, which from their great height or rocky and precipitous situation can only serve for the pasture of sheep, or of small black cattle in the summer season.

From the abrupt and mountainous nature of the country, clay is a very rare production. It is to be seen only in few places and in small parcels. Nor does it abound so much as to form any where what is called a clay soil. The soil of the cultivated land in general is a light and gravelly loam, and is thereby adapted to yield a forward, though not a very luxuriant crop.

CLIMATE.

The climate of that part of Britain which lies to the north of the Forth and Clyde is essentially different from that of the more southern parts of the island. The whole of England and the south of Scotland is surrounded on three sides by the narrow seas; by the Irish and German seas, and by the British Channel. All that southern and more extensive part of the island is also much surrounded and in some degree sheltered by contiguous land; hy Ireland on the west, and by the continent towards the south and east. But the case is different with the north of Scotland: It has the wide Scandinavian sea towards the east, the Atlantic towards the west, and the Hyperborean ocean towards the north, without any land so near as to afford any degree of shelter. This situation, with the narrowness of the country and the great height and inequality of the. land, renders the climate much worse than what could arise from the mere difference of latitude between the south of England and the north of Scotland.

The climate of islands, in the temperate zone is warmer in winter, and less hot in summer, than the continental land under the same latitude.

This is the case of Britain with respect to the continent; and the same is the case of the smaller islands adjacent to Britain compared to the main land.

The climate of the Hebrides, as in other places, varies according to its height above the sea. The summer heat, within three or four hundred feet of the level of the sea, though not so great as on the main land, is yet sufficient for the ordinary white and green crops, and for the plentiful production of cor n and cattle, the two great staple commodities which the earth any where affords.

The western coasts and islands are exempted from the great severity of the east and north east winds which are so intemperate on the eastern coasts of the island. In consequence of this, not only trees, of all kinds, but every vegetable production prospers better in these western parts than in the eastern parts of the kingdom under the same parallel.

On these western coasts, the wind seldom blows directly either from the north or south, but proceeds almost like a constant trade wind from the west and south west, and often with great violence. The winds from these quarters accompanied with heavy rains, form the worst part of the climate, and especially in autumn.

In winter the islands and western shores are not exposed to any great degrees of cold, but enjoy almost continued open weather. Snow never lies long, nor is the frost ever intense, or of long continuance. The potatoes, with only a slight covering of ferns, remain in the ground all winter without injury.

These circumstances both of soil and climate render the islands remarkably well adapted for the turnip and other green crops. The inhabitants are much given to complain of their climate, and especially of the autumnal winds and rain. These are no doubt at times hurtful, but not sufficient to prevent a plentiful produce both of corn and cattle. This, like other defects in a climate may, no doubt, be greatly obviated by skill and industry.

It is rather unfortunate for the country, that the people have so bad an opinion of their climate. It is a commonplace objection against every improvement. But it is certain that improvements M'hich, for this reason, are resisted in the Highlands, have taken place successfully in districts of Scotland, which are more unfavourable in point of climate.

INHABITANTS.

The proprietors and inhabitants of a higher rank are men of education, of a liberal mind, and fond of their country, from which, it is to be regretted, that they are too often necessarily abstracted. The lower ranks are composed of a sensible, virtuous, hardy and laborious race of people.

To call them laborious, is indeed contrary to an opinion frequently received; but it is only from a superficial view, that they are represented as unconquerably averse to industry and every kind of innovation. Beside other good qualities, their laborious assiduity, in various occupations, is well known wherever they happen to settle in the low country. No men were found superior to the Highlanders in digging the navigation between the Forth and the Clyde where their work was by the piece, and which was profitable according to their degrees of exertion. Their persevering labour has also been conspicuous in the numerous colony settled on Blair-Drummond moss. Nor is their spirit of industry, in many cases, less remarkable at home, especially in their field culture with the spade, which is the heaviest toil that any where occurs in the practice of husbandry.

In several other operations in their rude system of agriculture, they also exhibit patient and powerful, though indeed ill-directed efforts of industry. Their laborious and extensive cultivation of potatoes, their hardships and assiduity in the making of kelp, the success of the linen manufacture, wherever it has been introduced, and the unre-strained progress of inoculation, abundantly shew, that the Highlanders are as candid in their judgment, are as ready to embrace, and can as vigorously pursue any innovation that is advantageous or salutary, as any other people whatever. Unassisted exertions of industry are not to be expected from a people still in the pastoral stage of society; nor from unenlightened minds are we any where to expect the sudden discontinuance of old and inexpedient customs. But whereever the Highlanders are defective in industry, it will be found upon fair enquiry, to be rather their misfortune than their fault, and owing to their want of knowledge and opportunity, rather than to any want of a spirit for labour. Their disposition to industry, is greater than is usually imagined, and if judiciously directed, is capable of being highly advantageous both to themselves and to their country.

DESIGN.

»

It is proposed in this treatise, to give an account of the present state of husbandry in the Hebrides and Highlands; and of those improvements to be introduced, which appear to be most conducive to the prosperity of these countries. What is here delivered, is the result of all the agricultural observations that were made at different times, in travelling through the whole of the Islands, and of all the west Highlands, from the Clyde to Cape Wrath, by a tract of above 300 miles in extent. There is so perfect a similarity in the soil, climate, and agrestic management of all these countries, that though the observations here detailed, and the improvements proposed may immediately respect a particular district, yet they are generally applicable to the whole of these countries, and to many other parts of the kingdom which are in a similar situation.

Some of these improvements are of greater; and others of less importance: some of them are more easy, and others more difficult to be carried into execution. To trust as little as possible to the judgement of an individual, they have, for sev eral years undergone the examination of others; and have been sanctioned by the general opinion of the most intelligent and judicious of the inhabitants of these countries.

In the improvement here recommended, there are four separate interests to be regarded. The interest of the landlord, of the farmer, of the inferior people, and of the public at large. These are interests which deserve to be held in high estimation, and to be viewed with an impartial eye.

Some established customs, or proposed improvements may be friendly to the interest of one of these bodies, while they are prejudicial to the others. But the just man who loves his country, would never wish to see such customs retained, or such improvements promoted.

,

These four interests, though separate, are by no means incompatible, or placed at irreconcileable variance with one another. They are in most c?ses capable of being jointly advanced by the same means. In rural economy that measure will always be the best which unites and promotes these several interests; nor can any measure merit unreserved approbation that is calculated to advance only one of these interests to the prejudice of the others.

By wise and efficacious measures they may, almost at all times, be made to coincide; and it is this coincidence which ought to be the great object of every law, and every rule of police, respecting these, or any other countries. To unite and promote these interests, is the leading design of the following performance.

SECTION I. EXTENT AND POPULATION OF THE HEBRIDES AND HIGHLANDS. EXTENT.

The Hebrides comprehend all the islands situated upon the west coast of Britain, from the Isle of Man, to the extremity of the Lewis. They were for some centuries under the dominion of the Norwegians, and were then distinguished into the Nordureys and Sudureys. The former comprehending the islands lying in the Deucaledonian Sea, to the northward of the Promontory

of Cantire; and the latter, those islands which are situated in the Irish Sea, to the southward of that promontory. The Isle of Man Vol. i. a has been long under the dominion of England, and the Isle of Rachiine, from very remote times, has made: art of the kingdom of Ireland: all the others have been annexed to the crown of Scotland ever since the year 1263, when Alexander III. overthrew the Norwegian dynasty in these islands, at the battle of the Largs.

The Hebrides comprehend ninety-eight inhabited islands, beside a great number of smaller ones uninhabited, which only afford pasturage for cattle. The Isle of Man, with the small isle adjacent to it, and the Island of Rachline, being excluded, the inhabited islands belonging to Scotland amount to ninety-five in number.

The extent of these ninety-five islands in square miles, or acres, cannot be determined with any degree of precision. The dimensions, even of any particular island, can only be obtained by guess. Not one of them' has ever been measured, nor has the statute mile been applied to any of the roads. The length and breadth of each island can only be known by computed or Celtic miles; and by allowing these, on an average, to be one third more than dhe measured mile, a computation may be formed of the superficial contents. The result of this computation, indeed, must necessarily be inaccurate; and the great inequalities on the coast line of most of the islands, render it still more uncertain. As there is at present, however, no other method, the extent of the islands, determined even in this way, imperfect as it is, may serve to give a general view, and even to be in some degree useful, till more accurate measurements are obtained. «

From a calculation of this kind, made with respect to all the most considerable islands, it appeared, that the whole contain at least, and perhaps considerably more, than two millions of English statute acres.

As the whole extent of Scotland, according to Dr Templeman's computatifi, amounts to seventeen millions seven

hundred and eighty-eight thousand one hundred and sixty acres, the Hebrides belonging to Scotland may then be considered as forming about one-eighth of the whole kingdom.

The Highlands is a very general name for a large tract of the kingdom, which appears to be best defined by the boundary of the Gaelic language. On the main land of Scotland there are one hundred and thirty parishes in which the Gaelic is either preached or generally spoken. That great tract, known by the name of the West Highlands, extends from the mouth of the Clyde to Cape Wrath, the extremity of Britain towards the north, forming a coast of many hundred miles.

Its extent in breadth, from the West Sea to the water-shed of the island, or to that ridge or line of partition which determines the fall of the waters towards the west and east seas, being, in different places from thirty to sixty miles broad, and upwards. Those parts of the Highlands which lie to the eastward of the above line of partition, commonly pass by the name of the North Highlands.

It is difficult to form any estimate concerning the general extent of the Hebrides and Highlands, and the best that can be made must be very uncertain. These countries contain one hundred and sixty-two parishes, which compose what may be called the Gaelic part of Scotland. Several of these parishes are more extensive than some of the counties in the lowlands; and the one hundred and thirty on the main land, form a vast tract, of the most irregular dimensions. The one hundred and sixty-two parishes composing the Hebrides and Highlands, taken altogether, may be presumed to be considerably more than One-third, and to constitute perhaps nearer one-half of the whole kingdom.

It is supposed that the arable ground in the Hebrides does not amount to one-eightieth part of the untillaged land. Of course, there must be a great disproportion between the extent of country and the number of people.—The island of Jura was found to contain only four hundred and sixty-six inhabitants, and is computed to contain one hundred and

fifteen thousand acres, which is nearly two hundred and forty-six acres for each inhabitant. A similar melancholy proportion is to be found in many tracts on the main land, but no where else within the confines of Europe, unless in Lapland, or the country of the Samoiedes.
POPULATION.
The population of these remote and very extensive regions, and its progress or decay form an interesting subject, which well deserves the consideration of government and of the public at large. The western islands having been little attended to, there has never been any well grounded computation of the number of their inhabitants. Early in the last century, Martin supposed they might contain forty thousand people, exclusive of the Isle of Man. Soon after, the number was reckoned fifty thousand by Chamberlayne.
S

These computations, however, were but Ae result of conjecture; neither founded upon certain data nor particular inquiry.

The following table contains the number of inhabitants in these islands in the year 1764. It was formed from the particular reports of the clergy and catechists, and it is believed to contain a very exact enumeration of the people at that period.

1. It appears from this Table, that in the year 1764, the islands south of Cantire did at that time contain eight thousand and fifty-nine: And the islands north of Cantire, fifty-three thousand, four hundred and seventy-seven inhabitants. The whole ninety-five islands belonging to Scotland containing sixty-one thousand, five hundred and thirty-six. 2. At the same time, the people of the Isle of Man, with its small adjacent island, were computed at twenty-five thousand and seven; and those of the Isle of Rachline at four hundred: So that the number of people in the ninety-eight inhabited islands did then amount to eighty-six thousand nine hundred and thirty-seven. 3. The above ninety-six islands comprehend thirty-two parishes; the population of which, at four different periods, is contained in the following Table.

No. and Hum of 1 Rothsay,..
2 Kingarth, 3 Cumbray,. 4 Kilbride,.. 5 Kilmory,.. 6 Gigha, 7 KiFchoman, 8 Kildalton 9 Jura 10 Kilbrandoo,.. 11 Lismore, 12 Torosay, ¥3 Kilninian 14 Kilfinichen 15 Coll 16 Tirey, 17 Sleat 18 Strath, 19 Portree 20 Bracadale, 21 Duirnish, 22 Kilmuiiv 23 Snizort, 24 Small Isles 25 Earn 26 South Ui»t... 27 North Uist,... 28 Harris, 29 Stornaway,.. .. 30 Lochs 31 Uig.
".2 Barvat, OBSERVATIONS.

1. In this Table, the numbers of people in the Hebrides, at four different periods, are included in four different columns. The first column contains the numbers which were found in a record in possession of the church.

The numbers in this record seem to have been taken about, or within a few years before, the year 1750. In some cases, the numbers in this record are exactly the same with those of Dr Webster's list in the year 1755. But in most parishes they are less in this record than in the Doctor's list. The second column contains the numbers in Dr Webster's list, dated in the year 1755.

The third column contains the numbers in the year 1771, as I had them ascertained from the ministers of these parishes. The fourth column contains the numbers of people, in the same parishes, between the years 1791 and 1798, as stated in the Statistical History.
2. In the year 1750, the total number in these parishes, according to the above record, was fortynine thousand four hundred and eighty-five. In the estimate made by Dr Webster in the year 1755, of the number of people they contained, there are six parishes left blank. If we take the population of these six parishes as it then stood in the year 17o4, when it would not be much different from what it was in the year 1755, and add it to Dr Webster's numbers in the other twenty-six parishes, the whole amounts to fifty-two thousand, two hundred. It may be presumed, that this was nearly the number of people in our Western Islands in the year 1755. And that, between the years 1750 and 1755, there was an increase of about two thousand seven hundred and fifteen people. By

comparing the numbers in the year 1755, and the year 1771, it appears, that in these parishes there was an increase of ten thousand five hundred and thirty-eight people, during sixteen years. In like manner, by comparing the total number in the year 1771, with that about the year 1795, it appears, that the increased population of these parishes, during twenty-four years, amounted to about twelve thousand seven hundred and twenty-eight. Also, that during forty years, from the year 1755, to the year J 795, the increase of inhabitants in these parishes, amounts to twenty-three thousand two hundred and sixty-eight persons; approaching nearly to one-half of the original number of inhabitants.
3. Formerly the population of the Highlands was chiefly determined by the examination-rolls of the clergy. The whole number of inhabitants could then only be fixed by the precarious proportion between examinable and unexaminable persons. But of late, the Ministers in the Highlands, with a laudable zeal, have given us, in the Statistical History, a particular enumeration of the whole inhabitants in their respective parishes. From that enumeration it appears that, about the year 1795, the whole of our Western Islands contained seventy-five thousand four hundred and sixty-six inhabitants. This is probably a larger number than they ever possessed before; as the quota which they afforded in old times to the Scottish army, never exceeded six thousand men, when almost the whole fighting men were brought into the field.

The principal causes which, of late years, have so much advanced the population of the Hebrides, are, the introduction of inoculation, the manufacture of kelp, and the cultivation of potatoes. By the first, the lives of multitudes are saved; by the second, the quantity of labour, and by the third, the quantity of food, has been greatly enlarged.

It is even probable, if the people were provided with employment and sustenance at home, that, in their present state, and without emigration, they would double their numbers in little more than thirty years. TABLE *Highland*

Parishes on the Main Land of Scotland, zvith the Number of their Inhabitants in the Years 1755 and 1795' MO. Mid Names of Parishes 1 Drymen, 2 Buchanan, 3 Roseneath 4 Luss,, 5 Arrochar, 6 Dunoon, 7 Kilmodan, 8 Inverchal Un, 9 Kilfinan 10 Lochgoilhead,.... 11 Strachur,., 12 Inverary,., 13 Craignish 14 Kilmartin,........ 15 North Knapdale, 16 South Knapdale,. 17 Kilniichael 18 Campbeltown 19 South-End,. 20 Killean, 21 Kilcalmonel, 22 Skipness,,, 23 Glenurchy 24 Kilchrerun,

S5 Kilbrandon 2G Kilninver, 27 Kilmore 28 Ardhatton 29 Appin, 30 Abertarph 31 Urquhart, 32 Laggan

S3 Kilmanuivaig,...

34 Kilmaly, 35 Morven, 36 Ardnamurchan... 37 Ciirloch,... or THK

No. and Names of Parishes

ss Lochbroom

39 Applecrossy 40 Loch-Carron 41 I. och-Alsh, 42 Glenshiel, 43 Kintail, 44 Glenelg 45 Tongue......

46 Far, 47 Durness, 48 Edrachilis, 49 Thurso, 50 Reay 51 Latheron 52 Halkirk, 53 Dornach 54 Rogart, 55 Lairg, 56 Golspie 57 Loth 58 Criech, 59 Kildonan, 60 Clyne, 61 Assint, 62 Dingwal 63 Kilmorack, 64 Alness 65 Kiltaim 66 Urray, 67 Kincardine 68 Foderty, 69 Contin 70 Urquhart, 71 Tain, 72 Feara, 73 Kilmuir, Easter,. 74 Edderton,

Ann. 1795.

3500 1734 1068 1334 721 1000 2746 1489 2600 1182 f024 3146 2298 4006 3180 2541 2000 1350 1700 1370 1730 1365 1660 3000 1375 2318 11 til 1680 1860 1600 1730 2500 2901 2100 1600 1975 1000

Re. and Nana of Parishes.

75 Logie 76 Tarbat, 77 Rosskeen 78 Nigg 79 Kileamon 80 Avoch, 81 Callender, 82 Kilmuir Wester 83 Rosemarkie, 84 Inverness 3 pa-*l* rishes or charges. $ 8i KirkhiU, 88 Moy, 87 Durris, 88 Petty...... 89 Daviot,... 90 Kiltarlity, 91 Nairn 92 Ardclach 93 Croy, 94 Ardersier 85 Calder, 96 Edinkylie, 97 Abernethy,... 98 Kingusie, 99 Kirkmichael, 100 Alvie,. 101 Cromdale 109 Rothiemurcus,

No. snd Names of Parishes.

103 Knochandow 104 InYeraven, 105 Strathdon,. 106 Kincardine Oniel,... 107 Coldstone, 108 Crathie, 109 Glenmuck ScTulloch 110 Glenyla, 111 Alyth 112 Dunkeld, 113 Little Dunkeld, 114 Kirkmichael 115 Moulin, 116 Blair Athole, 117 Logierait, 118 Weem...... 119 Dull, 120 Fortingal, 181 Kenniore 122 Killin, 123 Crief, 124 Momie, 125 Muthil, 126 Comrie 127 Balwhidder, 128 Port 129 Aberfoil, 130 Callander

Total Ann. 1795, 250,100.

OBSERVATIONS. 1. The Highland countries on the main land, in which the Gaelic language is either preached or spoken by the natives, contains the above one hundred and thirty parishes. The number of people in these parishes, by Dr Webster's list, in the year 175. 5, amounted to two hundred and thirty-seven thousand, five hundred and ninety-eight. By the Statistical History, these parishes,, between the years 1792 and 1798, contained two hundred and fifty thousand one hundred inhabitants. The increase, therefore, of population in these parishes, during this term of forty years, amounted only to twelve thousand, five hundred and two. 2. This increase of inhabitants is much smaller than what is generally thought to have been the case in the Highlands during the above period. Their real increase in population has, no doubt, been much greater during these forty years, but in this period, these countries have, in different ways, been severely drained of their inhabitants. The ordinary egress to the low countries is always considerable. Great numbers of men have been drawn out to the army and navy, and many have emigrated to America. But the most depopulating effects have proceeded from the enlargement of grass farms, and especially those for the pasture of sheep. This unfavourable alteration has chiefly prevailed in the parishes next adjacent to the lowlands, in many of which the number of people has been deplorably diminished; but in the more remote parishes not affected by this depopulating cause, the people have increased onethird and upwards in the course of the above forty years. 0 3. For the same reason we find that the population in the islands has greatly exceeded that on the mainland. The one hundred and thirty parishes on the mainland containing two hundred and thirty-seven thousand five hundred and ninety-eight inhabitants, produced, during forty years, an increase of only twelve thousand five hundred and two persons; whereas the thirty-two parishes in the islands, containing only fifty-two thousand two hundred inhabitants, did, in the course of the same forty years, afford an increase of twenty-three thousand four hundred and sixty-six people. The islands during these forty years, sent a larger proportion of men to the sea and land service, than the parishes on the mainland, and likewise lost a larger proportion of their people by emigration to Ireland and America. But being freed from the desolating effects of immoderate grazing farms, their population has advanced in this great proportion, and along with it their prosperity. 4. In general, it appears from the above tables, that in the year 1795, the Hebrides and Highlands contained three hundred and twenty-five thousand five hundred and sixty-six inhabitants. 5. Of the one hundred and thirty parishes on the mainland, there are fifty-six, which, in the year 1755, contained one hundred and eight thousand three hundred and seventy-nine inhabitants. But in the year 1795, their number of people was reduced to ninety-four thousand two hundred and twenty-two. So that in the course of forty years, these fifty-six parishes have had their population diminished *by* fourteen thousand one hundred and fifty-seven people. These parishes are chiefly those which border on the lowlands: and this unfavourable alteration which has taken place in them has chiefly arisen from the establishment of extensive grazing and sheep farms 6. The Highland countries in general, are well adapted for the increase of inhabitants; they have a northern, but a healthy climate, and their soil may be rendered very productive. They are capable to afford cornj cattle, and fish, sufficient for a great degree of population.

The state of society in which the inhabitants are placed, is also friendly to their increase, their occupations are agriculture, pasturage and fishery. They have easy access to small possessions of land. Their sustenance is cheap and simple, and their manners virtuous. They marry early in life; the number of married servants is very great, and diseases and barrenness are very unfrequent. These positive causes of population subsist, while the depopulating effects of unwholesome situations, of great cities, of unhealthy manufactures, of luxury, vice, and dissolute manners are entirely unknown.

7. But the most favourable circumstances for population are sometimes counteracted and rendered ineffectual by other causes. Bad government and hurtful customs do often prevent the population of a country, though it may be destined by nature to overflow with inhabitants.

The infertility of the natives of the island of Madeira is highly remarkable: This arises not from any defect in the soil or climate, or other natural causes, but from the bad government and police of the country. There is only one birth annually for seventy one persons; and yet to shew the unparalleled healthfulness *of* the climate, the burials are to the births only as fifty-eight to one hundred.

8. In like manner, the thriving population of the Highlands has of late been obstructed, and is threatened to be destroyed, not by any natural, but an extrinsic and incidental cause, the great extension of grass farms, and especially those entirely allotted for sheep.

Though the farms in the Highlands are small with respect to rent, they are very extensive. Yet such large farms are not so hurtful to the population of the country as those in England or in the south of Scotland; for under the tenant or tacksman, there is always so great a number of subtenants and cottagers retained as to form a considerable degree of population. These two classes make up the great body of the people in the Highlands, and it is upon Vor.. I. c these that the populousness of the country chiefly depends.

Some considerable proprietors have, of late, either dismissed or considerably abridged the number of these inferior people upon their estates. This indeed may give an immediate rise of rent, but must destroy the population of the country. It would indeed be deplorable, if the interests of the proprietor and the public were in this matter really incompatible; but this is not the case, as it rather appears that such a proprietor proceeds upon a mistaken idea. He may imagine that this is the only effectual method to raise the value of land, and that this value must increase, or at least become permanent. But instead of a substantial tacksman, he may get upon his large farm an adventurer with a small stock, who is not able to withstand the losses arising from the death of cattle, or the fall of the markets. By dismissing his people, he cuts himself off from all other methods of improving his estate; he at one stroke, and by one rise of rent brings his estate to a value which it never can exceed; for a little immediate advantage, he renounces all prospect of progressive improvement and greater emolument.

ADDITIONAL REMARKS ON POPULATION. *Families.*—When the average number of individuals to a family is known, the number of families becomes then a certain rule for finding the number of people. This is a method commonly practised, but its accuracy depends upon the number of persons allotted to each family: an article which varies considerably in different pluees. In the country parishes of England, four and an half persons, and in the manufacturing towns, four tfnd three-fourths persons are assigned for each family. But a different proportion must be allowed for the Highlands.

The district of Coygach in Ross-shirc, according to an exact roll taken for me by the catechist, contained seven hundred and forty-live inhabitants, which composed one hundred and sixty-four families. This is above four and an half persons to a family. But in this country the people are living upon smaller possessions, and with less numerous families, than any where else in the Highlands. In the parish of Rothsay in the Isle of Bute, three hundred and twenty-eight families, situated in the country part of the parish, contain sixteen hundred and seventy-seven people. This gives upon an average, for each family, five persons and thirty-seven three hundred and twenty-eighths. The parish of Eig contains one thousand one hundred and fifty-seven inhabitants, whose possessions are also remarkably small, yet they compose only two hundred and seventeen families, which gives five persons and seventy-two one hundred and seventeenths to each family.

These three instances are taken from parts of the country where there is certainly the smallest number of persons to a family. Yet they afford above five to a family, which is the least number that can be allowed for the Highlands and Islands in general, and there is reason to think, that five and an half would be a nearer calculation. This indeed is a higher number than can be allotted to a family any where else in Britain. But the cause is obvious; which is a greater frequency of marriage. Among the two hundred and seventeen families in the parish of Eig, there were found to be two hundred and four marriages. The same proportion seems to hold over the country in general, which must occasion both numerous families, and a rapid population.

Sexes—From the want of registers of baptisms, the proportion between the males and females born could not be discovered. The following table shews how the two sexes arc divided in the parish of Eig; and the same proportion may be presumed to hold nearly in other parts of the country.

In the parish of Kilmaly, in Lochaber, the sexes are divided as follows:

Boys under 7 years. Girls under 7. Males above 7. Females above 7.
344. 312. 1071. 1211.

These numbers correspond with the observation frequently made, that a greater number of males is born than females. There is even reason to think, that the proportion of males increases till past the time of puberty. But after that period, the men leave the country, are called for to business or war, and exposed to many diseases and mortal accidents, from which the women are exempted. Before middle age, the women are superior in number, and the superiority increases to the extremity of life. In the Lewis, the women above sixty were three hundred and forty-eight, but the men above that age only two hundred and forty-two.

Number of' Children.—The precise number of people forms a most important article in the cconomical history of any country, but especially where industry and improvements are to be pushed by the publi. The only n ay to ascertain it in the Highlands, was by means of the clergy; who, in the course of their parochial visitations, make up a roll of all the persons who are of sufficient age to be examined on the principles of religion. In some of these rolb, I found all the people in the parish, young and old, enumerated to one person: the most satisfactory account that could be obtained or desired. But in others, only the examinable persons were recorded. And to fix, from these, the numbers of the whole, required a calculation of the persons omitted.

In order to determine this, the following trials were made. The district of Sunart, Moydart, Arisaig, and South Morar, in the parish of Ardnamurchan, in Argyleshire, contained two thousand five hundred and sixty-seven inhabitants. Among these, the number of children under seven years of age were exactly numbered for me by the missionary minister, and amounted to four hundred and fifty-seven. According to Mr Halley s Tables, the children between seven and eight make one-eighth of all the children under eight years of age: and in the country the proportion must be larger than in cities. But if the children between seven and eight are added to the above number, we have, even by his calculation, five hundred and twenty-two children, under eight years old, among two thousand live hundred and sixty-seven persons; which is more than one-fifth of the inhabitants.

The parish of Kilmaly in Lochaber, contains two thousand nine hundred and thirty-eight persons; and among these, the children under seven years amount

to six hundred and fifty-six. If to this number the children between seven and eight, even by Mr Hally's calculation, are added, which make ninety-three, the total is seven hundred and forty nine children under eight years old, among two thousand nine hundred and thirty-eight people, which, to a fraction not worth regarding, is one-fourth of the inhabitants .

The parish of Eig was found, by an exact enumeration, to contain one thousand one hundred and fifty-seven inhabitants. And among these, the number of children under eight years of age was two hun There are, perhaps, few parts of the world where the number of children bears a greater proportion to the number of adults. How different is the case in Madeira! Though an island the most friendly to health and population of any in the world, yet the children under seven years make only onetenth of the inhabitants t: an evil which arises, not from the nature of the country, but from bad government, from the celibacy of the religious of both sexes, who are extremely numerous, and from the bad morals of the people.

t Dr Heberden, Phile». Trans. Ann. 1767. Vol. 57. Part 1. p. 4S1 dred and seventy-nine; which is also, to a trifle, onefourth of all the people. By these trials in three parishes, it appears, that the number of children under eight amounts nearly to one-fourth of all the people: and the state of population is much the same in all the other parishes of the Highlands and Islands. Some of tiie ministers, indeed, begin to examine the children when they are seven years old; some when they are eight; but others not till they are nine or ten years old: The unexaminabje persons omitted in the ministers rolls may therefore be above, but cannot be under, one-fourth of the whole inhabitants. This it was necessary to remark, as many of the numbers in the above tables of population, were determined upon this principle. *Fcncible men.*—The number of people in the Hebrides being ascertained as above, the number of fencible men, or of those between sixteen and sixty, may be likewise determined. Be-

fore the union of the crowns, the islands were wont to send six thousand men to the war, and hands were left sufficient for raising the products of the country. But so few hands were then sufficient for the purpose, and in those days the ordinary levies made so great a part of the people, that this number seems to have comprehended every second person capable of bearing arms. For the islands cannot be supposed to have then contained above twelve thousand fighting men. 4

Dr Short allows thirty-four fencible men among each hundred of inhabitants. But, however it may be in other places, this proportion, which is onethird of the people is certainly too high for the western islands. For by an actual enumeration of the individuals, with their ages, in the five parishes of the Lewis and small isles, it appears, that the fencible men are nearly, but not more than one-fourth of the people. According to this computation, the whole Hebrides, exclusive of the Isle of Man, contain at present fifteen thousand three hundred and eighty-four fencible men.

A remarkable coincidence was discovered, in several instances, between the number of fencible men, and the number of children under eight years old, for each is nearly one-fourth of the inhabitants. The appearance of this fact, from accurate lists of the people, led to a proportional division, not hitherto noted, of the inhabitants of a country.

If we divide the whole people of a parish or district in the Hebrides into twelve parts, three of these are children under eight years of age; two are boys and girls from eight to sixteen; three are fencible men, between sixteen and sixty; three are women between sixteen and sixty; and the remaining twelfth part consists of men and women above sixty.

In the two following cases,. this proportional division takes place in a remarkable manner. The parish of Eig, comprehending the islands of Eig, Muic, Rume, and Canna, contains one thousand one hundred and fifty-seven inhabitants, who are thus divided.: 3. Children under eight 279 2. Boys and girls between eight and sixteen. 183 3. Fencible men between sixteen and sixty. 461

3. Women between sixteen and sixty... 336

1. Men and women above sixty.... 98

12 parts 1157

The twelfth part of the inhabitants being ninetysix, all the numbers do very nearly correspond with this proportional division. The greatest deviation is an overplus of forty-eight, among the women from sixteen to sixty.

The Island of Lewis, consisting of four parishes, contains seven thousand two hundred and eightyone inhabitants, who are divided as follows: 3. Children under eight 1820 2. Boys and girls between eight and sixteen 1673 3. Fencible men between sixteen and sixty. 1331

3. Women between sixteen and sixty.. 1867

1. Men and women abore sixty.... 590

12 parts 7281

The twelfth part of this number is six hundred and six, so that, here also, the inhabitants approach remarkably to the above proportional division.

The number of fencible men, indeed, falls considerably short. But a little before this list was taken, which was anno 1761, there were one hundred and seventy men drawn from the Lewis to the army, and more than that number went, about the same time, to the fishery and the navy. Were ail the men to remain in the country, the inhabitants, it is evident, would be very nearly divided according to the above arrangement.

The islanders being still equal to any of their countrymen in the warlike disposition, and being less occupied, furnished, it would appear, to the war between the years 1756 and 1763, a larger proportion of men, according to their numbers, than most parts of the kingdom. Scarce any of the islands, north of Cantire, sent less than one-eighth of all its fighting men: several of them sent almost one-third. And as the the proportion in many approached nearer to the latter, than to the former number, it may, in general, be concluded, that about one-fifth of the whole fencible

men was, at that time, drawn out to the army and navy.

In most of the islands, the precise number of men that went to the war was obtained; but, in others, no account, or, at least, no certain one, could be procured. It was found, that from islands containing forty-nine thousand three hundred and thirtyfive inhabitants, there had gone, in the course of the war, two thousand and eighty-seven soldiers. In the remaining islands, containing twelve thousand two hundred and one people, the number could not be exactly discovered; but if the same proportion is allowed as in the other islands, and there is reason to think that it was not less, the whole number of soldiers drawn immediately from the Hebrides to the war, amounted to two thousand five hundred men.

It is further to be observed, that, during the war, the navy was supplied with full five hundred sailors from the port of Campbelton, and upwards of three thousand from Port Glasgow and Greenock. But as these commercial places draw a great part of their sailors from the isles, it is judged, that of this number, there might be more, but could not be less than six hundred islanders.

The number of fighting men in the Hebrides is determined above to be fifteen thousand three hundred and eighty-four. And from the best information that could be procured, it appears, they afforded to the war, about three thousand one hundred and eighty-seven sailors, and soldiers:—that is above one-fifth of the whole. A country which, at that trying period, could afford such a number of wariors, is of no small importance to Britain, when we consider, that a thousand fencible men are accounted the full annual increase of a million of its inhabitants.

Neither was the employment of these men in the war so disadvantageous to the public, as if the same number had been collected from the more busy parts of the kingdom. Their absence did raise a little, and only a little, the price of labour; but their going to the field gave no stop to agriculture, nor interruption to any manufacture.—Matters went on

as formerly, and the islands scarcely felt the want of one-fifth of their fencible men.

The parishes of Kilmanivaig and Kilmaly in Lochabar, contain six thousand six hundred and sixty-one inhabitants, and about one thousand six hundred and sixty-five fighting men; of which number, five hundred and fifteen went to the army during the war. This was little under one-third of all the fencible men; and yet, notwithstanding the absence of so great a number, the whole labour of the country was as well carried on as before.

The detriment sustained by the Hebrides, in their present state, by parting with a large proportion of their inhabitants to the army, is comparatively small. Upon any great emergency, they may be considered as capable of raising five or six capital Highland regiments, without any loss to the country that would not soon be recovered: and if no events fall out unfriendly to their population, they would also be capable of suporting these regiments in the service, by a regular supply of new lev ies.

NUMBER OF PEOPLE COMPARED WITH THE EXTENT OF LAND.

In the Highlands, as in other countries, the most productive lands abound most with inhabitants; the least productive being always the least populous. Accordingly, wherever the rent is highest, the proportion of inhabitants is always largest, compared to the extent of land which they occupy. This proportion varies remarkably in different parts of the Highlands, as it does, indeed, in different parts of other countries; but, in general, the number is smaller, and the country they inhabit more extensive than is to be found in any other parts of the British kingdoms.

The number of people in the islands being exactly known, and a calculation made, as nearly as possible, of their extent in square miles and acres; it was from thence found, that some of the most fertile and populous islands, north of Cantire, contain about twenty English acres for each inhabitant.

Others were found to contain fifty, others a hundred, others a hundred and fifty, and some with extensive tracts on the main land, were found to contain above two hundred acres for each person.

RENT OF LAND.

An account of the rent of land cannot be obtained witli precision, in any of the remote Highland countries. The farms are sometimes estimated rather by their extent in computed miles, than by statute acres. No lands have ever been surveyed, and the inhabitants even know not what the measure of an acre is. The farms are valued, so far as it can be known, according to the number of black cattle which they keep, or rather according to the number of cows and their followers, every farm being entirely occupied by a breeding stock. The horses, the sheep, the goats, and even the arable land, which is generally indeed inconsiderable, are not taken into the account, but merely considered as necessary to the service of the farm, and the accommodation of the farmer's family. The black cattle are the only article upon the farm which affords money to the tenant, and payment to the landlord. The old custom of the payment of the rents in victual, and in services and casualties, does in some degree remain, but has of late years been much abridged, the rents in many places being now paid chiefly, if not en tirely, in money. From the state of the farms, however, as now described, no accurate idea can be formed of the rent payable from any certain quantity of land. From a general computation of the extent of many of the Hebridian isles, compared with their general amount of rent, it appeared, that in the year 1771, the most productive of the islands north of Cantyre, did not afford in rent above sixpence the Scots acre: In some, the rent turned out to be only fourpence, in others threepence, in others twopence, and in some of a great extent, the rent could not be estimated at so much as one penny the English acre. The case was found to be similar in many districts on the main-land. One proprietor, who may be considered as possessing more surface than any other subject in Britain, drew from his estate at that period, about nine thousand pounds a-year; yet, by the nearest computation that could be made, the whole was rented at less than, fourpence the Scots acre.,...

COMPARISON BETWEEN THE RENTAL AND THE NUMBER OF PEOPLE.

A comparison between the number of people and the rent of land, is another article worthy of observation in the economical history of any country. From this comparison, a general estimate may be formed of the natural fertility, or advanced im provement of any district. According as the soil is more or less productive, the rent of land bears a greater or less proportion to the number of people.

In some of the best of the islands among the Hebrides, and in districts on the mainland, it was found that each inhabitant corresponded to about twelve shillings of rent. In others this proportion varied from twelve shillings down to five shillings of rent for each person; but in some of the islands, and in some extensive tracts on the mainland, it appeared that one inhabitant corresponded even to four shillings of the rent of the land.

In the more fertile and cultivated parts of Scotland, five pounds sterling of rent for each inhabitant, may perhaps not be far from the average proportion. The above state therefore of the Highlands and islands in this article, does at least shew what great room there is for melioration in these extensive countries.

SECTION II. TENURE OF LANDS. LEASES. SUBTENANTS.

The state of agriculture, in every country, depends very much on the nature of the tenure, by which the labourers of the soil possess their lands.

The possessors of land/over the Highlands in general, are of three different kinds; tacksmen, tenants, and subtenants. The tacksmen hold their land of the proprietor, by lease; the tenants hold their farms, without any lease, at the will of the landlord; the subtenants have small possessions of land, let out to them from year to year, by the tacksmen and tenants.

The tacksmen are a superior order of people in the community. They are generally relations to the proprietor, and often men of education and of eonsidcrable endowments. In the year 1764, the farms they possessed, generally ran fioiri twenty to fifty-five poun s a year. The tenants again, are of a lower class, and their possessions are usually from five to twenty pounds per annum. The subtenants have small parcels of land let to them by the tacksmen and tenants, from fifteen shillings to forty shillings of yearly value, and resemble what are called cottars or crofters, in some other parts of Scotland.

A farm of thirty pounds a year, will have ten such subtenants upon it. Each of these has a family. The tacksman, besides his wife and children, has eight men servants, six women and two boys. The whole amounts to about seventy-one persons. Such a number of people, living by agriculture, upon so small a property, is not to be found any where else.

It appeared in general, that there was a Subtenant for about every four pounds of rent paid by a tacksman or tenant. On the Lochiel estate of six hundred pounds a year, the tenants in general rented only about five pounds each; and yet each of these, at an average, had two subtenants. This is a subtenant for every fifty shillings worth of land rented by the farmer; and the like proportion was found to hold in many other places.

This subsetting of lands is one great obstacle to the improvement of the Highlands—a relic of the old feudal system, which it were well was abolished, and that every person who holds land, should rent it of the proprietor. The progress of improvement, the advantage of the public, the revenue of the landlord, and the liberty and happiness of the people demand this. All the subtenants, who are the great body of the people in the Highlands, are tenants at the will of the tacksman or farmer, and are therefore placed in a state of subjection, that is not only unreasonable, but unprofitable, both to themselves and their superiors. Of all the people who Occupy land in the south of Scotland, the person most oppressed, or who has the hardest bargain and the least profit, is the tenant of a tenant. It cannot be supposed to be otherwise in the north, or indeed anywhere else.

It has been said, that were these small subtenants to be rendered more independent, by holding immediately of the proprietor by lease, that they would often, in, many respects, prove troublesome neighbours to the prjncipaLtacksman. They would not indeed be then so subjected to his power, as they are at present; a power which he might naturally wish to retain. But why should they be more troublesome neighbours than such small tenants, who are tradesmen and labourers, adjacent to a considerable farm, in any other part of Scotland, where the tacksman of a large possession, finds a number of such people in his neighbourhood, of essential service to him upon many occasions? At any rate, in every lease, all subtenants, or cottars holding land, should be excluded, except with the consent and under the authority of the proprietor..

Did the subtenants hold their small possessions by a more certain tenure, and enjoyed them by a lease from the landlord, there would be a far greater appearance of industry among them than there is at present; but their precarious situation must continue, as it has hitherto been, an effectual discouragement to every improvement of the soil . Their subjection to the tacksman or farmer, on whose ground they live, leaves them no more time than what is barely sufficient to support themselves and their families in life. The tacksman generally has one day in the week of the subtenant's labour the year round, It was found to be the opinion of a great proprietor in the Hebrides, that subtenants should not be totally prohibited, but that they should be allowed, wherever they can obtain a tack for nineteen years, or during the currency of the principal tacksman's lease. This opinion being liberal and rational, might be expected to be confirmed by experience. Such persons having their possession, and the terms by which they hold it, rendered certain, they become lessees, and arc no longer tenants at will. Accordingly, this gentleman has frequently found

the most material improvements made by sub. tenants in this situation. It was agreeable to find the same sentiments entertained by another person of very extensive property, who thought that the possession even of the smallest tenants, ought to be secured to them on the same footing with that of the tacksmen or tenants of a superior class.

which, with the spring and harvest work, and other occasions, will amount to more than a third of his whole annual labour He can therefore have neither ability nor opportunity to attempt any improvement, which many of those subtenants would undoubtedly do, were they but masters of their time, and independent in their possessions.

Here, as in other parts of Britain, it is necessary, that there should be a number of farms so consider able, as to invite men of education and intelligence to embark in agriculture; as it is from them that the improvement of the country is chiefly to be expected. But it is no less necessary, that a large proportion of the land, should also be occupied by smaller farmers, holding their possessions by leases from the proprietor. Without this degree of security, they never can be sufficiently useful to themselves, to their landlord, or to the public. There can also be no doubt but that the tacksman, holding a large farm, would find it far move profitable to have it managed by regular hired servants, than by the reluctant and careless labour of subtenants forced from their own occupations.

ALLOTMENTS OF LAND.

There is a very old valuation of the grounds in the Western Islands and Highlands, which to this day is scrupulously observed. By this, the whole country was divided into shilling, sixpenny, and three-penny lands of Scots money. But in later times, and at present, according to the English denomination of money, they are termed penny, halfpenny, and farthing hmds.

The large farms, held by tacksmen, contain a great number of those penny lands, sometimes twenty or thirty, and upwards. Where a number of tenants jointly occupy a farm, they pay rent ac-

cording to their separate valuation; some having a penny, some a halfpenny, and others only a farthing land. Each has his number of cattle soumed or proportioned to his rent, which go in a common herd. But they all join in labouring the arable part of the farm, and according to their valuation receive a proportion of its produce. As in this situation their separate interests must frequently interfere, the harmony in which they live, and the good will they bear to one another, is'truly surprising.

The souming, and the rent of the lands which pass under these denominations, vary much in different places.

The tenant of a penny land often keeps four or five cows, with what are called their followers, six or eight horses, and some sheep. The followers are, the calf, a one year old, a two year old, and a three year old; making in all, with the cow, five head of black cattle. By frequent deaths among them, the number indeed is seldom compleat; yet this penny land has, or may have, upon it, about twenty or twenty-five head of black cattle, beside horses and sheep.

The half-penny land is generally rented at about the half of the former; that is, at between five and six pounds. It supports eight or nine soum; sometimes four cows, three horses, and ten sheep; at other times, six cows and six horses. Yet the labour of these six horses, as it is employed, is scarcely sufficient to supply the tenant's family with meal.

The farthing land, in the most remote parts of the Highlands, is a very extraordinary possession. It supports sometimes four cows, with their followers, four horses, with some arable land, and a number of sheep. Yet the rent for the whole is but from thirty to fifty shillings. The grain raised by the labour of these horses, and assisted too by the spade, amounts not to above five or six bolls. All the disadvantages which such a country may lie under, from its climate and distant situation, cannot account for its being in such an unproductive STEELBOW.

There is another hurtful method of subsetting lands, which of late has become frequent, both in the islands and in the adjacent districts on the main land,—when a tacksman subsets his farm, with his whole stock of cattle upon it. This is called setting a farm in Steelbow; but for what reason it is so called does not appear. In this case, the whole stock upon the farm is valued, and at the expiration of the subtenant's lease he must either produce the stock in the same condition, or pay the value of what is wanting. By this sort of agreement, the tacksman often draws from the subtenant two rents of the farm, and sometimes three, and has besides from twelve to eighteen per cent, for the value of the stock upon it.

These high profits have induced many tacksmen to subset their farms in this manner. But it is plain, that all improvement must be stopped upon a farm in this state. Was the practice to become general, it would be highly prejudicial. The subtenants employed for the purpose never make any thing by it; and yet, for want of possessions of their own, and opportunity of employing their stock and labour otherwise, they are obliged to submit to this strange «ort of tenure.

HALF FOOT.

There is another method of occupying a farm, practised in Skye and the neighbouring countries, called Half-foot. In this case, the possessor of the farm affords the land and the seed-corn, and another person executes the tilling, sowing, and harrowing. After which, they divide the crop between them, in such proportion as they have agreed upon. Under these circumstances, it is not to be supposed that either of the parties can have much concern about any thing but the present crop: and in this way they endeavour to obtain it, as long as the lease or the soil will permit. This is a practice so contrary to the improvement of the farm and the landlord's interest, and likewise so inconsistent with the real advantage of the tenant, that it ought to be strictly prohibited in every lease where there is any risk of its being adopted.

LARCE AND SMALL FARMS

Large farms in the Highlands are not so prejudicial to the population of the country, as in England or the south of Scotland; there being generally maintained upon them so considerable a number of subtenants and married servants. Yet a err tain proportion of large and small farms is necessary in every part of Britain. It would appear to be useful in the Highlands, that about one-fourth of the land should be disposed in farms of a superior class, from twenty pounds to one hundred pounds per ann. fit to be occupied by men of stock and intelligence. And that the other three-fourths should be possessed by smaller tenants, paying from one to twenty pounds a year; but no subtenants to be allowed, either in the larger or smaller farms.

Though the rent of the largest farms in the Highlands is not considerable, yet their extent is often so great as to prevent all improvement. They require to be diminished with respect to their bounds, rather than with respect to their rental. Many farms axe estimated, not by the acres they contain, but by their miles in length and breadth.

The farm of Barrisdale, in Knoidart, consists of fifteen thousand acres and is rented for one hundred and fifty pounds, which is little above two-pence per acre. There are three farms on the Gordon estate in Lochaber, computed to contain forty-three thousand acres, and let for two hundred and fifty pounds, which is less than three half-pence per acre.

On farms so extensive, and yet so low in rent, there is certainly a favourable opportunity to settle numbers of the lowest of the people, much to their own comfort, and to the advantage both of the proprietor and of the public. Small parts detached frohr such farms, would be sufficient for the purpose, as a family in the Highlands can be supported on a Smaller rent of land than any where else in Britain. That parts of such large tracts should be disjoined, and appropriated for the accommodation of the inferior people, is on every account highly expedient.

An increase of population is indispensably necessary for the real impiovement of the Highlands. While the population is low, the Highlands must remain merely as a pasture-field for England and the south of Scotland. It is only by the number of people, properly employed, that the soil can be subdued, and raised to its proper value. Depopulation may bring to the proprietor a little immediate addition of rent, but it cuts off all future prospect of advancing the value of his property.

MONOPOLY OF FARMS.

The monopoly of farms is every where inconsistent with the interest of the public. The practice indeed is less prejudicial in the fertile parts of the kingdom, which abound in manufactures; but is destructive in those parts of the country that are destitute of manufactures, that are unimproved, and thinly peopled. There is reason to presume, that no farmer's possession should any where be of greater extent than what he can personally and daily inspect and superintend; and that all distant and led farms, as they are called, managed by the farmers servants or agents, ought to be discouraged. This rule is expedient even in the cultivated districts of the country, but is most necessary in those which stand in need of cultivation.

The ingrossing of farms has begun in some parts of the Highlands, and may at first be found profitable by the possessors and the proprietors. But the country is thereby depopulated, the hands which ought to improve it dismissed, and its ultimate interest sacrificed. All improvement of the soil must be abandoned, when the people by whom it should be accomplished are gone. The landlords will not judge wisely, if, for the sake of a little present profit, they prevent the permanent rising value of their property, and the general prosperity of the country.

LEASES TOR YEARS AND FOR LIVES.

It is impossible that the agriculture of any country, or that a country itself can flourish, where the possessors of the land are only tenants at will. No effort of industry is to be expected from people who have no security to enjoy its beneficial effects. Much of the land in the Highlands is occupied by the tenants and subtenants only from year to year. This precarious situation is the most effectual obstacle tc the spirit and industry of the people that could possibly be devised.

In former times, this was the case over Scotland in general, but is now happily altered. The experience of a great length of time has demonstrated, that landed property never can be advanced to its full value, without leases of considerable duration. Were the possessors of all the lands in the Highlands to enjoy the security of a lease, the country would then unquestionably assume a very different appearance. It is a privilege that ought to be communicated to the possessor of the very smallest tenement, as well as of the largest farm.

A considerable length of lease is peculiarly requisite in all lands that require improvement. It is therefore the opinion of some of the most skillful and patriotic gentlemen in the Highlands, that every lease should at least extend to the term of nineteen years. It is also supposed, that leases, very inviting to the commons in the Highlands, and fair and advantageous to all parties, might be formed, by combining one or more lives with a fixed number of years.

'CONJUNCT POSSESSIONS.

In old times, a large farm was usually occupied by a number of conjunct tenants, who cultivated the farm in common, and divided the produce. In this way, the interest of each became the interest of the whole. They were therefore ready, and were frequently called upon, to defend the common interest, the crop and the cattle, against depredations. There was then a necessity for such an allotment of lauds, especially in the border counties and in the Highlands. But though that necessity does no longer remain, the practice still continues in many places unaltered.

Nothing like improvement can be expected from farmers placed in this situation. Each of them has a negative on the rest, which must confine the whole, as it every where does, to the immemorial and aukward practice upon the farm. Neither is it to be supposed that the land can, by any practice, afford the greatest produce, or the highest rent, by this conjunct tenure. Such tenants have, indeed,

a common interest, but this never can be so strong as an interest that is personal. No community can ever equal the carefulness and industry of an individual in the management of his own affairs.

It appears, therefore, proper, on every account, that all such conjunct possessions should be disjoined, and that a separate farm, or portion of land, should be allotted to each possessor .

RUN-RIG.

Run-rig is another way of possessing'land, which was formerly very general in Scotland. It has been abolished wherever improvement has taken place, but still subsists in many parts of the north. A number of tenants on the same farm, have a common pasture for their cattle; and the arable land is divided among them, by ridge and ridge alternately, which each cultivates for his own behoof. This gives them all a common interest in the crop, and, where there was no inclosure, might be of some advantage, in guarding each person's lot of cornfield, against the encroachments of his neighbour's cattle.

A nobleman 6f large property in the Highlands, was clear, ly of this opinion,—that all such common farms ought to be! divided; and, that each possessor, according to his rent, should have allotted to him, a just share of the arable and pasture: But he knew it, from experience, to be a difficult operation, and that it could only be executed in a gradual way.

Vol. I. E

The disadvantages, however, of possessing land in this way, are so manifest, that the tenants arc every where well pleased to have it altered, and, by an equitable division, to be put, each of them in possession of their share of the land separately. This renders the operation easy to a proprietor, and should be every where practised, as it is the previous step, and indispensibly necessary to every sort of improvement.

STIPULATED IMPROVEMENTS.

In the cultivated parts of the country, the farmers are well acquainted with the most profitable methods of culture, and will not fail to prosecute them, for their own advantage. It would be unneces-

sary to stipulate with a Lothian farmer, that he should cultivate sown grass, or with a farmer in Berwickshire, that he should raise turnips; but the case is widely different in the uncultivated parts of the north: There, the labourers of the soil are unacquainted with the improvements that would be most beneficial to themselves and their country. Their knowledge is confined. They are naturally, and not blameably shy to alterations of which they have no experience. Their inclination is to proceed in the old beaten track; but from this they may be.'. allured, by the instruction "and example of their superiors; by reasonable prospects of profit; and by proper stipulations engrossed in their leases.

Whatever the intended improvements are, it will generally be found expedient, not to attempt their execution in a manner too rapid, nor. too violently to oppose the dispositions of the people. Those improvements that are gradual in their advancement, will always prove the most effectual in the end. To accomplish any general improvement, the people are the necessary instruments; they must, therefore, be rendered pliable and friendly to the work; their disinclination, and even their prejudices ought to be overcome, not by open combat, but by rational and persuasive means.

Though it is to be wished that all the farmers in the Highlands held their lands by lease; yet, such is their present situation, and that of the country, that even long leases will be of little avail towards improvement, unless they contain express stipulations for the purpose. Though the farmers Lad the inclination to improve their lands, they know not as yet how to do it. It is reasonable and necessary, that they should first be instructed, and then bound in their leases to pursue that practice in husbandry, which is most beneficial to themselves and others.

Long leases are constantly affirmed to be absolutely necessary to the improvement of the country, and sufficient of themselves to advance its progress, without any further encouragement given to the farmers. This maxim, however, cannot be safely assumed in general, but may be true or false, according to the knowledge and industry of the people, their opportunities of improvement, and the progress it may have already made.

A great many years ago, Archibald Duke of Argyll, with an intention to excite some persons upon his estate in Mull, to set a pattern of industry and improvement, let out three considerable farms, in leases of three nineteen years duration; but the attempt was not rewarded with the success it deserved: For these farms, after the leases were half expired, were found to be as little improved as any others in the island.

Mr Campbell of Shawfield, about the year 1720, ith very liberal views, let all his estate in Ila, in three nineteen years leases; but in the year 1764, that extensive estate had undergone no improvement, and was much in the same situation as when the leases commenced. The only prestation in these long leases was the sowing of flax, and that accordingly became a source of industry and advantage to the island.

The above reasoning, and these instances, may serve to prove, that no leases of any considerable duration ought to be granted in the Highlands, but on certain conditions of progressive improvement.

ENCOURAGEMENTS AND PRESTATIONS.
o

The agriculture of the Highlands and Islands being still in its infancy, it is entitled to be fostered, and to receive all the aid that can be given, from the parties interested in its advancement. The public is materially concerned, and, on every proper occasion, should lend its assistance.

The Board of Trustees for fisheries, manufactures, and improvements, have never bestowed much, either of their attention or revenue upon husbandry; though, if improvements lie within their commission, there are certainly no improvements more essential and necessary than those in agriculture. The manufactures have been their principal object, and in these indeed, they have done much good. But it was evident thirty-

years ago, and much more at present, that our agriculture has not kept pace with our manufactures, though the sound and solid foundation on which they ought to be established.

The views of the Highland Society are immediately directed towards these countries; and its efforts, from what has already appeared, promise to be very beneficial. It is to be hoped, that the husbandry of the Highlands, the most permanent source of prosperity, will continue to be their principal object. If the agriculture of the country can be made to flourish, and its population to increase, manufactures, and the erection of villages, wll then of course take place with the greatest advantage.

A Board of Agriculture in Scotland was long ago projected, and the excellent Lord Kaims chalked out a plan for it, which met not with the attention it deserved. Of late, Sir John Sinclair has had the spirit to call the attention of the public to the subject, and his Majesty's ministers have wisely and seasonably entered into his views. There could not be a more proper time to animate the people to promote the most laudable species of industry, and of course, their own happiness; nor a more eligible method to detach them from all ideas of pernicious innovations. In this light, the new Board deserves the approbation and assistance of every well wisher of his country, and especially of every person of rank and fortune.

The advancement of fisheries and manufactures in the Highlands, depends chiefly on the enactment of laws; and certain new laws for their encouragement are undoubtedly requisite. Agriculture is not directly the subject of law, but must depend for its progress on the energy of individuals, aided, if possible, by all the encouragements that can be given by public and patriotic institutions. Such encouragements are properly bestowed, in honorary and lucrative premiums to those persons, who signalise themselves by their knowledge and industry, in advancing the progress of agriculture and the public good.

The just and proper form of a lease is still a problem in husbandry. It is vain to

imagine, that the same form will answer every where, or even suit every district of the same county. To render the conditions of a lease equitable and useful, they must vary according to the state of the country, and the situation of the people. Even a single farm may require a form of a lease, different from what would be proper in its immediate neighbourhood.

The farmers in the Highlands stand in need of all the encouragements that their landlords can conveniently afford them; and the most important of these ought to be comprehended in the articles of their lease. Proper encouragements must vary according to circumstances; but in general, such advantages as the following, granted by the proprietor, must tend to promote both his own interest and that of his tenants.

1. To supply them with timber for the farm buildings, and especially for stables and byres. 2. To inclose for them a large kitchen garden. 3. To accept of money instead of payment in kind, 4. To convert all casualties and services into mo ney rent. 5. To give a premium, by the acre, for all wild land reduced to tillage. 6. To require no rent for fallowed land.. 7. To engage to advance money, at a reasonable rate, for improvements which jointly concern the interest both of landlord and tenant: such as sufficient march dykes between farm and farm; also for fencing the low arable grounds from the hilly pasture, and for inclosures within the farm. It would be a great point gained, if for these, or the like purposes, the Highland farmers could be brought to pay an interest, suppose about seven per cent, for money laid out by the landlord. 8. To render the terms of payment convenient for the tenant, and the rent not to be exacted sooner, than he can have the annual produce of the farm converted into money. But rent remaining unpaid, longer than what may be necessary, is prejudicial both to landlord and tenant.

The prestations in a lease, incumbent on a tenant, are generally restraints in favour of the proprietor. But if they are just and reasonable, they are not to be complained of.

It may be proper in a lease, 1. To exclude the subsetting of lands, without the consent of the proprietor. 2. To restrain the number of repeated crops of corn, and to establish the cultivation of green crops. 3. To confine the culture of potatoes to waste land. 4. To prevent the thatching of houses with straw; and the making of graddan bread. 5. To secure the preservation of inclosures, and of wood and plantations. 6. To ensure the raising of a certain quantity of flax.

Other restrictions of a local nature, may perhaps be proper, but whatever the prestations imposed upon a tenant may be, they ought neither to be too numerous, nor of difficult execution; not liable to doubt or dispute, but simple and well defined, and conceived in such terms, as to give no foundation for any questions in law. The disposition and ability of the tenant to perform what is required of him, deserve also to be well considered.

FARMERS STOCK.

Farmers frequently aim at possessions, too large for their funds; and none will offer a higher rent than persons of this description; whereas men of real substance are usually more cautious and less enterprising. Bad consequences, however, are always to be apprehended, when the farmers stock is inadequate to his farm.

This inclination in tenants to occupy possessions above what their stock can reach, takes place more readily in grass than in corn farms. Upon a farm in tillage, the necessary stock is small, compared to what is requisite, on a grass farm of the same rent, whether occupied by black cattle or sheep. The corn farm also, whatever its extent may be, requires the constant attendance of the tenant; but a grass farm, even of the largest size, may be easily managed by a few servants. This induces graziers, to add if they can, farm to farm, even beyond their stock, and tempts them to borrow money for the purpose, perhaps at a very heavy rate. Such an enterprise must become dangerous to all parties concerned. A tenant in this situation can never be able to stand the shock of a bad

season, the fall of markets, or an accidental loss, by the people with whom he deals. No advancement of rent should induce a landlord to prefer such a person, M ho is indeed rather an adventurer than a fanner. Whatever may be the nature or extent of the farm, the landlord should have evidence that it can be stocked by the tenant's own money. In every case, it is of great moment, that the farmer should not be weaker, but stronger than his farm.

PAYMENT IN KIND.

It was long ago a general practice in Scotland to have part of the rent of every farm, and sometimes the whole, paid in grain, which is called payment in kind. This custom still prevails in many places, and especially in the north, where two-thirds of the rent are often paid in grain and other articles, and one-third in money Sometimes the money rent makes but one-fifth of the whole.

In ancient times, this practice must have added to the power of the chieftain, by giving him the command of a great part of the sustenance of the country; but it seems chiefly to have arisen from want of markets. The markets in Scotland, were then, as at present, in the Highlands, very few and distant. The landlord for the support of his household, was obliged to stipulate for the delivery of so much corn and cattle from his estate. These necessaries of life could not easily be procured for money. Even at present in the Highlands, meal, meat, and malt, cannot be readily purchased for the support of a family. Every considerable family, to be furnished with these material articles of living, must either possess lands for the purpose, or be supplied with them by agreement with tenants. Though there is a sufficient circulation of money in all the Highlands, for the payment of the rents, yet for this reason, many of them are still paid in kind.

By the want of markets, the tenants also were at a loss to get the grain upon their farms exchanged for money; so that to deliver their rent in grain, was a matter of conveniency, and even necessity. The landlord was obliged to be

the salesman; and on large estates, to become a considerable corn merchant; a business which, it is probable, he seldom found turn to account.

The tenants are often obliged to carry this farm grain as it is called, to the distance of twelve or fifteen miles, and more, at the option of the landlord. This method of paying rent, is apt likewise to occasion disputes, as to the quality of the grain, between landlord and tenant, and indeed upon the whole, cannot in the present times, be agreeable or profitable to either.

Wherever the causes which occasioned this custom have ceased, the custom itself ought to cease of course. It is a paction from which all tenants wish to get free; and it is no less the interest of proprietors to absolve them from it. The practice accordingly has been on the decline for many years. In many cases of late, the grain has been converted into money; which should be the case in general, wherever the situation of the proprietor will permit.

CASUALTIES.,

On a Highland estate, there are many articles termed casualties, paid by the farmer to the proprietor, beside the stated rent in money and grtuh. In former times, this custom obtained over all Scotland. In the more populous and improved parts of the kingdom, it has gone gradually into disuse. But in the Highlands, and other remote parts, it still exists, and must necessarily do so, in some degree, from the state of the country.

The most common casualties paid by the tenants are, sheep, calves, lambs, kids, pigs, poultry, eggs, butter, cheese, wool, yarn, blanketting, and sacking. A gentleman's family may require a greater quantity of these articles than the lands which he himself possesses can afford. And as there are no regular mar kets, it is necessary that he should be supplied with them from his own estate. Such casualties amount frequently to one-fifteenth, and sometimes to more than one-twelfth of the whole rent of the lands. They are commonly said, and considered, to be so much over and above the rent. But they are in fact so much real rent; and there is not a tenant who would not rather pay money in compensation for them. Unless where the conveniency of the proprietor absolutely requires them, it is unquestionably both his interest and that of the tenant, to have them fairly converted into money rent.

Another casualty, though now unfrequent, deserves to be noticed, as extremely improper and unprofitable. A proprietor receives annually a sum of money, such as twenty guineas, from a drover, for liberty to buy his tenants cattle; and none of the tenants dare sell any of their cattle, except to that person. It is obvious that these cattle can by no means be sold to the best advantage. The tenants being forced to sell to an individual, all they can do is, to make the best of a bad bargain they can. Were they to have the choice of their market, they would undoubtedly turn their cattle to much higher account, and be able to pay a much higher rent. The proprietor, in such a case, by receiving twenty guineas, probablj robs himself of three times the sum.

SERVICES.

The services, as they are called, which are exacted hy a landlord in the Highlands from his tenants, are various and numerous. The tenants are obliged to plough and harrow the landlord's farm in the spring, and to plant potatoes; to work at his hay and corn harvest; to build fold dykes; to cut and dry peats; to weed the corn, and to thatch the houses. At different times of the year, their cattle likewise must be employed, on demand, in the carriage of corn, fuel, wood, and manure. These services, in different places, extend to every sort of labour that must be executed upon a farm.

In old times, such services came naturally into use, and were exacted when the rents were far from being adequate to the possessions, when the landlords stood more in need of the assistance of their tenants, and when the tenants stood more in need of the protection of their landlords, than either of them do at present. These services were not confined to the superior, but were claimed and possessed by inferior persons. The feudal arrangement, if it formed not a *beau systeme,* as Montesquieu calls it, formed at least a well connected chain. The tenant, though the vassal of a vassal, had, and has to this day, a number of vassals subordinate to him.

A subtenant, who pays in rent only thirty shillings a year, will pay sometimes to the tacksman, in the above casualties and services, to the value of three pounds yearly; the whole amounting to four pounds ten shillings. But for such a possession, was he freed from these incumbrances, he would willingly pay six pounds, or upwards. Beside the rent and these casualties and services, the subtenant sometimes pays so much a piece for every head of black cattle, horses, or sheep, in his possession. The labour, also, required of him, is not always restricted to a certain number of days in the year; but, at particular seasons, his services are demanded without any limitation. This state of servitude disconcerts him in his labour. Being at the call of another person, he can never depend upon having any thing done in proper time upon his own farm. On the other hand, it is impossible that the tacksman's work can ever be properly executed by people in this situation, employed in another person's harvest, while their own is neglected; and a great part of whose labour must be lost, by being mistimed and misplaced.—All parties, and especially the landlord, must therefore suffer by this method of management.

These services are called in some places by the name of bondage. For though the people are obliged to submit to it, they cannot, even in spite of ancient custom, but feel it. It is a practice which deceives with the appearance of conveniency and advantage; but it has, in fact, nothing in it either of the one or of the other. If the proprietor thinks that he has these services for nothing, or over and above the rent which the lands would give, he is egregiously mistaken. If they are judged to be absolutely necessary for his conveniency, that is a different case. But for this conveniency he must certainly pay a very high price. Nothing but necessity should persuade a proprietor to exact or receive these seeming advantages from a tenant. For he may depend upon it, that although they have a gratuitous appearance, they are all obtained at more than their value; and that every tenant would give more than their value in money rent, to be freed from them.. They form a sort of servitude, which may have had its origin in necessity, but which does not now answer any good purpose, and directly opposes the improvement of the country. As it is, however, a general and immemorial custom, it is not to be abolished of a sudden; but it is to be expected, that the proprietors and tacksmen in the Highlands will now find it their interest to suffer the practice to fall gradually into dissuetude.

FARM SERVANTS.

It is a great object in agriculture, to execute the work that is required with the least power, and at VOL. i. p the least expence. Any person acquainted with the state of husbandry in other parts of Scotland, must at once be surprised at the great number of servants retained upon a Highland farm. Many farms in tho south of Scotland, are exactly similar to many in the Highlands; consisting of hill grounds, with a stock of black cattle or sheep, and a certain portion of arable land. Yet, upon a farm of this kind in the north, you will find more than double the number of servants that are kept upon a farm of the same rent in the south of Scotland. In the south, the power of labour is adapted, and sometimes too narrowly adapted, to the size of the possession, whether largo or small. But, in the Highlands, the number of men and horses upon a farm are often found equal to what they are upon another farm, much larger both in rental and in extent.

A superfluous number of servants and horses must be a heavy load, both upon the landlord and tenant. It is not to be supposed, that the farmers in the Highlands subject themselves to this burden from choice, whatever they may do from the prevalence of custom. But there are circumstances in the present situation of the country, that naturally lead to the present practice.

In most places, three men are required to attend an ill-constructed plough. One to hold it, another to drive four horses abteast, and a third to follow with a spade, to rectify the imperfection of the tilth. Beside these, where the reestle is used to precede the plough, one man is employed to hold it, and another to drive one or two horses. By this aukward management, five men, and five or six horses, arc required for a feeble plough. Thus, by the want of proper instruments of husbandry, the number of men servants and horses is rendered much greater than is necessary.

The want of day labourers, also, obliges the farmer to keep more men servants than what he constantly requires, but whose labour at particular seasons is necessary. On a grasing farm, the management of the milk makes a considerable article; and this, with the labour of procuring peats in summer, calls for a number of hands. These causes, with the low wages of servants, their easy maintenance, and the established custom of the country, all conspire to render the number of servants upon a Highland farm far larger than any where else.

A man who rents five pounds a year, will be found to keep six horses. On a farm of twenty pounds a year, you will find twelve or fourteen men and women servants. Even when every allowance is made for the situation of the country, there certainly must be something wrong in this economy. Mr M'Aulay, minister of Ardnamurchan, who possessed a steclbow farm of one hundred pounds rent, executed all the cultivation upon it with four men servants, which employed eight when this farm was in the possession of a country tenant. Notwithstanding all the circumstances mentioned above, it is probable, that there are few farms in the Highlands which might not be equally well cultivated with onethird, and some with one-half fewer men servants and horses, than what are used at present.

The men servants not being properly or sufficiently employed, it has been found, that the want of a considerable number of them is not sensibly felt. The two parishes of Kilmalie and Kilmanivaig, from the year 1755 to 1763, afforded to the war full five hundred men, and yet the whole labour of the country was as well carried on, and the land as well cultivated as before. In a district in these two parishes, of seven hundred pounds rent, it appeared, that there were near seven hundred women, very imperfectly employed, all of whom might, in some degree, be profitably occupied in manufacture.

It is certainly most expedient, that every person who possesses land should have the command of his own time, and of his own labour; without which, it can never be cultivated with sufficient advantage, either to himself or others. This requires the giving up of all services from tenants and subtenants, by a just commutation.

But there is another custom which likewise requires to be considered.

The farm servants' in the Highlands who are married, generally have a possession of their own to cultivate, granted to them by their master, instead of wages. They have pasture to support from one to three or four milk cows and some sheep, with cultivated land sufficient to raise from three to ten bolls of meal, beside potatoes. By these means, their labour and attention must be so much divided between their master's work and their own, that both must suffer.

The improvement of Britain has been accomplished by servants hired upon wages in money or grain; not by people who were also employed in the cultivation of land upon their own account. It is therefore to be wished, that the same practice should take place in the Highlands; that all farm servants should be bound to their master's work without any other avocation; and that all persons who possess land, should have their whole labour secured to them without any infringement.

DAY LABOURERS.

In every country where the improvement of the soil is pursued, the command of day labourers is of great importance. In this situation, the farmer must have many casual operations to carry on, which cannot be overtaken by his hired servants, and which do not require servants to be retained through the whole year. These operations, however useful, he must either relinquish, or be obliged to keep supernumerary servants, if he has not temporary labourers at his call.

This is well known to all the farmers in the cultivated parts of Britain. The day labourers are a useful and meritorious body of people. Their labour usually is hard, and their earnings small. In many places, they have been drawn off' from this occupation, by fmding their industry more profitably employed in manufactures. Wherever this happens, the tanner very sensibly feels the wont of them. The price of labour comes to be raised, and sometimes fie cannot, at any price, have the work performed he would wish.

The small subtenants in the Highlands, who rent from one to four pounds a year, should all be in the state of day labourers. This, indeed, cannot take place while so much of their labour is exacted by their superiors. But if they held their little possessions by lease from the landlord, free of all services, their spare time, which would then be a great deal, would become their own. It would then be chiefly employed for days wages, in the service of the neighbouring proprietors and principal tacksmen, and turn to much greater account, both to themselves and their employers, than it can at present. The greatest improvements have been made, and both proprietors and tenants have been most enriched, in those parts of the kingdom where day labourers were most numerous. Without them, improvement must go On every where at a very slow pace.

The persons of the lowest rank in the Highlands, are more numerous, in proportion, than any where else, and form a vast body of people. In every reasonable and profitable enterprise, they are capable of great energy; but it has never been called forth. Their wants are few; they can be supported on little; and know not how to better their situation. Not half employed, these people must be considered as a burden, who, if properly managed, ought to be the strength and wealth of their country.

At present, it would be both more eligible and more easy to turn the industry of these people to the business of agriculture than to that of manufactures. There is one way in which, without much cost or care, they might all be beneficially employed, and that is, in reclaiming wild and untillaged land. This, however, can never be accomplished, but by making them their own masters. This might be done, were they to obtain from proprietors, small parcels of uncultivated land by lease, free of rent for a term of years, after which a stipulated and advancing rent should take place. This is a proposition calculated to the taste of the lower people, and would every where be gladly embraced by them. With such a holding as this, no common Highlander would ever think of deserting his country. Such people would be all retained, without expence, and with manifest advantage. Great additions would every where be made to the cultivated land, and in a few years every property increased in value; not by the fluctuation of prices and markets, but by a solid and permanent improvement.

There are few considerable farms in the Highlands and Islands but what contain a great deal of land, fit for this important purpose, and scarcely indeed for any other. The land to be set apart in this way, ought to be such, as has never been laboured, either by the plough or spade; such as mossy, moorish, and boggy grounds; such as are so incumbered with stones, as to be incapable of tillage till they are cleared; and some tracts of barren sandy soil which almost blows with the wind. Such lands, in short, as bring not to the proprietor, at present, above two pence or three pence an acre.

The quantity of such land to be granted to these possessors, would, no doubt, vary, according to its quality and situation; but in general, from ten to thirty acres for each, would seem to be the most proper for the purpose. Many patches of land of this kind might be thus detached, without any prejudice to the considerable farms. The remission of rent, on such possessions, perhaps from half a crown to three half crowns annually, for a few years, cannot be an object with a proprietor, considering the advantageous consequences that would follow.

The method of improving the Highlands, as now described, will readily occur to a stranger, attentive to the agriculture of the country, though it passes unnoticed by the inhabitants. One instance, however, which was observed in the Isle of Mull in the year 1764, deserves to be recorded.

A sensible and worthy gentleman, Mr Niel Macleod, minister of Ross, in the year 1760. subset during will, to a poor labouring man, fifteen acres of the wildest land upon his farm, at six shillings yearly, which he thought a good rent. The ground which was of the coarsest kind, and had never been cultivated, was moss covered with rank heather. The man, however, planted on it the first year above an acre of potatoes. He did the same the three tollowing years, and on the 5th of July 1764, besides his annual acre of potatoes, he had, upon four acres already reclaimed, as plentiful a crop of oats, as was any where in the neighbourhood upon land that had been immemorially in tillage. Mr Macleod was then offered one pound four shillings for this subtenement; but he would neither dispossess the poor man, nor raise his rent, who had thus quadrupled the value of the ground, by his industry, in four years.

From a calculation it was supposed that there were above fifty thousand acres in the Isle of Mull, of the same nature, and improveable in the same manner. But if this method of improvement, is thus practicable and profitable, in the hands of a tenant, it must surely be more so under the direction of a proprietor, who is better able to remit a trifle of rent for a few years, and to grant to the useful labourer, security for enjoying the fruits of his toil.

The experiment has also been successfully tried in other parts of Scotland, which should give encou«, ragement to the prosecution of it in the Highlands, where it can be more easily and beneficially accom plished, and to a greater extent, than any where else in the kingdom.

In the country of East Ross, a great deal of unprofitable land has been improved by persons whom they call there, mailers. These are poor labourers, who have small parcels of moorish ground let off to them for some years rent free, on which they build huts, and in a few years bring the land into culture. When the period expires, during which they pay no rent, their little possessions come to pay twenty, thirty, or forty shillings yearly, which before were of no value whatever. In like manner, the little crofters as they are called, in Aberdeenshire, encouraged by a liferent lease, or one of nineteen years, upon the most barren uncultivated ground, have come to raise on their small lots of land both sown grass and turnip. In both cases, these people do partly subsist, and with much advantage to the country, by working as day labourers to the neighbouring gentlemen and farmers. They would answer the same purpose in the Highlands, and be also of the greatest use, wherever fishery or manufacture came to be established.

Another instance, similar to those above stated, deserves notice in this place; the improvement of the moss of Kincardine. This was first projected by the worthy Lord Kaims, and with much ingenuity, perseverance and expence, has now almost been compleated by his son, Mr Drummond. This was apparently the most untoward subject of improvement of any in Scotland. A dead flat of fourteen hundred acres of moss, from three to twelve feet deep, bottomed with clay. It cannot be imagined, that this could ever have been profitably reclaimed, but by the means which have been employed. It was let out to common labourers, most of them people expelled from the Highlands, and upon such terms as were sufficient to induce them to undertake its improvement.

Each person has a lot of eight acres of the moss granted to him, by a lease of thirty eight years, with a proper quantity of timber, and two bolls of oatmeal, to support him while employed in rearing a house. The first seven years he pays no rent; the eighth year he pays one merk Scots; the ninth year two merks, and so on with the addition of one merk yearly, till the end of the first nineteen years. Upon the commencement of the second nineteen years, he begins to pay a yearly rent of twelve shillings for each acre of land cleared from moss, and two shillings and sixpence for each acre that is not cleared.

Upon these terms, this extensive tract, which scarce ever before could feed any thing but a moorfowl, and was of no value to the proprietor, is now peopled with six hundred and twenty inhabitants. These people have cleared and cultivated above three hundred acres of the moss, which afford two thousand four hundred bolls of grain, beside other productions. From the poorest hovels, they have now. got into good brick houses. They have cattle and carriages in abundance, and form a colony of industrious, virtuous, and happy people. The advantages from this plan, which accrue to these colonists at present, and which must in time accrue to the public, and to the proprietor of the Blair Drummond estate, are great and manifest.

There is not a considerable landholder in the Highlands, but who has a much greater extent of waste land than the moss of Kincardine, which might all be improved in a similar manner, but with more ease, and at far less expence. In any trial to be made in this way, there was a rule adopted by Lord Kaims and his son, which it would be worth while to observe. Every tenant in the moss has the liberty of selling his lease, provided he enters on the cultivation of a new possession. This liberty has been of great advantage, both to the settlers, and to the progress of the improvement. Many of them, after their lots were improved, have sold their leases to considerable advantage, and entered on the improvement of new possessions with fresh vigour.

Of all the proposals made for the improvement of agriculture in the Highlands, there seems to be none so simple, so practicable, so inexpensive, so effectual, and of such general utility, as that which is suggested in the above observations.

SECTION III. BUILDINGS AND INCLOSURES. HOUSES. . In the Highlands and Islands there is a great deficiency in the materials for building. Neither freestone nor brick are to be had; wood in many places is scarce; lime can only be procured at a high expence; and there is no opportunity to obtain foreign timber. In most places, whinstone, turf, and thatch, or sand to mix with lime, are all the materials for building which the country affords. Where wood is at hand, they erect what are called creel fiouses. These are formed of wooden posts, interlaced with brandies of trees, like wicker work, and covered on the outside with turf. For these reasons, the farm houses are inferior to those in other places, and must necessarily be so; though it is highly proper they should be of a better construction than at present, especially on the more considerable farms. The farmers have some reason to expect assistance in this article, as there is no part in Britain where the farm houses and offices cost the proprietor so little. 2. The cattle of every kind range the fields all the year round. The farmers, having neither stables nor cow-houses, form no dunghills. Sea weed is almost the only manure their grounds ever receive; and yet a great part of them has been immemorially cropped with oats and bear without intermission: a treatment which could never be productive of white crops, was it not for the uncommon natural fertility of the soil. The first step, therefore, to be recommended to the farmers is, to provide winter forage, to house their horses and cattle, and to preserve the dung. This is but the common practice of every country where agriculture has made any progress. Every improved country is a proof that this practice is the previous step to all other improvements of the soil. Without this, a farm is left destitute of artificial manure, the great support of cultivation. But though stables and byres are highly necessary, and universally wanting, it will be no easy matter to bring the common farmers to adopt them of a sudden. They have hitherto had no use for them, being destitute of a proper provision of winter pro vender: but wherever that comes into use, a demand for stables and byres will naturally follow. Whereever they are required, it is certainly the interest of a landlord to have them erected at his own expence, as it is from them chiefly that he is to expect the improvement of his land. Their expence would be very inconsiderable to be built of dry stone, or of stone and sod, and covered with a slight thatch roof.

The extent of these houses is not to be proportioned, as in other places to the extent of the farm, but according to the quantity of winter forage it affords. If this could be rendered sufficient for the milk cows, the labouring horses, and such young cattle as stand most in need of assistance to get through the winter, it would be of great advantage. The rest of the stock might keep the fields all winter, as they do at present, though with great risk, and often with great loss, till winter food was provided for them likewise. But the preservation of a considerable part would be secured, by being housed and fed, and a valuable stock of manure provided for the farm.

GARDENS.

At no very remote period, the common productions of the kitchen garden were unknown in the Vol. i. n

Highlands. Lochiel, on returning from abroad, with excellent intentions to improve his country, established a kitchen garden at his seat of Achnacary: and in August 1734 entertained his guests with hotchpotch, containing pease, turnip, and carrot; which was the first time these vegetables had been produced in that part of the world. Since that time, kitchen gardens have been formed at all the gentlemen's houses; but the common tenants and subtenants remain still destitute of a garden of any kind.

To every family, whether high or low, placed in the country, the productions of a garden are not only conducive to health, but of great consideration in domestic economy. A little meat, with plenty of garden-stu ft', goes a great way in the maintenance of a family. The Highlanders live entirely on fish, flesh, and the produce of their cattle; but have no vegetable aliment except meal and potatoes. The addition of garden-stuff would not only render their diet cheaper and wholesomer, but more plentiful.

All the lower people in the Highlands are still strangers to every sort of vegetable food, except meal from oats, barley, or rye; and potatoes, which, of late years, have made a happy addition. But the same was the case, at no very distant period, with all the lower people in the south of Scotland. They have begun, indeed, gradually, and continue more and more, to admit into their diet the productions of the garden. An alteration most beneficial, both with respect to their health, and their economy.

i

Above thirty years ago, there was an observation made on this subject by some of the ablest physicians in Scotland , who had practised in different parts of the kingdom, more than thirty years before that period; and who had seen the first introduction of kail-yards and potatoes in many districts of the country. They all agreed, that, in consequence of this' alteration, a most obvious improvement had taken place in the health of the people. Some prevailing diseases being greatly alleviated, and others almost wholly extirpated.

From want of habit, however, the lower people, both in the Highlands and Lowlands, are rather averse to any sort of vegetables, except the few articles to which tbey have been accustomed. That their health would be improved by a greater proportion *of* vegetable food, especially where they live much upon fish and salted meats, is an argument they may not readily understand. They know little of the difference between an alkalescent and an acescent diet. But it may be, and hag often been proved to their satisfaction, that, by means of garden-stuff, they may By Dr Cullen, in Clydesdale; Dr Gilchrist, in Dumfriesshire; Dr Mitchell and Dr Campbell, in Galloway; Dr Dalrymple, in Ayrshire; Dr Stirling, in Stirlingshire, and Dr Ma-

clean, in the Isle ef Skye.

have greater plenty of wholesome food, and that their scanty income may be enabled to go much further than it does, in the way of living.

There arc many articles to be considered as the luxuries of a garden, which may be proper only for people of wealth. But there are others, which may be most beneficially raised by every small farmer and cottar, as they yield a large quantity of provision in a little spot of ground, and with little labour. These are, cabbages, savoys, and curled kail, turnips, carrots, parsnips, the root of scarcity, and the Swedish turnip. To these must be added, onions, leeksi and cives; which are not only useful in rural cookcry, by adding to the quantity of nourishment, but necessary to improve the relish of the above articles. These eleven plants, with a little care, may all be raised in the garden of the meanest farmer or cottar, and at a small expence, in plenty and perfection. Wherever they are in abundance, they add greatly to the support of a poor family. On many occasions, they may be used only with bread; on others, they make a little salt fish, or flesh, go far in the way of sustenance, and not only improve the health, but in reality add to the income of such people. At one time, in the gardens of some small tenants in the Highlands, there were observed, in the beginning of September, some plots of luxuriant tobacco plants, as well hoed and dressed, and as clean, as any that ever were raised in Virginia or Berwickshire. There can, indeed, be no doubt, that the common people in the Highlands are capable of raising every garden crop to perfection in which they are interested.

For this purpose, however, it is necessary that they should have a piece of ground effectually inclosed. This must vary in extent, according to the size of the possession; but in general it ought to be large. A space of ground, from half an acre to two acres, or perhaps more, allotted to this use, would be well bestowed. What part of it was not necessary for the use of the family, might be profitably employed in raising red clover, turnips, and cabbages, for the

use of the cattle. The perfection of husbandry is, to introduce the productions of the garden into the field. In this way, more readily than by any other, the Highland tenants might be brought to, cultivate these useful crops upon a larger scale.

WINTER HERDING.

In former times, the cattle over all Scotland roamed through the fields, and over all the adjacent farms, through the whole winter, without any restraint. They were herded only in summer, for the safety of the corn crop; but when that was removed, the herding ceased, and they were then allowed to stray as they chose, not only over the farm, but in all the neighbouring grounds. In the lowlands, this custom has been gradually abolished, as altogether inconsistent with good husbandry, hut still continues to prevail in the Highlands.

On every open grasing farm, whether stocked with black cattle, or sheep, it is proper to preserve some tracts of saved pasture, as a relief for the cattle late in winter, and in early spring. But this cannot be done, when such reserved pastures lie open to the encroachments, not only of the cattle upon the farm, but of those in the neighbourhood. This, beside other reasons, renders the careful herding of cattle no less necessary in winter than in summer: without it, indeed, the farmer can neither do justice to his stock, nor to his own interest.

Even at present, in the Highlands, winter herding is therefore requisite, to make any grasing farm turn out to the most advantage; but it would become still more necessary, if green winter crops were to be introduced. In many of the uninclosed parts of Scotland, tlie neglect of winter herding has been the chief bar to the cultivation of clover and turnips, and must be an insurmountable obstacle to their cultivation in the Highlands. With attentive winter herding they might be preserved; but this is not to be expected where the practice is yet to be introduced, and where it is even undervalued. Sown grass and green winter crops cannot therefore be attempted, but in inclosed grounds.

QUARRYING.

Some parts of the Highlands and Islands may be advantageously inclosed with hedges; walls of stone and lime are utterly unattainable; but in general these countries must depend for inclosures chiefly upon dry stone dykes. The proper construction of such dykes, though of the greatest importance, is quite unknown. The inhabitants have neither implements nor skill in the previous art of quarrying. The stones used for their houses or walls, are such as are found loose on the surface of the earth, and which can be got without the assistance of levers, wedges, or hammers. But with these instruments they might be easily provided, and all the skill that is necessary may be soon acquired, to procure stones sufficient for the purposes of building and inclosure. There is no free-stone, and very little flat bedded rock of any kind in these countries. The rocks in general are whin-stone, disposed in vertical strata, or edge seams; they are extremely hard, and require a particular method of working. Among the numerous varieties of whin-rock, there are some much more suitable for the purpose of building than others; which can scarcely be described, but which are at once known by a skillful quarrier. Such a person, who has had experience in working whinstone quarries in the south of Scotland, for the pur pose of building, would be of great use in any part of the Highlands, SNAP DYKES.

The snap dyke is usually composed of whin-rock. It is built of dry stones, to a certain height, generally from three to five feet, a double wall, and coped with large flat stones. Upon these a number of loose stones are piled up, sloping like the ridge of a house, which is called the snap. The dyke at bottom should be from thirty inches to three feet in breadth, and from fifteen to eighteen inches at top. These dykes began to be built in Galloway about the year 1720, and since that time the greatest part of that country has been inclosed with them. On this account, they are known in other places by the name of Galloway dykes. To this practice the inhabitants were led by the nature of the stone of the country, which is excellently adapt-

ed for the purpose.

These dykes have been attempted in many other parts of Scotland, but no where with such success as in Galloway. Either from want of proper materials, or want of skill, they are generally ill constructed, and form a very imperfect fence. The snap dyke when well formed is the only good inclosure to be had, where free-stone and lime are wanting, and where the soil, climate, or other circumstances, will not admit of hedges. For these reasons, it is the most proper, and must be the general inclosure for the Highlands, which abound in most places with stone fit for the purpose. All that is wanting is sufficient skill in quarrying the stones and in constructing the dyke.

The snap dyke should never be built of any stone that either splits or moulders in the air. It may vary in height, according to the disposition of the ground, or the purpose intended. But on level ground, a well built dyke of six quarters high, exclusive of the snap, is a sufficient fence against black cattle or sheep. To build it of small or rounded stones, is but to frame a rope of sand. They are constantly tumbling down, and do never again compleatly repair the dyke. It ought to be built double and strong, with large angulated stones firmly bedded. It should have as many band-stones as possible; nor is there any disadvantage, though they project upon one or both sides of the wall. The cope-stones should be large and flat, and extend from six to nine inches over the wall on each side. The snap ought to be about eighteen inches high, formed not of small or rounded stones, but of a large size, and cornered, and To obtain these cop-stones of a proper size and form, is the most important article in building a dyke of this sort. It is on the length, strength, and weight of these flat stones that the strength and stability of this dyke must depend.

so piled up as to withstand any force of wind. Some dykes built in this way have lasted fifty or sixty years, without needing any repair. The stones of the snap being ready to tumble upon any attack, render this sort of fence very formida-

ble to cattle. Even dogs of sport tremble to pass over it, many of them being often lamed and sometimes killed in the attempt. Though the building of such a fence, may appear easy, it requires much observation and practice to do it properly. In most parts of the Highlands, a person who has been trained to this work, and who understands it thoroughly would be highly useful.

Strong march dykes of this kind ought every where to be established between different properties and between different farms. Every farmer's pasture would then be secured. His cattle would not be annoyed and driven, as they now are, much to their prejudice, on passing a march, and his expence in herding would be greatly abridged.

Most Highland farms consist of hilly pasture, with tracts of arable land in the adjoining valley or about the bottom of the hills; but there is no fence between the pasture and the arable part of a farm. To divide the one from the other by a strong snap dyke, would be of the greatest advantage to every Highhnd farm so situated. This is the general situation of the farms in the mountainous parts of the south of Scotland. There, it is found both by proprietors and farmers, that a sufficient dry stone dyke between the mountain pasture and the arable grounds, is one of the most beneficial improvements upon such farms. The tenants are always willing to pay a reasonable rate of interest for money laid out by the proprietor for this purpose; and the proprietor, on the other hand, finds it very advantageous to lay out his money in this manner.

But beside these important purposes, the snap dyke is the only proper fence, in most parts of the Highlands, for subdividing and inclosing the arable lands. Till this is done, there can be no proper system of tillage, no sown grass, no green winter crops, nor any proper provision for cattle in winter. Such inclosures ought to be adequate to the size of the farm, but in general, they should not be too large. They may extend from two to ten acres. But inclosures from twenty to sixty acres of pasturage which cannot be rendered arable, would in many places be highly beneficial. Such inclosures we find formed at a high ex pence, in the mountainous parts of Cumberland and Westmoreland, where the pasture is not superior, to what is to be seen upon the generality of the Highland hills.

INCLOSURE OF INFIELD.

On every Highland farm, there is a certain portion of infield land, which is always, without exception, a piece of excellent soil. It varies in extent according to the situation and extent of the farms. On some, it is under ten acres; in others, it extends from ten to thirty, to forty, and even to fifty acres.

To establish a proper system of agriculture in the Highlands, this is the land that ought to be first inclosed. It should be divided into small inclosures from two, to eight or ten acres, with dry stone dykes, as it requires both a sufficient and immediate fence. It is the most valuable land on each farm, and therefore deserves the first attention; especially, as it is the proper foundation for the improvement of all the rest of the farm.

This land, thus divided, should be entirely occupied, at all times, with sown grass and green crops, and with only one crop of barley at every proper period. Being naturally fertile, and already in good tilth, it might be kept constantly in this train of culture, and rendered highly productive without the assistance of manure, or, at least, with but a very little dung at distant intervals.

The infield land thus managed, would afford clover and rye-grass hay, with an after-growth, horsehoed potatoes, turnips, beans, coleworts, and a barley crop, forming, altogether, a produce double in value to what it yields at present; but this is not the principal view, nor the principal, ad vantage to be obtained from this alteration.

A large stock, both of dry and green food, would be provided for the cattle in winter. The quantity of dung would be greatly enlarged, and the whole might then be bestowed on the outfield land, which should be gradually inclosed and cultivated in a similar manner.

This material alteration upon a Highland farm, requires, indeed, a certain degree of information and skill in the farmer: but all the skill necessary, is no more than what is now possessed by every farmer in Scotland, where cultivation has made any progress. The expence requisite for this alteration, is by no means great, nor attended with any risque. It consists entirely in the inclosure of the infield land with dry stone dykes. In return for it, every Highland farmer, who understands his business and his interest, might safely pay ten per cent.; but it would be the interest of any proprietor, to defray this expence at a much lower rate of interest.

HEDGES.

Though the Highlands and Islands in general, must depend for inclosures, upon dry stone walls, yet there are many tracts of ground, which might be profitably inclosed with hedges. These are not nearly so expensive as walls, and if properly planted and managed with care, have great advantages over walls, especially in countries w here shelter is required.

Of all the trees and shrubs now known, there is not one possessed of the excellent properties of the hawthorn for a hedge. It is a native of the Highlands, and grows vigorously in every proper situation. It should not, however, be planted young, which is The hawthorn is in tllls view a very singular plant. Of all the trees and shrubs, either native, or that have been brought into Europe; there is not one yet known that is equal to it for a hedge. The Rosa Eglanteria, Sweet Briar or Eglantine: Prunus *spiHoxaLi.* the Sloe, and Ulcx *europaeus* L. the Whin; have been used in several parts of Scotland.— Hedges also are formed in Sweden of the Hippophae *rham. noides* L. or Sea Buckthorn: and in Russia, of the Robinia *spinosa* L. or Siberian Acacia. These shrubs are indeed armed with spines or prickles, but they are all deficient in somo properties, and deserve not to be regarded, wherever a fence, can be formed of the hawthorn. Some of the American shrubs of the Crataegus kind are the most promising to be of use for this purpose.

too frequently the case. The thorns ought at least to be five years old, and it will be often advantageous, to have them six, seven, or eight years old, in order speedily to establish a good fence. If thorns so old, cannot be obtained, it will be the interest of the planter to keep young thorns in a nursery, till they are of that age, rather than risk them in a fence, when they have had but two or three years growth. It is also expedient, that they never should be planted without a faced dyke, which according to the disposition of the ground, may be from eighteen inches to three feet high. To form a strong fence, they should always be planted in a double row, and never mixed with any other shrubs whatever; as these never fail in time to form so many gaps in a hawthorn hedge. Previous to planting the thorns, the best preparation of the soil is to form it into a lazy bed of potatoes, about four feet broad, in the line of the intended hedge. The potatoes to be raised in October, and the thorns to be planted in February.

HEDGE-ROWS. .1

When hedges were first planted in England, they were always accompanied with a hedge-row of trees. The trees were generally placed, though very improperly, in the line of the hedge. The consequence of this is the decay of the hedge, when thfl trees grow up to a considerable size. But notwithstanding this, the English farmers, by their great care in pruning and splashing, preserve both the hedge and trees, so as to form a sufficient fence.— For two centuries past, the trees in the hedges of England, have afforded the chief supply of timber for the use of the country. The hedge-row trees grow to a large size, and are sufficient for every purpose. They are sometimes equal in value to the land which they inclose. In many places, oaks are cut out of the hedges, which are fit for ship-building. Not less than three-fourths of all the wood in England grows at present in hedge rows. The rest is contained in the royal forests and parks and plantations about the seats of noblemen and gentlemen, which cannot be commanded for common use. Was it not for this stock of wood in the hedges, the whole kingdom, for the most common purposes, would require to be supplied by foreign timber. From this state of the case, the planting of hedge-rows must appear to be a matter of great moment to the proprietors of land and to the public: especially in Scotland where wood in general is scarce, and which by the decay of the natural woods, and the progress of manufacture, has of late risen to a very high price.

The farmers are usually averse to hedge-rows. By being free of them they are freed from any charge of the trees when young; and from the alleged detriment, they are supposed to occasion to the adjacent crop when they are old. It is likewise urged that they ruin the fence; yet this is not the case in England, even where the trees are planted in the line of the hedge. To avoid this however, the trees should never be planted in that line, but in a line parallel to the hedge, and three feet distant from it. The hedge, when full grown, will extend thus far, so that the three feet are not lost. If a line of trees is placed at this distance, and the trees fifteen feet asunder, a hawthorn hedge will receive no injury from them, but with proper management, may continue for a century to be an effectual fence. It is alleged, that a full grown hedge-row of trees affects. the next adjacent ridge, and diminishes the crop. But this is amply recompensed by the superior growth of the whole field in consequence of the shelter. That a hedge-row is unfriendly to the drying of corn in harvest, may happen in very small inclosures in a flat country. But there can be no such effect in fields extending from six to twenty acres on a declivity, or of a very unequal surface, which is the case of most of the inclosures in Scotland.

In some places, the hedge, to appearance, destroys the trees, but this is always owing to the trees being planted in an improper situation, and would therefore fail, whether they were in the neighbourhood of a hedge or not. In other places, the trees not only seem to destroy the hedge, but actually do so; yet this is always occasioned, either by an injuVol. I. H dicious selection of trees, or by their being planted and trained in an improper manner. There can be no doubt, as hundreds of instances might be adduced, that in every proper situation, a sufficient hedge, and a profitable hedge-row of trees may be raised together, without prejudice either to the one or the other.

Rich land, from thirty shillings to four pounds an acre, cannot be profitably employed in plantation of any kind. Land of this sort, is usually in such a. climate, as to stand in no need of shelter for producing the common crops. Hedge-rows, in this case, may perhaps be improper, and they have accordingly, in many such places been laid aside. — But on all land to be inclosed with hedges, which may be in value from two shillings and sixpence to thirty shillings an acre, a hedge-row of trees is certainly most expedient; especially in those fields which require shelter, and in those parts of the country where there is a scarcity of timber.

In the hedge-rows in Scotland very little judgement appears in the choice of the trees. The larch, though hardy, requires more shelter than it can usually have in the line of an inclosure. The same is the case with the New England pine. Wherever the alder, the abele, or the willows will grow well, the black poplar, a much more valuable tree will succeed. The ash is to be avoided, because of the spread of its roots. The Scots fir and Scots elm, because of the spread of their heads; and the pitch and silver fir because of the spread of their branches.

The most eligible trees are those which afford the best timber, which will answer to the soil and situation, and be the least hurtful to the hedge and the adjacent field. Such are the oak, the beech, the plane, and the English elm. In deep and wet grounds, the black poplar is the best tree for a hedge row. In grounds at any considerable height, the birch, the rowan, and the laburnum may be chosen.

In Tirey, and other islands, many of the fields are inclosed with walls of earth, very broad at the foundation, five Of six feet high, and covered with grass from top to bottom. Without answering, in any tolerable degree, the purposes of inclosure, being built of a dry loamy earth, they are perpetually crumbling to pieces, and create to the husbandman a constant annual toil, much greater than what is occasioned by the best fences. But were these mounds of earth covered with coarse robust hedges; by being filled with black and white thorns, crabs, brambles, the dog and buract rose, whins, and other hedge shrubs and trees, they would then become extremely useful. All the old hedges in England are of this kind, and preferable to the neat hawthorn hedge, in a country that stands so much in need of shelter as the Western Islands. This would not only supersede the labour of repairing these earthen mounds, and fence the fields from all inroads, but would improve the climate by affording shelter, and protect the crops from the strength of the winds, which is almost the only danger they have to en- counter.

For the right cultivation of the soil, for the purpose of plantation, and of inclosure by means of hedges, the inhabitants of the Western Islands and Highlands lie under great disadvantages. For these ends, it is necessary that nurseries of trees and hedge plants should be formed in proper places; and that the people should have easy access to purchase garden seeds, the seeds of clover and rye-grass, of turnips and other green winter crops. From all these they are at present excluded. But the proper methods of supplying them with these necessary articles of improvement, must be left with the proprietors and the public.

EMBANKMENT OF RIVERS.

Where the channel of a river is rocky, it is usually deep, and the river seldom overflows it banks, being confined between two walls of rock; but where a river runs rapidly upon a gravel, with soft banks, little elevated above its level, on these it never fails, in a flood, to commit great devastation. This last case is very frequent in the south of Scotland, and also in some parts of the north. The crop upon rich haugh ground is often destroyed by the overflowing of the river; sometimes they are entirely stripped of their vegetable soil; at other times, they are covered with a thick bed of sand and gravel. Frequently, too, the river deserts its course, and cuts for itself a new channel through fertile fields.

Several contrivances have been executed to prevent these hurtful effects. 1. Large banks of earth have been formed, sloping to the river. 2. Perpendicular ramparts of stones and sods have been constructed. 3. Bulwarks of stone contained in a wooden frame are built to defend the banks, and sometimes a large sloping caul of loose stones is formed to divert the course of the river, where it threatens an irruption. These contrivances are sometimes successful, but most frequently otherwise; and they are always laborious and expensive.

There is another method I have often practised, and which answers all the ends sought for by the above contrivances, whenever a rjver runs over soft bottom.

It is by forming a single or double line of stakes in the bed, or on the bank of the river, of the branches of trees. These stakes may be from the thickness of one's wrist, to that of a man's leg; they are to be driven into the Boil between two and four feet deep, and reach above the ground, or above the water, a little higher than the rise of the greatest flood. They may be from six to twelve inches distant from each other; and if there is a double row, they are to be placed in the quincunx order.

Such stakes, thus situated, can neither be displaced nor shaken by any force of water; they stop and entangle every sort of refuse brought down by the river; they intercept the mud and the gravel, which gradually form a bank, and force the river to establish a barrier against its own incursions;—a barrier, likewise, far more efficacious, and more permanent, than any that can be formed by art with earth and stones.

It is an obvious property of this mode of defence against the encroachments of rivers, that it is easily and quickly executed, and at a mere trifle of expence. A single cart-load of such stakes, in some situations, might effectually preserve many acres of rich land. Every river, by the above method, may be thus turned

and directed in its course at will. It would always be advantageous if the stakes employed in this way, were of the different sorts of willows.

These take root, grow, and form a strong living fence against the river. But if stakes of willows cannot be provided, cuttings or truncheons of willows ought to be sunk in along with the stakes, and intermixed with them.

For which purpose, the shrubby and low growing willows, are more proper than the mast willow, the osier, the crack willow, or any others which grow up to a tree.

A different method, though founded on the same principle, has been successfully practised in slow running rivers, flowing through soft, deep earthy strata. The encroachments of such rivers are slower in their progress, but often more prejudicial than those of the former.

When the bank and the adjacent ground is threatened by such a river, the hurtful consequences apprehended may be prevented in the following manner:—Let a large quantity of the small brandies of trees, of broom, brambles, or such like brushwood, and especially of whins, be placed in the river, near the side where it threatens to encroach.

If the river runs slow, they require merely to be thrown in; but if its current is considerable, they must be stuck into the bottom. This heap of rubbish intercepts the slime and mud of the river, which quickly accumulates into a bank, and becomes a most effectual defence against any further encroachment in that quarter.

SECTION IV. INSTRUMENTS.

The instruments of agriculture in the Hebrides, are of a very early and unimproved age of the world. They are apparently the same that were used when the art of tillage was first introduced into these countries. They must necessarily, therefore, be simple, and must, to persons of the present aera, appear very imperfect. Their imperfection, however, cannot be so much ascribed to the want of ingenuity in the inhabitants, as to the situation of their country, and the disadvantages to which they have hitherto been liable. Having no command either

of wood or of iron; uninstructed in the mechanical powers; and strangers to the progress of the mechanical arts, in the more improved parts of the kingdom; it is no wonder that their implements of husbandry should stiil remain extremely defective.

All that are at present in use, require either to be laid aside, or to be considerably altered. It is well known how much of the labour of men and horses is prodigally thrown away, where bad instruments of agriculture are used, which is at present the case in the Highlands; and, on the other hand, how much that labour is facilitated and abridged, and the crop enlarged, by instruments of a proper construction. The common instruments have now been brought to a very considerable degree cf perfection in many parts of the Lowlands. They have been thoroughly tried, by the experience of many years, in the hands of the common farmers, and found by them to be effectual and highly profitable. These instruments are equally applicable to the arable lands in the Highlands, and would there produce the same beneficial effects. Their introduction, therefore, ought to be a principal object with all proprietors, and with all the considerable farmers. To be brought into use by the general body of the people, they require only to be fully known.

PLOUGH.

The Highland plough is a very singular and feeble instrument: Its whole length is about four feet seven inches. Like the plough used by the ancients, it has only one stilt or handle, by which it is directed; a slight mold-board is fastened to it with two leather straps; and the sock and coulter are bound together at the point with a ring of iron. To this plough there are four horses yoked abreast; their traces are thongs of leather; the driver, with the reins fixed on a cross stick, walks before the horses backwards, and strikes them on the face to make them proceed forwards. The ploughman holding the stilt, walks not behind, but by the side of the plough, directing it with one hand; another man follows with a spade, to lay down the turf that is torn off. The want of a proper mold-board, is the reason why the labour of this additional man is required to finish the furrow. In other places, they have a plough similar to this, but with two stilts, which are almost erect; so that the man who holds the plough, walks upright between them. All the work executed by this plough, which occupies four horses and three men, ought to be performed by one, man and two horses: so far behind are the Hebridians in the improvements of the plough, and so uninformed they still are, in the value of the labour of men and cattle.

The two-horse plough, held and driven by one man, is the most useful improvement in husbandry, that has been introduced into Scotland for forty years past. Its usefulness is so great, that it must, in time, universally prevail; and the sooner the better: It promises more than any thing, to correct the bad system of tillage in Scotland. It is of sufficient power for all the old arable land in the Highlands, which is, in general, of a thin and light soil. Where wild land is to be broken up, a stronger plough, and a stronger team will be necessary; but for all the land already in tillage, the light Scots plough for two horses, as improved in many places, is the most proper instrument, and ought to be universally used in the Highlands.

REESTLE.

There is a very singular instrument used in the Hebrides termed the reestle, and called in English the sickle plough. In its use, it resembles the modern instrument called a scarificator, or sward cutter; which is intended to cut a tough sward, or tough roots in the soil, in order to make the %vork of the plough easy. The scarificator has four or five or more coulters, but the reestle has only one. It is an instrument of the shape, and nearly of the size of the Hebridian plough, with a beam and one stilt. It is usually about three feet long. It is drawn by one horse, which is led by a man, and another man holds and directs it by the stilt. It has no sock, and only a single iron coulter, of the size and shape of a reaping hook, but stronger, which is drawn through the soil about eight inch-

es deep. It is drawn before the plough, in order to cut the strong twisted roots of the creeping restharrow, the sandy Ouonis *repens,* Linn.

carex, and other repent plants, with which the sandy soil of many of the islands is particularly infested. These are powerful enough to obstruct the progress of so weak a plough, as that which is commonly used, and therefore the reestle is employed.

In this way, five men and five horses are taken up in the tillage of a ley field, not very old, and of a light sandy soil, which with a proper plough should occupy only two tolerable horses and one man. If the reestle is at all necessary, it should be changed in its form to a simple scarificator, with a streight coulter, and to be held and driven by a single man.

CASCROME.

A great part of the land in the Highlands and Islands, instead of being ploughed by cattle, is cultivated with human labour, and dug by an instrument called the Cascrome, in English, the crooked foot, or crooked spade. This is a strong coarse spade, about six feet long, with a thick flat wooden head, anned at the extremity with a sharp narrow piece of iron. The iron serves the purpose of a sock, to penetrate the soil, and the wooden head, that of a mold-board to turn over the turf. The great length of the shaft, and the bulky wooden head, which Carex *arenarius,* Linn.

serves as a fulcrum, form a lever of considerable power. This instrument is exceedingly well adapted to cultivate the earth among fixed rocks, where the plough cannot go, or where the soil is so filled with large loose stones as not to be arable.

To a stranger, it may appear a very uncouth instrument, and it might, no doubt, be much better' constructed than it is at present. But even in its present rude form, it is highly useful, and indeed necessary in many parts of the Highlands. In the parish of Ederachilis, there is not as much arable land as would give employment to three ploughs; though a parish near thirty miles long with above one thousand in-

habitants. The parish of Uig in the Lewes, equally extensive and more populous, has not in it one plough. In the island of Bernera, containing above two hundred people, there is not one ridge where the plough could go, it is so encumbered with fast rocks. In tracts of the country, such as these, there can be no culture but with the spade, and the inhabitants cannot subsist without corn and potatoes.

With this instrument, a Highlander will open up more ground in a day, and render it fit for the sowing of grain, than could be done by two or three men, with any other spades that are commonly used. He will dig as much ground in a day as will sow more than a peck of oats. If he works assiduously, from about Christmas, to near the end of April, he will prepare land sufficient to sow five bolls. After this, he will dig as much land in a day as will sow two pecks of bear; and in the course of the season, will cultivate as much land with his spade, as is sufficient to supply a family of seven or eight persons, the year round, with meal and potatoes.

The land dug with the cascrome, always affords a more considerable increase, than that which is laboured with the plough. If a boll of bear, raised with the plough on good land, yields ten bolls; raised by the spade, it would produce better than thirteen; and on poorer land, the proportion in favour of the spade is still larger. In general, the dug land yields in bear above two seeds more of increase, than land of the same kind when ploughed. As an instance of the extraordinary produce of this grain, sown upon ground cultivated with the cascrome; a farmer in the parish of Bracadale, in the year 1 763, being in scarcity of seed bear, sowed five lippies extremely thin, upon rich dug land. From this he had five bolls in return, which amounts to sixty-four fold. On poor ley land, a boll of oats, after the plough, will bring only three bolls, but will produce five after the spade. In such land, however, it is observed, that the third crop on what is ploughed, is sometimes better than the third crop on what is worked by the spade. It appears, in general, that a field laboured with the cascrome, affords, usually, near one third more crop, than if laboured with the plough. Poor land will afford near one half more. But then it must be noticed, that their tillage with the plough is very imperfect, and the soil scarcely half laboured.

In Barra, and other parts of the Long Island, they sow their bear in the same way as they plant their potatoes in lazy beds. They lay sea ware on the green sward in winter. In February they dig trenches, and cast out the earth, on each side, upon the beds. When it is perfectly dry, in the beginning of May, they sow their bear, and then harrow it with a hand harrow, which is an instrument like a garden rake with wooden teeth. In this way, they obtain exceeding good crops of that grain, and as they sow it very thin, they have a large increase compared to the quantity of seed.

But though a field, laboured by the spade, may produce a larger crop than by the plough, this advantage must be greatly overbalanced by the difference between the value of the labour of men and. cattle, at least, wherever human labour can be profitably applied. In the Isle of Skye, a plough with four horses and three men, was found, in five days, to labour only so much land as would" sow a boll of bear, or five firlots of oats. The same quantity of land was dug by twelve men in the same time. The expence of this plough to the farmer was estimated at six shillings and nine-pence per week, and the labour of the twelve men, at nineteen shillings per week. Without attending to this price of labour, though to many it must appear very extraordinary; it is sufficient at present to observe, that the culture with the spade, must therefore be three times more expensive than with the plough; and that the return of one third more crop can never be equivalent for this great difference of expence. Besides, their culture with the spade, is much more perfect in its kind, than what is performed with their plough. The difference between them, as now stated, is great; but was the operation of the spade to be compared to that of a well equipped plough; the difference against

the spade would be three or four times greater.
i

A tenant on a large farm, with much arable land, ploughs a considerable quantity of it in winter; but as his horses never taste a morsel either of corn or dry forage, and have only what they can pick up in the fields, they are so wasted by the winter labour, that they are incapable of going through the spring work. The making of the bear land, therefore, falls to be executed by his servants with the spade: the frequency of this case has rendered it customary to sow all their bear upon land so cultivated. The custom is followed, but the cause of it being forgot, they now look upon it, not as proceeding from necessity, but as an eligible practice. The digging of land, where it is necessary, leads the inhabitants to pracVol. I. I tise it in places where there is no necessity for it at all. Many fields are to be seen worked by the spade, which might be much more profitably cultivated by the plough. It is even manifest, that no land in the Highlands, where the plough can travel, should be cultivated with the spade.

The cascrome, therefore, should unquestionably be laid aside upon all extensive arable fields; yet there are situations, in which it is a convenient and useful instrument. Many possessions have not employment for a plough. Many of them are too small, even for the fourth part of one. In this case, the small tenant keeps no horse, and finding it difficult to procure the use of a plough, manufactures the little arable land he has with his own labour. It is a beneficial instrument likewise in cultivating; those rocky tracts which are inaccessible to the plough.— They are thereby brought to yield profitable crops of corn and potatoes, and afterwards much better pasture than they would otherwise do. It is an excellent tool in the hands of the cottager or day labourer, who possess a little land, and friendly to the culture and population of the country.

The cascrome might be rendered useful in many places as well as in the Highlands; particularly on steep hills

and places, where the plough cannot go. Sue h places, by means of this instrument might b brought into tilth for two or three crops, the surfac e smoothed, and the succeeding pasture greatly mended.

Marrow.

The harrows commonly used in the Highlands are still more imperlect, if possible, than the ploughs. Some of them, which are but like hay rakes, are managed by the hand: others, drawn by horses, are light and feeble, with wooden teeth, which may scratch the surface and cover the seed, but can have no effect in breaking the soil. The grounds that have been kept in constant tillage, are easy both to plough and harrow: but where ley land is broken up, the tillage is so ineffectual, that it would require the aid of harrows of greater power. The harrows, therefore, should be made much heavier, and none should be permitted with wooden teeth.

There is great opportunity in the Highlands of breaking up moorish and mossy land, and of reducing it into culture; but this cannot be atchieved entirely by the plough; the stress of the work must lie on the heavy break-harrow. After such ground has been opened by the plough, the heavy break will at one time, during drought, do more execution in subduing the soil, than what could be accomplished by repeated ploughings. It is an instrument, therefore, that ought to be provided, wherever any improvement of this kind is intended.

CL0UMA1T.

The island of Lismore is of a very peculiar soil, and different from that of all the other Hebrides. The island is composed almost entirely of black limestone. The soil above this rock is thin, of a black colour, and very full of calcareous earth. In consequence of this, the corn fields are over-run with several very rank and hurtful weeds; particularly the Spear-thistle , the Hemp Agrimony f, and especially by the Way-thistle This has led the inhabitants to a contrivance very well adapted for destroying them. It is a pair of large strong wooden pincers: their jaws are ten inches, and their handles two feet ten inches long; the whole instrument being three feet eight inches in length. The handles, when expanded, are at the extremity two feet asunder. It is called in Gaelic the clou-mait, or timber tongs. When the thistles are of a proper age to be destroyed, a man traverses the field with this instrument, and draws them out by the root, more expe Carduus *lanceolatus*. Linn.

,i. Eupatorium *Cannabinum.* Linn.

J Serratula *arvensis.* Lion.

ditiously, and with less detriment to the crop, than when pulled by the hand, covered with a thick glove, which is the practice in other parts of Scotland.

It is an instrument of considerable power, and so well calculated for the purpose, that it deserVes being brought into use in other places. Beside the above weeds, it is well suited to eradicate the Sowthistle , the Com Sow-thistle f, the Burdock J, Mugwort §, Knapweed , Cow Parsnip Blue Bottle, and others, which generally make too great a figure in our corn fields.

CART.

The want of proper carriages in the Highlands is one of the great obstacles to the progress of agriculture, and of every improvement. Having no Sonchus *oleraceus.* Linn.

+ Sonchus *arvensis.* Linn.

Arctium *Lappa.* Linn.

§ Artemisia *vulgaris.* Linn.

Ccntaurea *nigra.* Linn.

! Hcracleum *Sphondylium.* Linn.

Centaurea *Cyanus.* Linn.

carts, their corn, straw, manures, fuel, stone, timber, sea-weed and kelp, the articles necessary in the fisheries, and every other bulky commodity, must be transported from one place to another on horseback, or on sledges. This must triple or quadruple the expence of their carriage. It must prevent, particularly, the use of the natural manures, with which the country abounds; as without cheap carriage they cannot be rendered profitable.

The roads in most places are so bad, as to render the use of wheel-carriages impossible; but they are not brought into use even where the natural roads would admit them. In the dry dale country of Cantire there are few carts; and even at the royal burgh of Campbelton there was not a cart of any kind till the year 1756. In the islands of South Uist, North Uist, and lienbecula, the country is so flat, and the natural roads so good, that every heavy article might be transported on wheels; yet no cart has ever yet made its appearance in these islands. This must be a great drawback on the profits arising from the valuable manufacture of kelp. Wherever the farmer cannot employ a cart, he must not only retain a much greater number of horses and servants than would be otherwise necessary for his ordinary work, but he must also be excluded from the numerous advantages that arise from that common but most useful machine.

The remedy must lie with the proprietors of the country, whose interest loudly calls on them to render, wherever it is practicable, the roads of every parish, and indeed upon every farm, accessible to carts, and to establish the use of them among all their tenants.

/ SECTION V. MANURES. NATURAL MANURES.

Natural manures are such as are provided by nature without any care or preparation on the part of the farmer, and are generally substances of the fossil kingdom. Artificial manures, on the other hand, are the various sorts of dung, quicklime, animal and vegetable substances, composts, ashes, water manure, and others which are to be obtained only by being carefully preserved, or in consequence of some process of art.

The natural manures to be had in the Highlands and Islands form one of the greatest advantages which these countries possess in agriculture. They are, clay, sand, shell marle, stone marie, clay marle, sea shells, shelly sand, coral, sea sleech, and sea weeds. These are valuable wherever there is no manure to be obtained, except the artificial manure produced upon the farm. But they are still more valuable and necessary where there is no sufficient stock of artificial manure provided, which is the general case in the Highlands, where the cattle are not housed, nor dunghills of any consequence formed. Excepting sea ware, the whole of these natural manures have hitherto been neglected, though in other countries they would be accounted a treasure.

Were but the common farmers once initiated in the practice of these manures, there is no doubt but they would employ and pursue them with assiduity. For though there are no people more backward to any new improvement where they see not the certainty of the event, yet there are none who can more steadily pursue any branch of industry, when once they are persuaded to adopt it, and especially when convinced by finding that it is advantageous.

These manures deserve to be separately considered...

CLAY.

The most essential property of a soil is to possess a right proportion of clay and sand. When this is the case, and the soil otherwise well situated, though never so poor, it can be advanced by manures and culture to the greatest perfection. But if the clay and sand.re in undue proportion, much of the manure and labour bestowed upon such a soil will be but ill rewarded. The addition of sand to a clay soil, and of clay to a sandy soil, has therefore been a rational practice, wherever cultivation has made any considerable progress;

The soil in general in the Highlands and Islands is deficient in clay. It is overloaded either with gravel or with sand. There are many tracts of sandy soil so light, that, when turned up by the plough, it is apt even to blow with the w ind. An addition of clay to such soils would add greatly to their fertility. It is true, indeed, that strata of clay, such as prevail in champaign countries, are rarely to be met with in the Highlands. But there are everywhere to be found, hollow grounds and morasses, which are dry in summer, filled to a considerable depth with the most fertile of all clay, the sediment of water. These do in most places afford an excellent material to fertilise the lighter soils, and require only cheap carriage and a degree of labour that would be amply rewarded. The benefit of this practice, or of forming feal middings, as they are called, is well known in other parts of Scotland, where the price of labour and the value of land are very considerable.

SAND.

Clay soils, capable of being improved by an addition of sand, are very unfrequent in the Highlands. But there is another soil which common sea sand seems to meliorate to a great degree. It was observed on several occasions, that where the sea sand was blown from the shore on a mossy soil, a considerable alteration took place. The moss covered with from half an inch, to two, three, or four inches of sand, assumed a very different appearance: wherever the sand reached, the moss became green. The Heather , the Ling f, the Deer's Hair J, the Wire Bent §, and other plants of a mossy soil, gradually gave way, and were succeeded by a growth of the very best pasture grasses, which communicated a verdure to the soil which was never seen before. These effects probably proceed in a great measure from the saline, but especially from the calcareous matter contained in the sand. This process of nature, however, may possibly in some places be imitated to advantage by art.

Erica *vulgaris.* Linn. + Nardus *stricta.* Linn.

J Scirpus *caespitosus.* Linn.

Juncus *squarrosus.* Linn.

SHELL MARLE.

Wherever shell marle is found in abundance, it becomes a most valuable acquisition. It not only improves the soil, but it becomes the parent of every other improvement. The Stewartry of Kirkcudbright, and the counties of Wigton and Forfar, are instances of this. The surprising and solid improvements now to be observed in these countries, are all to be dated from the discovery of the shell marle. It is the purest, and consequently the strongest of all the calcareous earths; and is applicable to a greater variety of soils and situations than any other manure. It is not only the most effectual, but where it is found in plenty, it is also the cheapest of all manures.

Shell marle has been little enquired after in the Highlands and Western Is-

lands; yet there is reason to believe that it is to be found in many places, as the fresh water snails, from whose shells it is formed, abound in many of the standing waters. It was observed in the island of Ila, in strata from three to six feet deep, and of considerable extent, under a cover of moss. It has also been discovered in some bos in the island of Lismore, and used by some of the formers, though in a very injudicious manner.

When the ground is marled, they take one crop of oats and three of bear; they then surfer the field to continue ley three years, and sometimes only two; after which they again take the crop of oats, and three crops of bear, as before. These crops, which have hitherto been considerable, say a great deal both for the groodness of the soil and the manure. But what soil, with the assistance only of a forcing manure, can go on to be scourged with eight white crops in ten years, without being destroyed? Were these farmers but acquainted with a proper rotation, and with the cultivation of green crops, they might reap from their marle great and lasting advantage. By their present practice, their profit will be but temporary, and the loss in the end certain, both to themselves and their landlords.

Wherever there is access to shell marle in the Highlands, it cannot, perhaps, be more properly applied, than upon pasture grounds over-run with heath. There it will have its ordinary effect, of extirpating the heath, and of producing a rich growth of the best grasses and of white clover in its place.

STONE MARLE.

Though stone marle, or rock marle, is rather a rare production in Scotland, and especially in the

Highlands, it abounds in the island of Ila in an inexhaustible quantity. The centre of the island is a dale country, where there is 'a fine valley, about six miles long, and three or four in breadth, extending from Lochindaal to the Sound of Ila, which is all arable and well inhabited. Besides abundance of limestone, this tract contains a great number of little hills, which are composed from top to bottom of rock marle

of an excellent quality. It is so soft as to be easily dug, is richly impregnated with calcareous earth, and falls to powder upon exposure to the air; properties which render it extremely valuable. Though this part of the island is naturally fertile both in grass and corn, there is no doubt but that a proper application of this manure would produce a great change upon it for the better.

Clay marle was not observed any where in the West Highlands or Hebrides in sufficient quantity to be useful, excepn the Isle of Man. In the low grounds in that island there are in some places beds of an excellent clay marle, of a red colour, and the same with what has produced most beneficial effects in Cheshire. It is precisely adapted for the light dry grounds which abound in the island: but it is the disadvantage of clay marle, that it cannot bear the expence of a very distant carriage.

i MARBLE EARTH.

There is another natural manure which may be noticed in this place,—the marble earth of the Isle of Skye. This might readily be considered as a marle, but in its nature and properties it is widely different from any thing of the marle kind. No earth precisely of this sort has anywhere else been discovered in Britain. In its district of Strath in this island there are extensive strata of a pure white marble. In its neighbourhood there are strata of this earth. The earth is white, like the marble, and as purely calcareous. It may be dug with a spade. It is friable and powdery when dry, rough to the touch, and exactly resembles the suhstance of the marble when reduced to powder. To a person on the spot it must appear to be either the white marble decomposed and reduced to an earth, or the earth of which the white marble consists, that has not been consolidated into the form of a stone.

Whichsoever of these may be the case, it forms a great body of pure natural lime, and a most valuable manure. It is disposed in thick strata, which reach near to the surface of the earth, and are in Paractonium *album.* the same position as the marble, being ittclined to the hori6on at a small angle. It is from strata of this earth that the strata of the white marble are evidently formed. Though it is of the greatest value as a manure, it has hitherto been neglected. It is to be had in inexhaustible quantity at the easiest rate, and is capable to enrich to a high degree all the adjacent country.

StiVTJER.

There is a sort of lime, or calcareous earth, found, not only in the Highlands, but in many other parts of Scotland, which has hitherto been overlooked as a manure. It is that earth which is deposited by calcareous or petrifying springs, and is known by the name of sinter . It is sometimes hardened to a considerable degree, but is frequently a white earth so soft as to be dug and spread on a field with the spade. It occurs in many parts of England, where it is not neglected, as it is with us. There is a meadow near Worsley in Lancashire, which contains a considerable body of this earth. There it is not only used as a manure, but it is burnt for lime by a very laborious operation. To make it cohere, it is first formed, with an addition of clay, into bricks, and these, when dried, are calcined into quicklime Undukijo *font turn.* VOL. III. K for building. There are large quantities of this earth in several places in Scotland,—in Clydesdale, and especially in Eskdale, where it has never been Used either as a manure or for building, though in a country where there is neither marle nor limestone.

If this be the case in the south of Scotland, it is not surprising that the use of this earth should be neglected in the Highlands. There are considerable quantities of it in the island of Lismore and especially in the island of Upper Sheuna. This island is composed entirely of limestone; all its springs are heavily loaded with calcareous earth. This they dcposite in their channels, and it has accumulated in the course of time to a prodigious quantity. The island is of a richer soil, and lets at a higher rent, than most parts of the Highlands. Its soil being formed on limestone, it stands little in need of a calcareous manure. But this earth might be employed with great advantage on the adjacent lands of Appin, from which the island is separated only by a narrow sound.

SEA SHELLS.

The use of sea shells as a manure was first niadr known in the north of Ireland about the end of the seventeenth century. The practice came to be adopted 1 soon after on the opposite coasts of Galloway, where it has ever since been pursued to a great extent, though still neglected, and almost unknown, in the other parts of Scotland. Beside other places in Galloway, there are remarkable shell banks at the mouth of the river Cree. Here there are above thirty sail of vessels, from thirty to one hundred tons, constantly employed in transporting the shells from this place to the other parts of Galloway, to Ayrshire, Dumfriesshire, Cumberland, and even to Ireland. The experience of above half a century, and in the hands of the «iost skillful farmers in these countries, shows them to be a manure that deserves to be purchased even at a high price.

By the want of information, and by supineness among those who cultivate land on the shores of Scotland, the advantage to be reaped from sea shells has been quite overlooked. ' There are, indeed, tracts of bold shore where shells are not to be found; yet even in such tracts, there are generally small bays and inlets, where shells are to be had in abundance. When thrown in by the tide, they ought immediately to be cast up in heaps beyond flood mark, and there reserved for use, as the shells thrown in by one tide, are apt to be swept away by another. The labour to obtain them, even in this way, is small, compared to what they cost in other places, by water carriage.

Upon most of the coasts of Scotland, and in all the Hebrides, they are to be had in greater plenty, and at an easier rate. Where the shores are flat, there are generally beds of them, between floodmark and the lowest ebb. In other places, there are banks of shells, above flood-mark, overgrown with grass, which have been left there by extraordinary tides, or by the retreat of the sea. In one or other of these situations, a great body of shells is to be found in many places, which is not only sufficient for the grounds immediately adjacent, but for aU the neighbourhood.

In the Island of Barra, there is an extensive sand, called the Cray-more of Kil-barra. It is several square miles in extent, and contains a quantity of sea shells of the best kind, sufficient to manure a county. With these, the inhabitants might raise their land to the highest degree of fertility; but they are wholly unacquainted with the use of them. The labour they employ in a couple of years, io giving their ground a straggling cover of sea weeds, which lasts but one season, if laid out upon shells, would communicate a much greater fertility to the soil for fifty years.

All sorts of shells may be applied as a manure; but those of a small size are to be preferred, because they mix more thoroughly with the soil: They are likewise to be chosen as free as possible from any mixture of sand or gravel. When situated in banks above floodmark, where they have remained long, and though apparently in a decayed state, they still have the same fertilising, effects.

They appear to be the most durable of all manures. Some extensive fields were shelled by Mr Craik of Arbigland, fifty years ago, with shells found on his own shore. Above thirty acres of these fields soon after afforded twelve successive crops of horsehoed wheat. They have since been employed in a proper succession of white and green crops. They still retail their fertility, and are greatly superior in their produce to the neighbouring lands, of a similar nature, that never were shelled. One of these shelled fields yielded, for a number of years, the heaviest crops of lucerne that have been raised in Scotland, i

Sheila have also been most successfully applied to meadow land in Galloway. This was' first done by Mr Heron of Heron, about eighty years ago. He then shelled plentifully some of his meadows on the Cree which are never in, tillage: A great increase in the hay erop was the immediate consequence; and k has always, continued to be about double the quantity, compared to the hay produced on the same sort of meadow land that has never received any shells.

SHELL SAND.

There is to be found, almost everywhere, upon the sea shores, another material of improvement, equally neglected with many others. This, to appearance is sand, but is chiefly composed of the substance of shells. Much of our sea sand consists of the hard particles of siliceous stones, which cannot be dissolved; and which, as a manure, can act only by rendering an adhesive soil more friable and porous. A great deal of that sand, however, is mixed more or less, with the matter of shells reduced to powder; and so far, it is capable of acting in a different manner, as a calcareous manure. In some places, if the sand on the sea shore is examined by a good eye, or by the help of a magnifying glass, it may be perceived to be composed, almost entirely, of the particles of shells. This can never fail to be a valuable manure. It is more so, indeed, than even the shells; for, by being reduced to powder, it is capable of being incorporated more intimately with the soil. It acts not only as a calcareous manure, but likewise as a sand, in rendering the soil more pervious. Wherever this shelly sand, therefore, occurs, which it does in great abundance, in many places, the farmer grossly mistakes his interest, if he does not apply it to use.

CORAL.

On several parts of the British coast, there is a small species of coral, which grows in the sea; and nowhere in larger quantities, than upon the shore of some of the Hebrides . It is usually from half an inch, to two or three inches in length, of the thickness of a small quill, and considerably branched. Like all other coral, it is of a calcareous substance; it is a natural lime; and, of course, a powerful manure. It is dredged out of the sea at Falmouth, and on the adjoining shores in Cornwall; where a barge-load of it, which will dress an acre, is usually delivered at a price, from ten to fifteen shillings; but, in many parts of the Hebrides, this manure is to be

had in abundance, without such expensive labour. In some places, it is thrown out in heaps by the tide; in others, it forms banks above flood-mark, deposited there by former inundations:—In both cases, it requires only to be removed, and spread on the adjoining fields.

Millepora *Britannica.*—Coralliura album pumilum nolira. Raji Syn. iii. p. 32. o. 1. 8EA SLEECH.

The great improvements which have been made in the course of forty years, in the extensive country of Galloway, have been chiefly owing to the application of natural manures. Among these, sea-sleeeh has been most advantageously used, though Uttle employed, and oven scarcely known as a manure, in other parts of Scotland

It is the sediment of the ocean, It is taken up in most harbours upon the flukes of the anchors. It abounds, especially, about the mouths of rivera, and upon those shores where the beach is of a clayey, not of a sandy consistence. It is a mass of all the animal and vegetable substances of the sea, in a. putrid state, accompanied with a considerable; pojf tion of calcareous matter and sea salt, all wcorpch rated with the fine clay which subsides from the waters of the ocean. It must therefore be an enriclnng manure, and this has been found to be the case, wherever it has been tried.

It is to be had in great plenty in many parts of the Hebrides and West Highlands, and in all other places in Scotland where the shores are commonly called sleechy. "Its effects on the thin, dry, hazely soils on the coasts of Galloway, have been very be neficial. On the surface, it is of a grey colour; but at the depth of a foot or two, it is of a blueish or blackish cast; the usual consequence of putrefaction. When dug, it is soft and smooth like the most tenacious clay, but falls to powder in the air or in the earth, i

Much depends on its being mixed with the soil when it is recently dug. The putrid animal and vegetable substance it contains, is in a great measure lost by long exposure. It smells strong of volatile salts when hrst dug, but this

smell goes off when it has been long spread abroad to the air. If it cannot be ploughed into the soil soon after it is dug out, it should be thrown into large heaps, mixed with shells, sea weeds, and all the refuse of the sea that is within reach; from thence it should be transported to. the field that is tq be immediately pkugbd.

Sea weecb, sea wrack, or sea wajre, as they ai» sometimes called, are everywhere known as a manure, and it is almost the only one that is used in the Western Highlands and Islands. It is formed chiefly by four plants:—These are the sea oak, the sea Fucus *vaiculosus,* Lion. cracker , the serrated wrack J, and the tangle . All the other plants growing in the sea, and which are very numerous, are of a similar substance, and capable, in some degree, to answer the same purpose; but they are either inconsiderable in quantity, or attached to particular places. The above four plants universally occupy the British shores; and form the chief material, both for manure, and for the manufacture of kelp.

The good effects of this manure are very considerable, but they are not durable. As used at present, it adds greatly to one, or even to two white crops, but its influence in the soil seems then to cease. It is usually applied to the barley crop. The grain produced, is distinguished by the name of ware barley, and is generally reckoned to be of the best quality. But though this manure, in its operation, is not very permanent; yet, while it lasts, it forms a very enriching addition to the soil, and desei»ves to be held in repute. It is to be had in great cjuantities, at a small ex pence, and often in places w here other manures are not to be obtained. Wherever it abounds, it ought to be more carefully and copiously collected than at present, and more judiciously applied: for though universally employed, it is very grossly mismanaged.

+ Focus *nodosus,* Linn. X *terrains,* Linn. *digitatus,* Linn.

There is a remarkable property in all plants that grow under water, whether in fresh waters or in the sea; that, in the air, they dry more suddenly than any others. The sea weeds, though gross and succulent when taken out of the sea, by exposure to the air in dry weather, soon shrivel away to a mere film. If an acre of land is compleatly covered with them, and they are allowed to remain on the surface for a few days, during drying weather in the month of May, the whole would not weigh five hundred pounds weight. The valuable part of their substance, which constitutes their bulk and weight, evaporates. The slender fibrous parts of their substance, reduced to mere threads, only remain; so that it is like manuring land with cobwebs.

By inattention to this, more than three fourths of the value of all the sea weeds used in Scotland, as a manure, are lost. 1 he obvious remedy, is to plough them down immediately when laid on the land; by which means, their whole substunce, and their whole value are secured in the soil.

As the appearance of a quantity of sea weeds on the beach is somewhat casual, depending on the tides and winds: when they happen to be thrown up, they are carried from the shore and spread on the land, till they can be overtaken by the plough; but were they properly managed, they would never be carried from the shore to the land in their recent state. They should be thrown into large heaps, in the form of dunghills, above flood-mark, and there reserved for use. They ought to be mixed, if possible, with, sea sleech, nor suffered to remain long in these heaps; only from one to four months, as their putrefaction is very rapid. When taken fresh from the shore, they are so bulky, compared to their weight, that an ordinary cart cannot contain a sufficient load for a horse; but wlen kept for a little time in such heaps, they become compacted; much heavier in proportion to their bulk; and more easily transported. By this method, likewise, the sea weeds may be obtained from the sea at all times of the year, as opportunity offers; and from the heaps in which they are lodged, may be transported to the land where they are to be used, and when they are immediately to be ploughed in.

It has been a matter of doubt, with some proprietors and farmers, whether sea weeds on a shore, can be most profitably employed as a manure, or in the making of kelp. One great proprietor in the Hebrides, from excellent motives, resigned his profits upon kelp, and prohibited the manufacture of. it, that his tenants might be accommodated, and the lands hnpimed with the sea weeds. The manufacture of kelp, and the use of sea weed as a manure, are by no means, however, incompatible.

Kelp cannot be manufactured to much advantage, but from sea weeds that are quite fresh. It is true, indeed, that on the coasts of England, some kelp is made from drifted sea wrack; but it cannot be a very profitable operation. The kelp obtained from such weeds, can neither be great in quantity, nor of a good quality. The float wrack, or drifted sea weeds, are always, in some degree, advanced in putrefaction. In proportion as they are putrid, their yield of fixed alcaline salt must be less; and the proportion of other salts , which debase the quality of the kelp, greater.

The best kelp we have, is that "which is manufactured in the Hebrides. There, it is made from sea weeds, cut fresh from the rocks, and transported to the shore with great labour. But though sea weeds in this way, may be profitably employed in making kelp, they could not afford such a degree of labour and expence, to be applied as a manure. It is certain, at least, that to convert them into kelp, is a more advantageous way of using them; but the float wrack, which, in its half putrid state, is improper for kelp, is equally valuable as a manure with the fresh sea weeds. There needs, therefore, be no interference, in the application of sea weeds for the These salts are chiefly sea salt, Glauber's salt, and the two bitter salts formed of Magnesia with the vitriolic and muriatic acids.

purpose of making kelp, and for the purpose of manure. The fresh weeds, cut from the rocks, answer best for kelp:— The drifted weeds, thrown in upon the shore, answer best for the fields; but neither of the two can answer the op-

posite purpose with much emolument. Sea weeds may therefore be employed in agriculture, to their full extent, without encroaching on the manufacture of kelp. All the sea weeds, growing on any tract of coast, form a small quantity, compared to the drift weeds thrown in, were they but carefully collected. BRA RESTS.

The braken may also be considered as a natural manure, and is a plant that deserves particular attention in the Highlands, where it abounds in immense quantities. The roots of it, which are strong and succulent, when they happen to be thrown up, are poisonous to cattle. Its stems and foliage arc not touched by any quadruped, nor even by the caterpillar of any insect. It may therefore be reckoned inimical to all animals. It always occupies land that produces good grass. In the height of summer, all the pasture it overshades is shunned by cattle and lost, and it is generally of that soft kind which is of little use in winter. It is particularly hurtful in Pteris *aquilina.* Linn. The female fern. sheep walks; and to this the farmers who raise sheep in the Highlands should attend.

That disease in sheep, called the braxy, so well known in the south of Scotland, and now so bitterly complained of in the Highlands, is partly, if not chiefly owing to this pernicious plant. The disease prevails most in the grounds that are over-run with it. Immediately after the rise of the braken, in the beginning of summer, and after its fall, late in autumn, the braxy is most prevalent and mortal. In both seasons, the sheep are tempted from scarcity to devour the fresh succulent grass, reared under the thick shade of the braken, which brings on the disorder. It is a plant, thus noxious, in all grasing farms, and should by all possible means be extirpated.

To destroy it, however, is more than can be expected, unless by its destruction, it can be converted to some use. There are fortunately three purposes which it may be made to answer. It makes a durable and excellent thatch, but its consumption in this way can never be considerable. It may in some places be burnt,, and converted into ashes, with sufficient profit. But to cut it for the purpose of manure, seems to be the most extensive and effectual way of getting the better of it.

It is soon greatly diminished, and would probably, in time, be fully exterminated, by being repeat edly cut. It is well known to the people who have made fern ashes, that when they have cut the hraken for two, or at most, for three years successively, it becomes so diminished in quantity, that it is not worth their while to pursue the work another season, on the same ground.

There can be no doubt, that if the braken was cut early in summer, in its most succulent state, thrown into great heaps, and permitted to rot till the following spring, that it would furnish a valuable feeding manure to any soil. By this practice, the farmer might not only add to his stock of manure, but increase the quantity and improve the quality of his pasture. For these purposes he might find it profitable to cut down the brakens longer than the manufacturers of fern ashes can do, and thereby eradicate this hurtful plant compleatly from the soil.

ARTIFICIAL MANURES.

The natural manures which have now been mentioned, are the best calculated for a country which is but just emerging from pasturage to tillage. The manures procured by the toils of art, are the effects of advanced knowledge and advanced industry. The most obvious of these 'are dunghills and compost middings, the neglect of which is inexcusable where«ver tillage is pretended to be pursued.

But there are other artificial manures which are most advantageous, and which lie within the reach of most Highland farmers. They, no doubt, require a degree of industry and art, but they will always abundantly reward any art or industry that is bestowed on them.

QUICKLIME.

It is remarkable that quicklime is generally applied as a manure, with more industry, at a great distance from the lime kiln than in its immediate neighbourhood, where the lime may be had at the easiest rate. Lime is transported from Yorkshire to Aberdeenshire, at a high expence, for improving the soil; while the lands in Yorkshire, well adapted for this manure, and adjacent to the lime works, never receive the advantage of it. Lime is brought by sea, from the coast of Cumberland to Galloway, and after this, carried sometimes by land to the distance of ten miles; yet the use of lime in Cumberland is neglected. In tracts of Clydesdale and Ayrshire, where it might be had at the very least expence it has never been applied to use. Draw-kilns may be seen in Mid Lothian, surrounded by wild land which might be highly improved with lime, but which has never received any; while from these very kilns, the lime is carried with great advantage to Berwickshire, by an expensive carriage of sixteen or eighteen miles.

VOL. I. L

Though it may scem unaccountable, it is certainly true, that lime is most neglected as a manure, in those parts of Scotland where it is in the greatest abundance, and to be procured at the lowest price. The county of Fife is perhaps the chief exception.

Though calcareous strata are not so frequent in the Hebrides and West Highlands as in many other places: yet there is a sufficiency of them to supply all these countries with quicklime, both for building and for manure. There is abundance of limestone in Ila, in Lismore, in Sheuna, in Skye, and on the coast of Morven, Loch Caron and Gareloch. There is abundance of marble, fit to afford the finest lime in the islands of Garviloch, Tirey, Icolumbkil and Skye, and on the coast of Appin and Assint. From these places, all the adjacent countries might be supplied with lime by a short navigation. But it is proper, that the use of lime as a manure should begin at the places now mentioned, where it may be had, without any distant carriage, and at an easy rate.

All uncultivated land, when first broke up, stands in need of a forcing manure; and of this kind, quicklime, if it can be afforded in sufficient quantity, is certainly the best. There has, accordingly, been more wild land in Scotland, reclaimed by means of lime, than by any other manure. This is the moat proper, and the most profitable w ay in which it can be applied. To old arable land that has lain long ley, it is capable to communicate great additional fertility. But this fertility, if not cautiously managed, tends to make a rich tenant and a poor landlord. When moorish land, moderately dry, is brought into tillage with a proper quantity of lime, there arises the most profitable improvement of the soil that is made in Scotland, to the proprietor, to the tenant, and to the public. All that is afterwards requisite is a right succession of crops.

In most parts of the Highlands there are favourable opportunities for carrying on this essential improvement. Wild land fit for the purpose occurs everywhere. Limestone and marble are found in sufficient quantities in many places. It is only necessary to convert them into lime, and to apply it as a manure.

For these purposes, the w ant of coal, is, no doubt, a great disadvantage. Even the abolition of the duty on coals will not render them sufficiently cheap for the burning of lime. But there are few places In the parish of Linton in Twecd-dalc, which is a later country than most arable tracts in the Highlands, jive hundred and thirty acres of wild land, were, by means of lime, reduced to tillage, within less than *twenty* years.

in the Highlands, where limestone and marble are found where there is not also abundance of peat.

In a kiln, properly constructed, good limestone may be burnt and calcined sufficiently with peat.— This has been long an established practice, in several parts of Scotland, where there is no access to coal. But in the remote Highlands and Islands, it is either not known or not practised. The Highlands, however, in this article, are not behind other parts of the world. Some years ago, a Danish gentleman travelled in this country, at the King of Denmark's expence, and at the rate of some hundreds a year, for the purpose of importing into Denmark the useful occonomical practices of other countries. He observed in

Scotland, and with great attention, the custom of burning limestone with peats. In the countries of Jutland, Sleswick, and Holstein, they have plenty of limestone and plenty of peat; but no lime, except what is made with coal, brought from afar, or with wood. He judged that the communication of this single practice, of calcining limestone with peat, would, to the inhabitants of these countries, repay more than tenfold, all the expences of his travels.

The great addition which may be made to the arable land in the Highlands, by means of lime, is a matter of such moment, that the burning of limeatone with peat, should be universally known and practised. It would perhaps be right to employ a skillful limeburner to travel through the country for this purpose; a man who has had full experience in burning limestone with peat, turf, and Avood; who might instruct the inhabitants in quarrying and breaking the stone, in constructing and filling the kiln, and in the management of the fire. Such a man might be most beneficially employed for two or three years in this way. The expence could not be any great sum; and was it defrayed by the Highland Society, would be amply repaid in promoting their views.

If limestone is broke down, and reduced so small as to mix intimately with the soil, it must become a valuable and lasting manure, as well as when reduced to quicklime. In Ireland, there are strata of limestone gravel, which is advantageously applied as a manure, without any preparation. In Scotland we have no limestone but what is disposed in fixed rocks. But it has been supposed that limestone might be made to answer as a manure, by being ground into a coarse powder. With this view, a trial was made several years ago upon one of the Annexed Estates. A machine was erected, which was moved by water, for grinding limestone to powder. It executed the work, but not sufficiently cheap. Its construction, indeed, was reckoned defective; and ns it is rash to prescribe bounds to the mechanical powers, a machine to answer this purpose compleatly, may perhaps still be practicable.

Upon the farm of Aird, in the parish of Kilmuir, in Skye, there is a great body of limestone, very soft and easy to be reduced to powder. There is a rivulet hard by, sufficient to drive any mill, and great abundance of land in the neighbourhood, well calculated for this manure. Such a favourable situation, for erecting a machine of this kind, occurs in many other places.

FLOODING.

The sediment of water consists of the matter that is minutely diffused in it, which is chiefly vegetable and animal substances, and the finer parts of clay. — This sediment must therefore be a rich feeding manure for any soil, and is to be obtained by the farmer, in three different ways.

It is to be found in the form of mud, at the bottom, and on the margins of lakes, pools, and slow running rivers; in all hollows, where water stagnates in winter, in ditches, at the side of high roads, and many other places. It is therefore to be had almost everywhere, but is nowhere so much valued and used as it ought to be. It may be laid upon land, without any preparation, when immediately dug from the places where it has been deposited. But in general, it is best managed, when it is made to form the most bulky material, in compost dunghills. and to be mixed in tbem, not with dung, but with lime, or other calcareous manures.

This sediment is also to be obtained, by allowing water to stagnate for a time, on the surface of the ground. The sediment of the Nile, which is almost proverbial, and which gives to the lower Egypt all its fertility, is of this kind. To procure the sediment of water, in this way, is the privilege of low flat countries, nor are there many opportunities for it in Scotland. There are some, however, and especially those meadows which are cut annually for hay, but are never in tillage. If flood water can be made to stagnate upon them for some time, the crop of hay is greatly increased. This is the process of nature, and deserves to be imitated by art. Those meadow grounds that are casually overflowed in winter are always the

most productive; but the continuance of the water upon them, at least at one time, should not be long. When the flood water has stood about two or three days stagnant, all the benefit it can afford is received. If it is continued much beyond this time, the herbage or sward, it is intended to improve, will be apt to be hurt.

There is yet another way in which the sediment of water may be applied as a manure, and in which it may be procured at an easy rate in many parts of Scotland, especially in the Highlands: this is, by flooding the ground with running water, called in some places where it is practised Water-tathing. For this purpose, a ley field that is apt to be over-run with water from higher grounds, is traversed with furrows made by trie plough in different directions. The master-furrow at the head of the field, like all the others, should be led in a very gentle slope, that the water may no where run with rapidity. The plough should go as deep as possible, and the furrow be always laid up to the declivity. When a field is properly furrowed in this way, the flood water coming upon it is made to flow slowly, and to deposite its sediment. The most fertile parts of the soil, which are naturally carried down from the higher grounds into the valleys, or into the sea, are by this means intercepted. The dry hanging grounds, which would otherwise be impoverished, are enriched by every flood. The most proper subject for this improvement is poor outfield land. Where there is not water running naturally upon it sufficient for the purpose, any neighbouring burn may be led off' while it is in a flood, and the water dispersed over the field in the manner now described.

The great advantage of this practice is well understood in many places, and it should be known and generally followed in the Highlands, where most of the farms afford a favourable opportunity for it. When a field has been watertathed in this way but for one w inter, the growth of grass upon it is more early, and continues much more luxuriant through the whole season, than it would otherwise be. The moss or fog, with which the grass is oppressed, likewise disappears. Any parts of the field which have not been reached by the water, are backward, and continue for the whole season comparatively barren. When the field is broken up, it never fails to yield a hearty crop of oats, superior to what is obtained by the laborious and circumscribed practice of folding.

Water-tathing needs but a very small degree of labour, and only requires the farmer to suffer the water to run on his ground in a proper manner. It is certainly the most beneficial and the least expensive of all manures.

The practice of flooding with stagnant water requires an extent of level ground which in the Highlands is rather unfrequent; but that of tathing by means of running water is more applicable to Scotland in general, and especially to the higher parts of the country. Most of the grounds to be improved in the Highlands by means of water are situated on a declivity. The practice will always be most beneficial where the soil is naturally dry. The dry soils in the Highlands on a declivity are chiefly of two sorts. The one consists of arable outfield land, the other of wild land on the sides of the hills, covered usually with heather. These two form the most eligible tracts in the Highlands for water-tathing. On the arable land the water is to be conducted by furrows made by the plough: on the wild land, by furrows formed, or rather torn up, by the cascrorae, or crook spade. On the wild land, this water manure not only increases the quantity of grass, but alters its nature and improves its quality. On poor dry arable land its enriching property is most conspicuous. It not only increases the quantity and improves the quality of the grass, but in the course of one year renders the soil better prepared for a crop of oats than it would be by lying seven years as a dry pasture.

BURNBAITING.

The practice of burning the superficial parts of a wild soil, for the melioration of what is below, is commonly called Burnbaiting, or sod burning: in England it is called denshiring, or Devonshiring,

from the county of that name, where it was first extensively used.' and with us it is frequently termed paring and burning. It is certainly a most effectual method to subdue many wild soils, that are of the most barren and stubborn nature, and is especially requisite where there is no command of lime, or any other rich calcareous manure. It should be restricted, however, entirely to uncultivated land, nor ever extended to any soil that has ever been in tillage.

The most advantageous opportunity for this operation is where there are moorish and mosBy grounds, bottomed by a good clay, which is a case, indeed, that very often occurs. In this situation, every thing should be burnt, the more the better, till you come within three, four, or five inches of the clay. But so much of the moss or peat earth should be always suffered to remain, as a proper mixture of clay and moss forms an excellent basis for a soil.

The common custom is, to raise with the plough, or to tear off from the surface, large turfs or sods, with a daughter spade or breast spade, and when they are sufficiently dry, to burn them in heaps. But there is one thing in this process that deserve to be particularly noticed.

When burnbaiting, soon after the year 1720, first came into use in Scotland, it was chiefly pro moted by the authors of the Select Essays in Husbandry. These Essays have ever since been a sort of directory to Scots farmers in this and in other matters. It is there enjoined to burn all the sod, turf, and vegetables with a smothered fire, in order to obtain more ashes and salts. This accordingly has been generally practised; but the reverse is true. By this practice little either of ashes or salts can be obtained.

The.lands subjected to burnbaiting are generally covered with heather, willows, gale, juniper,, and other shrubs peculiar to a mossy soil, and the soil itself rilled with their roots. In other places, there is a tough superficial sod, filled with the strong matted roots of coarse aquatic grasses. These, with peat!earth, form the general mass that is to be burnt, and the chief design of the

operation is to turn all these vegetable matters to the best account as a manure.

If they are burnt with a smothered fire, and intermixed, as must necessarily happen, with a good deal of earth, much of their bulk may indeed be preserved, but they can only be charred, not calcined. They are not reduced to ashes, but only to charcoal; and of course no fixed alkaline salt can be formed; for it can only be obtained by the calcination of vegetables in an open fire. They are reduced by this smothered heat to a substance which of all others is the most indestructible and the most useless in a soil; for all charcoal, and every charred vegetable substance, is not only indissolvable in water, but impregnable even to putrefaction.

,

In the process of burnbaiting, the whole mass should therefore not merely be burnt, but calcined, or reduced to white ashes, with an open and as strong a fire as possible.. No part should be left black, or in a charred state. What remains after the conflagration will indeed be less bulky; but, so far as it goes, will be of real value. All the fixed alkaline salt which the vegetable substances can yield will be procured, and, even exclusive of this, the true ashes, or the earth of vegetables, obtained by thorough calcination, must always form a fertilising ingredient in a soil.

There is another case in which burnbaiting has been found very advantageous: when, in a barren clay soil, which has never been cultivated, the soil below is of the same quality with what is within four or five inches of the surface. In this situation, three or four inches pared off, consisting of mere clay, with some straggling roots of grass, and thoroughly dried and calcined, have produced an alteration and a degree of fertility not easy to be accounted for .

In either of these cases, when the operation of burning is over, and the ashes are spread, the plough has generally a very tough piece of work to encoun Iron, bituminous matter, and other substances, are often embodied with clay, but they are only accidental ingredients.

The only essential principles of clay are, siliceous earth, the earth of alum, and an unctuous substance. The unctuous matter flies off in the fire, the siliceous can serve only as so much sand in the soil; so that whatever fertility is communicated by calcined clay, it must proceed from the earth of alum.

ter. The object, then, should not be the attainment of a *few* immediate white crops; this method would soon even make the land worse than it was at first, and has on many occasions rendered burnbaiting rather a destructive than a useful practice. The chief view should be, to bring the land as soon as possible into tolerable tilth, and to an even surface. This may be done by means of one, or at most two crops, after which it should be resigned to grass.

This absorbent earth is the most friendly of all others to vegetation, and forms a great part of the substance of all vegetables. In clay it is so strictly combined with the siliceous earth and an unctuous matter, that it is not acted upon by weak acids. But when by calcination it is disengaged from these principles, it is then left open to the action of acids, and capable to form neutralised and soluble matter in the soil. It is probable that the value of clay, as a manure, when com. pleat I y calcined, is not as yet fully understood.

SECTION VI. TILLAGE. INFIELD AND OUTFIELD.

The division of a farm into infield and outfield, was the ancient and universal custom in Scotland, and still subsists, not only over all the Highlands, but in most parts of the kingdom; and yet, every proper plan of agriculture requires that it should be universally abolished: It has accordingly been laid aside, in all those parts of the country where husbandry is best understood.

The infield is, in general, a piece of land that is naturally good. The farm house always stands upon it: and this seems to have determined the situation pf all the old farm houses in Scotland. It receives all the manure that the farm affords. It is usually distributed into three divisions, or kevels, as they are called. Each of these is manured once in three

years; and for this, it must produce a crop of bear, and two crops of oats. These crops are usually but of a very middling sort; and by no means equivalent to the manure and labour that is bestowed upon them. Sometimes there is a fourth division, which is suffered to remain ley, or is used for potatoes; but, in general, the infield is kept constantly in tillage, and in white crops.

The outfield, again, though all arable, is regarded as a waste. When the infield or croft land is worth twenty or thirty shillings, the outfield will not be worth above two or three shillings an acre. It never receives any manure, except a small part which has the cattle folded upon it in summer. It yields grass of the poorest quality; and when it has remained ley from four to seven years, and is over-run with mosses, it is ploughed for three crops of oats. No land should be laboured by the plough for oats, unless it afford an increase of five fold: but it is well known, that these outfield lands do not yield near so much; they seldom yield four, and frequently not even three seeds.—It is plain, they should, therefore, be cultivated in some other manner. This is a scene of husbandry that is really deplorable; especially, as it is carried on by a sensible, frugal, and laborious set of people: But, un fortunately, thev have no knowledge of any thing better. To change their practice, they want only proper instruction, and proper example.

The alteration of this old custom of infield and outfield, in a proper manner, and for the conveniency and profit of the farmer, depends on many local circumstances; but, in general, the two following rules seem to be the most expedient:—— 1. To throw all the infield into sown grass, and into other green crops, to he horse-hoed, as turnips, beans, and potatoes. The poorest infield land is well calculated to produce these. In consequence of frequent manure and perpetual tillage, it is remarkably free of all root-weeds, and is of easy culture These crops it would yield in abundance. By a continuation of these crops, and of the horse-hoeing culture, the infields, at proper intervals, would come to afford,

and with little assistance from manure, more luxuriant crops of grain, than ever they did before.

2. To employ all the manure that can be commanded upon the farm, in the cultivation of the outfield.

The infield is usually but a spot, compared to the extent of the outfield, upon a farm. This land is poor, worn out, and its produce very inconsi VOL. III. M derable; yet, as at certain intervals, it has been imnieniorially in tillage, and is generally of a dry light soil, it is certainly capable of great melioration, by proper culture. At present, when in pasture, it is worth from two to five shillings an acre; when in crop, it yields but from two to four seeds of oats In order to recover this exhausted land, and to advance its fertility with profit, the following method appears, in general, to be the most proper.

1st Year, fallow, with lime, marle, or shells.

2d Year, oats.

3d Year, potatoes, beans, or turnips, horse-hoed. 4th Year, bear, with grass seeds. 5th Year, clover hay. 6th and 7th Years, pasture.

This course, which contains only two white crops in seven years, will, exclusive of the fallow, afford a beneficial return each year, and bring the land into proper heart and tilth without dung. If lime, marle, shells, or other calcareous manures are not to be had, dung must then be given the third year, to the horse-hoed green crop.

The land being thus brought into continued culture, and into a meliorating state; the following rotation, excluding local circumstances, seems to be the best.

1st and 2d Years, oats. 3d Year, potatoes, beans, or turnips, with dung, horse-hoed. 4th Year, bear, with grass seeds. 5th Year, clover hay. 6th and 7th Years, pasture.

This rotation contains three white, and four green crops; and this, it is believed, most of the outfield land in Scotland will not only bear, but continue, by this method of culture, in an improving state.

It may be left to every intelligent

farmer to determine, what would be the produce of outfield land, under this management, compared to what it is at present. There is no outlay required, nor any extra expence, except the lime and tallow of the first year. It is not a piece of improvement that requires the fanner to wait long for a return:—His emolument from it must appear the very second year, and must annually increase. It is a method of culture, which every farmer, who has a nineteen years lease, may safely and profitably undertake. The value of the ground and of the crop might, in three or four years, be doubled or tripled. As the outfield land forms above four-fifths of all the arable soil in Scotland, even a much smaller improvement upon it, would be a great public benefit.

Such a change, however, in the management of the infield and outfield land, cannot take place all at once; hut if the infield is divided into three or four kevels, one of these, with a suitable proportion of outfield, might be undertaken each year, and cultivated in the manner now described: so that the whole alteration might be accomplished, on any farm, large or small, in the course of three or four years.

EARLY TILLAGE.

The old Scots tillage was all confined to one season. Ploughing did not begin till after old Candlemas, the 13th of February, and concluded in May. This is still the case in many parts of the country. In the Highlands they do not in general begin to plough till March. Since the introduction of potatoes, they begin in some places more early; but not till the month of January. They have been led to this in order to have time between the oat and bear seed for planting their potatoes; and the practice has been conducive to render the inhabitants more industrious.

Where husbandry is in an improved state, tillage must go on through the whole year; every season being proper for particular crops or soils. The advantages of autumnal tillage are great. By exposing the soil long to the air, and to the influences of frost and thaw, it is always the most effectual. There is even

reason to think, that in order to do full justice to any soil, it should be ploughed immediately after the removal of every white crop.

Whenever it is requisite to give land two or more furrows, one of them should certainly take place in autumn. All the crops in the Highlands are raised with one furrow; but there is much of the land that would require more tillage; and where this is the case, the first furrow should undoubtedly be given early in winter. Was autumnal ploughing introduced, it would also accelerate the spring work, and enable the Highland farmers to sow more early, which is highly necessary.

It was urged indeed, by a gentleman of great knowledge and good judgment in the agrestic economy of the Highlands; "That as a great deal of "the ground lies upon declivities, and is of a thin "staple; if it was ploughed early, much of it would "be washed down into the rivers and lakes by the "frequent rains." The remark is certainly well-founded, with respect to all such lands. But there are others, of a different nature, not liable to this objection, which might be safely ploughed for oats early in winter. There are also grounds, which, if properly cultivated, would require both a winter and a spring furrow; especially all such as have been recently reclaimed from a wild state.

Tillage, often repeated, is the life of agriculture; but this is not to be obtained, unless the tillage can be executed at a cheap rate. The price of tillage again depends chiefly on the mechanism of the plough, and the nature of the team. Both tiiesc articles require to be greatly amended in the Highlands before the soil can receive that degree of tillage which is necessary for producing good crops.

TILLAGE SUBSERVIENT TO PASTURAGE.

The Hebridians complain that every fourth crop is almost entirely lost by the lateness of the harvest, and the inclemency of the weather. They are rather apt, indeed, to aggravate this circumstance, as an apology for their want of industry in agriculture; yet it is certainly so far true, as to make it evident,

that their country is more adapted for yielding grass than grain; and that cattle, not corn, should be the chief object in its cultivation. Instead of discouraging their industry, this defect in point of climate, should rather direct them, not to exhaust their lands, as they do at present, with poor white crops, but to render their tillage entirely subservient to the production of green and dry forage for their cattle in winter and spring.

The tillage of the western Highlands and Islands is so scanty and imperfect, that even with the assistance of potatoes, it is not sufficient to supply these countries with bread corn and malt spirits. Whereever there is any cultivation at all, it is certainly a great object to supply the inhabitants, with what grain is necessary for their own consumption. The Highlands, it may be said, is a pasture country, and that it is better for the natives to rear cattle and to import grain. But there is a fallacy in this common and superficial opinion. By proper cultivation, these countries may not only be amply supplied with grain and rendered independent upon distant markets; but this very cultivation would, at the same time, enable them to rear, to support, and to sell a much greater number of cattle than they do at present.

Upon a Highland farm, with a breeding stock, there may be sixty cows, which with their followers, as they are called, will amount to above two hundred head of black cattle, old and young. Upon this farm, there may be from ten to twenty acres of oats and bear. The straw of this crop is all they have to depend upon. This pittance of winter provender, is totally insufficient for such a herd of cattle, where all the pasture is blasted by the inclemency of winter. In consequence of this, numbers of the herd must fall, as they actually do every year, by hunger and diseases, during winter and spring.

i

The extent of cultivated land in the Highlands, is totally inadequate to the number of cattle. To sup ort them properly, and indeed to save their lives, the management of the land already in culture, should not only be altered, but its quantity should be greatly enlarged. To supply the inhabitants vvitli grain, would be a matter of great advantage, but it is only a secondary consideration. The great object is to prevent the cattle from dying of want, which they so frequently do at present in great numbers. This can only be prevented by extending the cultivation. It is only by this means, that sufficient winter provender can be provided for the cattle, and those great losses avoided, which are now every year incurred, by their perishing for want of food in the spring season.

RIDGES.

The crooked direction of ridges, which was universal over all Scotland, seems not to have arisen from design, but merely from the path of the cattle, which when left to themselves, naturally proceed in a curved line. This curvature of the ridges, is incommodious in ploughing the ground, and also in sowing and reaping the crop. It has therefore been abolished, wherever cultivation has made any considerable progress, and the ridges arc all laid out in straight lines.

In the remote parts of the country too, the ridges are generally of an unequal, and of an inconvenient breadth. They are often fifteen, twenty, or twentyfive feet broad; but it is well known from experience, that the most proper breadth of a ridge, is about twelve feet; and this rule is accordingly adopted in all the places where tillage is best understood.

It is also usual to gather ridges, and to form them immoderately high in the crown, whether there be any reason for it or not. In deep and wet soils, this practice is in some degree necessary, but even there, it is often carried to a hurtful excess. Soils of this kind in the Highlands, are very unfrequent, and yet the ridges are often coombed to a great degree. There can be no reason, however, for the practice on dry and thin soils. It is in these, evidently prejudicial. The arable lands in the Highlands being generally of this kind, the ridges ought every where to be lowered in the crown; and in most plac es, to be brought either to a level or to be formed with a very slight declivity.

These pieces of attention, in the article of tillage, are not only of moment in themselves, but tliey are every where followed with other desirable consequences. They bring the ploughmen to pursue their business with carefulness and accuracy, instead of the slovenly manner they were accustomed to before. They tend to introduce a polished culture; and serve to improve not only the other branches of tillage, but the whole husbandry of a country.

WASTE LAND.

To increase the quantity of cultivated land, is evidently the first, and most important point of improvement in the Highlands and Islands. This may be done in a variety of ways; but the easiest, the most general, and the most effectual, is by a potatoe crop, raised with the spade. All the reclaimable land may be subdued and brought into culture, by means of this crop, which is the very best preparation for tillage. During fifty years past, there have been no additions made to the cultivated land in the Highlands but by this practice; and it should every where be further and further extended.

It has been questioned, whether potatoes are in fact advantageous to the Highlands, or ought to be encouraged, as they tend to discountenance industry, by affording so great a quantity of sustenance with so little labour. But there is little foundation for such a surmise. There are sufficient reasons for thinking, that on every account they cannot be too extensively cultivated, provided they be confined to waste land.

Potatoes were first planted in the Lewes only in the year 1753, and in the year 1764, they supplied the place of bread to the inhabitants for near one half of the year.

In the island of Ila there are many fields of potatoes, of ten, twelve, and even fifteen acres each, all planted with the spade. The quantity raised, is greater than what is consumed by the inhabitants, and the overplus is transported to the ports in the Clyde and other places. This abundance, is not only of great use in reclaiming the wild land; but has also a very friendly influence upon the

progress of the linen manufacture in the island, and must certainly have the same effect in every other country.

Potatoes were first introduced into the island of South Uist, about the year 1743. By planting them on waste land, there were in the year 1764, above nine hundred acres under spade and plough culture in that island, more than at the former period. The quantity of corn, grass, and cattle, upon several farms, being thereby increased one third in the course of twenty years. In like manner, in the year 1764, there was not a possession in the Isle of Skye of twenty pounds rent, which, during the twenty years immediately preceding, had not at least twenty acres of corn field added to it, by planting potatoes in ground never formerly cultivated. In the farm of Ardnafuaran, in the country of Arisaig, there were raised in the year 1763, no less than four hundred bolls of potatoes, all on land which had never before been in any culture whatever. The farm of Cappoch, in the same country, sowed, in the year 1749, between twelve and fifteen bolls of oats and bear, and kept only forty cows. In the year 1764, this farm sowed thirty-seven *boh* of grain, and maintained seventy cows, which were not only of a larger size but better fed. This great alteration, in the course of fifteen years, was entirely owing to the bringing in of wild land with potatoes.

These, and many other instances of the same kind, make it questionable, whether any single rule in agriculture can be established of greater utility in the Highlands than this: "That, in every farm, where "there is land to be reclaimed, it ought to be ex"pressly stipulated in the lease; that no potatoes "should be planted upon any ground, wherever the plough or spade have formerly been employed."

If the good arable land, instead of being occupied by potatoes, is set apart for oats, barley, and green crops; and the potatoes planted on land not formerly cultivated, the quantity of sustenance upon a farm, both for men and cattle, must be greatly enlarged.

The Hebridians first received the

potatoe from the north of Ireland; and they have always continued to raise it in the manner of the Irish, by means of lazy-beds. The potatoes cultivated in this way, are always of the best quality. It is indeed a laborious method of culture; but the inhabitants think no labour too much, for obtaining this valuable crop. This method has for a long time been laid aside, in some parts of the Lowlands; but, for many reasons, it is still an expedient practice in most places in the Highlands. A plentiful crop of potatoes may be raised in lazy-beds, without the assistance of dung from the stable or byre. This gives an additional value to the potatoe crop; as it permits the dung of the farm to be bestowed on other lands.

Any manure used for potatoes, is always the best which is most open and pervious, and allows the young fibres of the root, which are extremely tender, to expand themselves with ease. The manures of this kind, are straw, litter, haulm, the thatch of old houses, and of stacks; and, indeed, all herbaceous vegetables in a half putrid state. Among these, the fern, might be usefully applied to this purpose; to be cut in summer, thrown into heaps, and reserved as a manure for the potatoes in spring. Upon all wild ground, planted with potatoes in lazybeds, the crop is always the best where the surface is roughest, with fern, heather, bushes, and decayed herbage: even a rank foggage is sufficient manure, for a tolerable crop of potatoes raised in this way.

As the planting of potatoes should be confmed, as much as possihle, to waste land; so, the use of the cascromc, on every considerable farm, should be restrained to this particular crop. It is an instrument well adapted for tearing up a wild and rough soil, but very improperly used upon any land that is arable, except in some of the smallest possessions.

FALLOWING.

Fallowing was in use among the ancients, and has been practised by all the moderns, who have made any remarkable progress in the cultivation of the earth. Of late years, it has indeed fallen properly into desuetude in many places, since the introduction of the horse-hoeing husbandry. A horsehoed green crop is now found, in some degree, to answer the purpose of a fallow, and without the temporary loss of rent and labour. In the most improved lands in England and Scotland, the practice of fallowing has therefore been laid aside.

Fallowing first took place in Scotland between the years 1700, and 1?2(», and was justly thought to be the highest improvement, even upon our best Soon after the Earl of Haddington settled at Tyningham, in East-Lothian, which was in the year 1700, he brought some farmers from Dorsetshire, by whom he first introduced lands. In those parts of the country where the advancement of agriculture has been greatest, a horsehoed green crop is now substituted in place of a fallow. The practice is certainly right, where land is clean and in perfect tilth; where the horsc-hoeing husbandry is well understood; and where an accurate culture is followed: but it is well known, that, as yet, this is the case with but few parts of the kingdom. In all other places, a fallow is most expedient and necessary; yet the practice is still very confined. There are extensive tracts, perhaps threefourths of the whole country, where fallow. has never been used. It is the introductory step, however, to a thorough improvement of the soil; and it may be presumed, that the progress of husbandry in Scotland, must continue very much to depend, as it has hitherto done, on the progress of fallowing.

Summer fallowing has not as yet reached the Highlands, and is every where introduced with difficulty among the vulgar, who are not easily brought to submit to the loss of a crop, in view of future emolument. It is most beneficial, no doubt, where the soil is deep and adhesive. Land of this sort, does not, indeed, occur very frequently in the Highlands; yet, there are four cases in which into Scotland, the practice of fallowing, and the culture of rye-grass and red-clover: He became thereby, a real benefactor to his country.

fallowing would be of great advantage in these countries.

The first, is of those lands kept in perpetual tillage, which, though naturally good, are worn out, and choaked with annual weeds, by constant white crops and bad cultivation. In this case, tallowing would give to the soil that relief which is necessary, and free it from those weeds, which at least destroy one half of the crop.

The second, is wherever wild moorish land is to be broken up, and reduced to culture.

The third, is of those fields which are designed for flax. This crop requires a soil that is in good heart, in good tilth, and free from weeds; which, without fallowing, is not to be had in many parts of the Highlands.

The fourth, is where coarse outfield land is to be brought into a state of constant and regular culture, in the manner already described.

The practice of fallowing is still very much confined to those parts of Scotland where wheat is raised. Farmers in other places erroneously suppose that it is an operation too expensive for any less valuable crop. In any of the above cases, it will be found highly profitable, even where no other grain is sown but bear and oats. Fallowing is not to be considered as necessary and useful only for winter grain, such as wheat or rye. In those parts of the country where the rent of land and the price of labour are comparatively low, it may be advantageously pursued for raising summer grain, and especially a crop of barley. The beneficial effects of a fallow are not confined to one year, but extended to several successive crops.

Farmers unacquainted with this process in agriculture, and ignorant of its beneficial effects, are naturally averse to it. They are apt to consider the want of a crop, and the expence of labour during a fallow, as so much dead loss. Some care is necessary, and it is well bestowed, to undeceive them in this. So far as their knowledge goes, they are abundantly quick-sighted in discerning their own interest; but through ignorance they are often apt to mistake it. They require to be instructed and encouraged, and even bribed, to pursue their own advantage. Some encouragement may be proper from a proprietor in the Highlands, to excite his tenants to the practice of fallowing. To remit the rent of the fallowed land would probably be a prevailing inducement. The rent of the land to be fallowed would generally be something between two and five shillings the acre. A few acres at this rent, and but for one year, could not amount to any great sum. There is reason to think that this encouragement would effectu VOL. I. N ally introduce the practice of fallowing; and when once introduced, it would of course be pursued without anv premium.

CLODDING.

In some places in the Highlands there is a piece of cultivation carried on which is unknown any where else in Scotland, and is called in English clodding. After a grass field has been tathed by the cattle during summer, they dig a trench, a spade deep, along every ridge, sometimes on the crown, and sometimes in the furrow. The earth dug out of this trench is spread over the rest of the ridge, so that the whole field comes to be covered with earth and clods. This is done commonly about the 1 st of August. These clods are suffered to remain on the surface till after harvest, when the field is ploughed. It is ploughed again in the spring, and then sown with bear.

This is an operation more laborious than profitable. It could only take place where a man's labour is of small value, and the labour of cattle with proper instruments but ill understood. It must be more expensive, and far less productive, than a summer fallow. It is to be regretted, that people capable of so much industry were not better directed. If they can pursue this practice, it certainly would be no difficult matter to bring them to the practice of fallowing.

SUCCESSION OF CROPS.

The succession of crops in the Highlands and Islands varies in the infield and outfield grounds, but in both cases requires to be totally altered.

The infield land is generally a light dry black loam, which is made to afford crops of grain without any respite. They raise alternately upon it a crop of bear, and another of oats, and ail the assistance it gets is a thin covering of sea weeds, or a little dung, to the bear crop. Sometimes even a second and a third crop of oats is taken. But these, as may reasonably be expected, are always of a poor quality. In Lismore, where they house some of their cattle, the dung is bestowed on the infield once in four years; and without any other aid it is made to produce the constant alternate crop of bear and oats. In Glenelg, where they have a little dung, they give it to the bear crop, and then take two crops of oats. After this they suffer the land to be ley for one year, and then break it up again for a bear crop. In Badenoch, when they dung a piece of infield, they raise from it, without intermission, two crops of bear and four crops of oats; alter which it is either dunged again, or tathed, and the same crops taken. In Canna and other islands the infield is cropped one year with bear; the next year it is allowed o remain ley; the following year it is again sown with bear; and this alternation goes on without any manure, and witliout the intervention of any other crop.

The crops afforded by these infield lands, even under this severe treatment, are surprising; hut they owe their lertility more to nature than to the skill of the i? habitants. They are naturally of a good soil; some of them are full of shelly and calcareous matter; others are repeatedly spread over in the "inter season with sea spray; and some are annually waterfed by floods from the higher grounds. *By* these means they afford such crops as could not be expected in other places without sufficient manure and proper culture. There are even some spots of what may be called perpetual soil, which yield a crop either of bear or oats every year, and that immenioTially, without any manure whatever. The crop, no doubt, is light, but it is of sufficient advantage to induce the people to raise it.

The oatfield land is commonly a thin, dry, hazelly, poor soil, full of stones, and situated most frequently on the sides of hills. From this sort of ground, in Lochaber and other places, there are generally taken four and sometimes five crops of oats, without any manure. It is then allowed to remain 4 ley *fat* three years, after which the game oat crops Hfe again resumed. On the west coast, where they have wood, they tathe part of the outfield in summer hy mean's of oar folds. After this, three crops of Oats are taken. It is then left ley fof three years-, when it is again tathed and cropped in the same manner. In the Long Island the outfield land is generally of a light sandy soil. The farmers give it a covering of sea weeds, and take a crop of bear and two crops of rye; it is then thrown out ley, and at the end of four or five years the same practice is again renewed. In Skye and other places, where untillaged land is planted with potatoes in lazy beds, they usually take two and sometimes three successive crops, each crop beihg manured with sea weed, or a little dung. These are succeeded by a crop of bear, and two or three crops of oats without manure; and when the soil is thus exhausted, rather than reclaimed, it is left to run to natural grass.

Such is the succession of crops in the Highlands and Islands; but to this sort of management, bad as it is, the inhabitants are in some degree constrained, from the small proportion of arable land upon their farms. From necessity, they are forced to raise what little grain they can, though at a great expence of labour, the produce being so inconsiderable. A crop of oats on outfield ground, without manure, they find more beneficial than the pasture. But if they must manure for a crop of oats, they reckon the crop of natural grass rather more profitable. But the scarcity of bread corn, or rather indeed the want of bread, obliges them to pursue the less profitable practice. Nor are we to expect that it is to be essentially altered till the quantity of cultivated land is enlarged. Oats and bear being necessary for their subsistence, they must prefer them to every other produce. The land at present in tillage, and fit to produce them, is very limited, and inadequate to the consumption of the inhabitants. They are therefore obliged to make it yield as much of these grains as possible, by scourging crops.

There are no crops at present in the Highlands but those already mentioned, bear, oats, rye, and potatoes. The potatoes are planted commonly on wild land; and this, as far as possible, should continue to be the practice. Having no fallow, nor any other crops to form a rotation with the above grains, they are obliged to raise them repeatedly on the same ground, with the little manure they can afford, and the' assistance obtained by permitting the land to remain for a time ley. This train of husbandry, poor and unprofitable as it is, the inhabitants are obliged to follow in their present situation. It cannot be materially changed till certain considerable alterations take place in the country; especially till fallowing and green crops are introduced, and the quantity of land kept in a regular course of culture is greatly enlarged. Repeated white crops, which form bad husbandry in every country, would then be discontinued. One or more green crops would take place between two white crops; by this alteration, the quantity of grain would not only be increased, but the winter provender; an article so necessary in a country that must chiefly depend on a breeding stock of cattle.

EARLY SOWING.

As the late sowing of all the grains is everywhere ne of the greatest defects in our Scots husbandry, we cannot be surprised that it should prevail in the Highlands. Many reasons are alleged by our country people for this practice; but none of them can with reason be admitted. It is a general but erroneous apprehension, that any of 'the grains, if sufficiently covered, can be killed by frost, and especially by any frost after the st of February. Oats and barley committed to the soil in October or November, are as capable, even in their infant state, to resist all the frosts of our climate, as wheat and rye, and would be still less liable to be injured, if sown in February or March.

In the Hebrides and West Highlands, the summer is abundantly favourable for all our common crops. But after the autumnal equinox, the weather does certainly become more liable to violent winds and rains than in the south. A late harvest is everywhere detrimental; but *in* these countries it is, *aii* this account, peculiarly hazardous and destructive, and ought by every means to' be avoided by the inhabitants. The easiest and most effectual measure for this purpose is, to sow all their crops,mote early than they do at present.

With proper care, there might be as early crops in the remote Western Islands, and on the opposite coasts, as in most parts of Scotland. But though they are subject to no considerable degree of frost or snow, and though the soil in general is light and dry, yet the people sow *nb* grain till after the beginning of April, from that period, till near the middle of May, they continue to sow oats aftd rye; and though the bear is not put into the ground till the end of May, yet in a good season it is often reaped yvitlrirt the month of August.

In Lochbrooth' and Garelocn, the oats which were sown on the 10th of April were ripe on the 8th of September. In the year 1762, in the island of Tirey, the common bear, or square barley, produced a crop in eighty-five days; being sowrt the 28th' Of April, and reaped the 22d of July. From such In the year 1732, Lfnnieus + found the' ffctrtic grain, TtiS Hordenm *vufgare,* to ripen in Lsplitnd in fifty-eight dsrys. Jieing sown the 31st of May, the crop was arrived at maturity f I.inn. Flor. Lapp. Prolegmen. instance's *H* wOold appear, *that* tf thtf faffhers coinplain of the destruction of their crops by the winds and rains of October and November, it is not the fault either of their soil 6f climate. While they per sist in delaying to sow oats till the end of April, ahd bear till the end of May, they must always, unless" ift a Tery favourable year, meet with the misfortunes of which they complain; and the fault is entirely their own. Their harvest must then frequently be thrown into October and November, and consequently be greatly damaged, if not entirely destroyed.

But they are by rid means' necessarily exposed to the disasters of a late harvest. Their weather during spring and summer needs be no obstruction to proper agriculture. Their arable lands are in general near the level of the sea. Their soil is every where of a sharp forward nature. Even though drenched with rain, it is capable, by a few fair days in February or March, of being rendered sufficiently ii the 28th of July. . This was in a latitude where the sun was in the firmament during almost the whole time that the crop was upon the ground, which occasions a great accumii. Jation of hetft even in the Arctic regions. But there are fe places in Britain capable of ripening this grain in less than (he bate-mentioned period of eighty.five days. The greater length of the day during summer, in the most northern parti of Scotland, is no inconsiderable advantage in favour of the crops of these countries.

dry for sowing. To remove the complaints of a late harvest, the easiest and most obvious remedy is, to put their crop in the ground about six weeks earlier than they do at present To take the first opportunity of sowing oats after the 12th of February, and of bear after the 12th of March. Sown at these seasons, an earlier harvest of these grains might be expected, than can be obtained in most parts of the south of Scotland.

DRAIN ISTG.

There are several ways in which draining might be turned to great account in the north.

One is, by excluding the sea. Though this has never been attempted, there can be no doubt of its being practicable in many places to a great extent, and with much advantage. In the islands of Skye and Ila, and especially in South and North Uist and Benbecula, there are extensive flats, covered at flood only with shoal water, and in some places by narrow inlets, which might be recovered from the sea by embankments. The principal material for this purpose, large loose rocks, are everywhere at hand in abundance. But in a country where land as yet is so low in value, and so much of it uncultivated, it is likely that enterprises of this kind will remain to be executed in after times.

Another is by draining fresh water lochs. Many opportunities of this kind occur, where lands which elsewhere would be reckoned estates, might be obtained by this operation. This is the case, not only on the main land, but in Skye, Ila, and in many parts of the Long Island. In South Uist, there is a tract of arable land near thirty miles in length; yet there is a quantity occupied by fresh water lakes nearly equal to all the arable land at present in the Island. Many of these lakes are not only extensive, but shallow, and with a sufficient fall to be drained. The richness of the soil, obtained from such pieces of water, and its easy culture, are well known.

The farmers, however, labour under some mistaken ideas on this subject, which prevent them from any attempts of the kind. They are deterred from draining any loch upon a farm, from the persuasion that their rent would be raised, even though they hold their farm in lease. This again is founded on a notion which prevails among them, "that all lochs, "rivers, and waters, belong to the superior." These were found to be the ideas of a very respectable clergyman, who had a loch on his farm, that by draining, might have afforded above sixty acres of rich land, at an expence of about ten pounds.

The third and most common method of draining is where land is to be cleared, either irom surface or under water by open or covered ditches.

It is but little of tire present arable land in the Highlands that stands in need of draining in this way. Kut there is great room for the practice in other places There are extensive tracts of wet pastures, which might be greatly improved by draining. They are ndw chiefly covejred with rushes, sprets., deers hairf, wire bent J, lingU, and the numerous Species of carex, or one pointed grass. Merely by laying the ground dry, with wed directed drains, these plants which form the poorest pasture for cattle, find are the inhabitants only of a wet soil, would gr« dually disappear, and be replaced w ith grasses of a much better quality. AH the wild land

likewise, which is naturally wet, must be previously drained, before it ean be reduced to cultivation. These are the two situations in which the draining of land is most necessary, and in which it may be rendered most profitable in the Highlands.

Utiderdrains in arable land, must be covered so *deep* with earth, that tle plough can go over them. These are necessary, however, only in fields kept in culture. They are of three different sorts: Some are so formed with sods as to leave a canal for the water to run below, which must necessarily bs .1 uncus *articulalus.* Linn.

+ Scirpus *cespitosus.* Linn.

J Juncus *squarrasus.* Linn.

U Narc!us *stricta..* Linn.

soon filled up*:* Oihers are filled with brush wood, a material too perishable Dor the purpose;,and some with stones. Of tljese, tlje covered drains with stones, if well constructed, are undoubtedly the best. But like the others, they are expensive, and liable to perpetual obstructions. When they are choaked, which inust generally happen, the water stagnates, rises to the surface, and becomes often more prejudicial than ia fc natuj-al state.

A few well conducted drains, will clear a field ftf fwface water, but to free it of under water is ano#e laborious operation. Where water rises through h# soil and pervades it, a great number of covered drains, and in various directions, is necessary. Jo «his case, draining has sometimes been executed, at an ex pence, almost equal to the value of the land, and which ne*ver* could be returned. This may be done in pleasure grounds, or on account *Q* the regularity of beauty of a field, but is not to be undertaken by 41 farmer.

On valuable land, from one to three pounds per acre, a good deal of labour js well bestowed U draining, especially, if the stones for filling the drains, can be removed from be soil. Put land pf a low salue will not bear a high.expense for thjs purpose. There is but little.geoujui in tin: Highlands which requires to be drained that will allow of the cost and care of covered drains; nor are they

necessary. In extensive and low rented lands, the open drain will always be found to be the least expensive, the least troublesome and the most effectual.

There is a simple and easy operation, not generally practised, which ought always to be performed, previous to the ch aining of any land whatever.

Before any attempt is made to drain a field, it is certainly of consequence to be as well informed as possible concerning the state of the water under ground. The easiest and the most effectual way for this purpose is to dig a number of small pits, about three feet deep, in different parts of the field. These should be suffered to remain open for a whole year.

«. By these pits, the depth of the soil, and the nature of the subsoil, will be every where exposed to view.

/3. They serve also to show, whether the water passes between the soil and the subsoil, or rises and pervades the soil, from a greater depth. *y.* It will then also be seen how near the underground water reaches to the surface, and at what height it stagnates in the different seasons.

These are important points of intelligence to be gained, before the operation of draining is begun. They are to be obtained, by what scarcely can be called any expence, and must be of great use to direct the execution of drains in a proper manner.

The circulation of the subterranean waters, and especially of those near the surface of the earth, is exceedingly various. They are obstructed and accelerated, they, a/e turned and directed in their course by such a variety of causes, and especially by the nature and inclination of the different strata, that the rules which may be proper for draining the soil in one place become inexpedient and entirely useless in another.

The operation here suggested is applicable, however, to every case where draining is to be practised.

INTRODUCTION OF GRAIN.

As it is very uncertain at what aera grain was first introduced into any of the European countries; it does not appear when its cultivation first took place in the Hebrides and Western Highlands.

There is no evidence of its having been in use, before the departure of the Romans from North-Britain. Grain was probably introduced here, and in other northern countries, by the first Christian missionaries. These appear to have come first from Ireland, and to have visited the Hebrides before they arrived in the NorthWest Highlands of Scotland. The most early authentic account we have of the use of grain in the Hebrides, is in the time of Columba, about the middle of the sixth century. The Hebridians have Vol. i. o been in immemorial possession only of three sorts of grain:—These are the grey oat, the bear, or four rowed barley, and rye. Any others they may have, are introduced but of late years, and in a few places.

It is probable that they owe the acquisition of rye to the Norwegians. This grain was anciently, as it is indeed at present, much more cultivated in the Scandinavian countries, than in the other parts of Europe. ' Its cultivation is of a more ancient date, and has always been more pursued in the islands which were long under the Norwegian government, than upon the main-land. There is no tradition, however, concerning its introduction; but it is certain, that no other grain, except the three above mentioned, has ever been sown in the Western Islands and Highlands for many centuries, till of late years.

The oats, bear, rye, and lintseed, sown in the Highlands, are generally either of bad kinds, or much degenerated. They ought, therefore, to be replaced by better sorts, and frequently changed for others, brought from the south of. Scotland, or from England. But the farmers, beside being uninformed on the subject, have no opportunity for such intercourse with distant places. The best sorts of these grains, and others fit to be introduced, ought to be imported by the proprietors, and sold to the tenants, at the price they cost. This would produce a most material alteration for the better, in the crops of the country. It would require, indeed, a little skill and attention, but might be executed without incurring any great expence.

As an instance of the importance of such an alteration, Mr Campbell of Dunstaffnage, a gentleman remarkable for his good sense, imported bear from Glasgow, which he sowed upon his farm of Icolumbkil. Beside a much larger crop, the grain which it produced, was so superior in quality, that he sold it one third dearer than any other bear that was raised from the grain upon the island. Those who do the same, may be always assured of similar success, both in the quantity and quality of their grain.

INCREASE OF GRAIN.

Before any improvements are suggested concerning the grain of the Highlands and Islands, it may be proper to take a view of the produce and quality of the grain at present in these countries.

Much of the arable land in the northern parts of Argyllshire; in the western parts of Inverness-shire and Ross-shire; and in most of the islands, when sown with the grey oat, affords only an increase ©f about three to one, in that grain. From m boll sown, there is only a return of the seed, and about one Linlithgow boll of meal. Nowhere in Britain, nor perhaps in Europe, is there so much labour exerted, to procunrsuch an inconsiderable crop. The labour to obtain it, would not be bestowed by the people, was it not on account of obtaining a little straw, for preserving their young cattle in spring. So poor a harvest, would be anywhere deplorable, but especially in these countries where there is both soil and climate to produce much better grain, and in far larger quantity.

In many places, the increase from the grey oat is less than what has now been stated: in others, it is something more; but, at most, amounts not to above five seeds. Over the Highlands and Islands, in general, the increase of this jrain cannot be estimated so high as four to one. A boll of it seldom affords more, and often less than eight pecks of meal. Where a Scots acre is sown with a boll of the grey oat, the utmost produce, in general, is the seed, and a boll and an half of meal:—A miserable return! for which, neither the soil nor the climate are to be blamed.

The usual produce of rye is four seeds. When this is the case, the inhabitants think it a more profitable crop than the grey oat, having the same increase. It affords, indeed, a larger proportion of 3 meal, but it is a more injurious crop to the soil, than the grey oat. For this reason, rye has been given up, of late years, in several places where it had been raised for many ages.

On the arable grounds, the produce of beat is often under five, and seldom exceeds eight seeds. In South Uist and other islands, they do not account their bear crop good, if it is not above ten; and it is usually, indeed, between that and fifteen seeds: even twenty, or twenty-five fold have been known to be produced, upon some of their richest sandy grounds. But this remarkable increase of bear, takes place only in those lands which are cultivated with the spade; which are plentifully supplied with sea ware; and are sown very thin. Bear being a grain of very expeditious growth, their short summer is capable of bringing it to great perfection.

QUALITY OF GEAIN.

Not only the increase, but the quality of the grey oat, as to the meal it affords, has already been noticed; from which it appears to be the most unproductive and unprofitable grain that is cultivated by mankind. The bear affords a much better crop, and a far larger proportion of meal; yet, in Skye, and trie neighbouring parts, there is not above one boll of bear sown, for thirty or forty of the grey oat.

These grains are of a different quality, however, in the Highlands, as in other places, according to the nature of the soil. In the Long Island, and other parts, the land sown with bear is of two kinds:—The one, a sort of outfield, consisting of a light sandy or gravelly soil, which is but occasionally in culture; the other, is infield, composed of a black loam, which has been cropped immemorially without intermission. There is a remarkable difference in the quality of the grain raised upon these two different soils. A boll of bear, of twenty pecks, which is produced upon the sandy soil, will afford twenty, and even sometimes twenty-five pecks of meal; but the same boll, from the black soil, kept constantly in tillage, yields usually but fourteen, and often only twelve pecks of meal.

It is evident, that the grain growing on the sandy soil, should, therefore, be always chosen for seed corn; but the weaker grain, produced on the black soil, is generally and injudiciously used for that purpose.

All the bear, in general, is of a thick husk. Of many parcels, examined in different places, that in the Uists and Harris was found to be the best bodied grain. Bear produced in the Isle of Ensay, raised with the spade, on their black land, yielded meal for bear, which is seldom the case in other places.

It may now be proper to take some further notice of the white crops which are at present cultivated at large in the Highlands; the grey oat, bear, and rye; and then describe those which ought to be introduced and propagated.

I. THE GREY OAT.

The grey oat, or small corn, as it is called in some places, is certainly the worst oat and the least productive grain that is anywhere raised in Europe. A boll, consisting of sixteen pecks, has been known to afford only four pecks of meal: and yet, at no very distant period, it was the only oat sown in Scotland.

How long it has been laid aside in Fife and the Lothians does not appear: but in the shire and Stewartry of Galloway no other oat was raised till about the year 1720. In several tracts even of the south of Scotland it is still retained; and, in many places, it is intermixed to a great degree, with oats of a better kind.

This wretched grain continues to be the prevailing crop in all the Highlands and Islands, where o 4 both both soil and climate would answer for white oata as well as in most parts of Scotland. No other oat is sown in the Island of Tirey, though suited by nature to be a good corn country, and to be as a granary indeed in that part oi the world. Yet here, the grey oat produces a crop only of two seeds and an half, that is, the seed corn, and perhaps half a boll of meal.

It is a grain, indeed, not very liable to shake. This makes the Hignland people imagine that it is the only oat fit for their high country and stormy climate. But white oats are sown in the south of Scotland, and indeed within the shire of Edinburgh, at a much greater height above the sea than anywhere in the Highlands. Upon the hills of Galawater, which are indeed of a good soil even to the summits, there are extensive fields of oats, from eight hundred to more than twelve hundred feet above the level of the sea. These consist chiefly of the Blainslie oat, which, in every tolerable season, affords beneficial crops, even at that great height, and in the most shelterless situation.

From what has been said of the grey oat, it must appear to be a heavy reflection on the agriculture of Scotland, that there should be a field of it sown in any part of the kingdom.

II. BEAR.

Bear, or four-rowed barley, called in the north of England big, is the only grain of the kind sow» in the Highlands The preference due to the twoirowed barley over the bear, in point of quality, is not very considerable; seldom above a shilling or eighteen pence in the boll, when they grow upon the same land. Its ordinary increase in the year is superior. A good head of barley contains thirty grains; but a good head of bear has often above fifty. Yet on a, proper soil, the barley affords a grain of a fuller body, and a larger quantity on the acre, which renders it a more eligible crop in many places.

The bear, however, will grow upon a poorer soil; it is a more early crop, and will stand rough weather with less damage. It is, therefore, a valuable grain in a severe climate; and the only one at present cultivated in the Highlands, that deserves to be retained. It is peculiarly useful in affording a good crop upon land dug with the spade. Many spaces on a Highland farm are thus laboured and rendered highly productive, which, from inequality of ground and intervening rocks, cannot be cultivated by the plough.

III. RYE.

Rye is not much sown upon the mainland, but to a considerable extent in the Hebrides. It is there raised in the spring, upon the sandy grounds manured with sea-weed, and accounted more profitable, which it may easily be, than the grey oat. On such a soil, and with such manure, it is certainly but an impoverishing and unprofitable crop; and to obtain it with most advantage, it should be sown in autumn. The natives have been in possession of this grain for ages: they have an attachment to it, and are unwilling to part with it; but, was it a new grain, its real merit would not probably induce them to raise it. Accordingly, of late years, a few of the most intelligent persons have given it up, being persuaded that it is very detrimental to the soil. There are but few parts of the Highlands that are well adapted for this grain. Its straw is of little value as a fodder, and wherever it can grow, more beneficial white crops may undoubtedly be raised.

We come next to consider the different sorts of grain which may, with advantage, be introduced into the Highlands.

I. WHITE OAT.

The white oat was little known in the Highlands till after the year 1746. In Gairloch, Loch broom, and the adjacent countries, it was not anywhere sown till the year 1760. In the Isle of Skye, Sheriff Macleod made the first trial of it in the year 1763. He sowed white and grey oats in the same, field, and at the same time, in order to make a fair comparison between the two. He was not sensible that the former were either later in ripening, or more hurt by the weather in autumn, than the grey oats. In consequence of this and other similar trials in different places, the white has continued to gain ground upon the grey oat, and must reasonably do so by its superior value. Its progress, however, to this day is very limited, and, upon the whole, inconsiderable; there being many extensive districts where it has never yet been introduced.

Of the different varieties of the common white. oat, the Blainslie oat may be presumed to be the best calculated for the Highlands. It is raised upon lands in Lauderdale, which are neither of a very rich soil, nor situated in a very favourable climate. It has always had, and still retains a great character with the farmers of the south, and is carried to very distant parts. It succeeds remarkably in high and exposed situations. It is an early oat, but the cup of the grain being more closely shut, it can stand violent winds without shaking, better than any other oat of the early kind.

II. FRIESLAND OAT.

The Friesland or Dutch oat, is sometimes called the Polish oat. It is in reality but the Polish oat raised in Holland. In several parts of Scotland, where it is now cultivated, it is termed the air or early seed corn, and in some places the barley corn.

It ripens sooner than any other of the oat kind. It affords also a full bodied and hearty grain; but it is not equal to some other oats in weight of crop, and it is easily shaken.

Notwithstanding these disadvantages, it has now been found by experience, to be a valuable acquisition, in some of the higher and later tracts of the country.

In this present year, a field situated five hundred feet above the level of the sea, was sown partly with Friesland, and partly with Blainslie oats. The first were reaped the 22d of August; the last, not till the 16th of September. This is a difference of twenty five days, which is a matter of great moment in any part of Scotland, but especially in the Highlands.

There can be no doubt then, that pains should be taken to introduce the Friesland oat into many parts of the Highlands. It would afford a hearty, and by much an earlier crop of oats, than has ever been reaped in that country. It should first indeed be tried in the lowest and best sheltered places.— Many farmers in the Lothians are now in possession of this grain; but for high lands, Tweeddale is the country from whence the seed corn should be brought. It was first sown in that county before the year 1748, by Mr Montgomery of Magbiehill, and has ever since been cultivated to a considerable extent. In a worse soil and climate than most of the arable

parts of the Highlands, they, now raise in Tweeddale beneficial crops of the Friesland oat, where, in most years, they cannot bring the Blainslie oat to a sufficient degree of maturity.

III. BLACK OAT.

The black oat is so called, because of the black colour of its husk, for its meal is as white and good as that of any other oat whatsoever. It is much sown in Forfarshire and the Mearns, and intelligent farmers in Lothian, who have lately brought it from these countries find their account in it. It is more liable to shake than the Biainslie oat, but upon land comparatively poor, it yields a more early and more valuable crop than any other oat. It is vvell adapted for many places in the Highlands, and its introduction would be an improvement also in many parts of the south country, where the arable land is under ten shillings an acre.

IV. TARTARIAN OAT.

It does not appear, when, or from what country the Tartarian oat was first brought into England.— It has only of late years been known in Scotland, but has now been cultivated in several places. Hitherto it has been sown only in the Lothians, and in the lower and more fertile parts of the country; but it seems to be a grain better calculated for a poorer soil and a more stormy climate. It approaches nearest in its characters to the old Scots grey oat; but is a much more luxuriant plant, yields a greater increase and a better grain. It grows tall, and affords a heavy crop both of corn and straw. By its pendulous head or panicle, leaning all to one side, it resembles the grey oat, and is thereby of a very different appearance from every other sort of white or black oat. In consequence of this, its grains are always directed from the wind, and cannot easily be shaken But it is rather a late grain, being more than ten days behind the Biainslie oat.

The first time I had the opportunity of procuring this grain, the season being far advanced, it was not sown till the 1st of June, and was not reaped till the 1st of November. It grew upon a poor gravelly soil, and afforded a better crop

than could have been expected from any other oat. It was sufficiently ripened, and though it had been exposed to much tempestuous weather, there was not a grain of it shaken. These qualities should render it a valuable grain in many parts of the Highlands.

It may be safely affirmed, that by the introduction and cultivation of the four sorts of grain now described, the produce of all the arable lands in the Highlands, at present occupied by the grey oat, might be more than doubled.

V. TWO ROWED BARLEY.

From what is said above, of the common bear or four rowed barley f, there seems not to be any pressing call at present, for the introduction of the two rowed barley mto the Highlands. All Europe, and all the East seem to have been originally supplied with this grain, from the Lower Egypt, where it is in the greatest perfection, and where no other Hordeum *distichon*. Linn.

+ Hordeum *vulgare*. Linn.

plant of the kind is raised. But the four rowed and six rowed barley, have been derived from some more northern countries, and are therefore better adapted for northern climates. If the two rowed barley was to be tried in the Highlands, the Lincolnshire and Aleppo barley, the best grains of the kind in England, ought to be avoided on account of their lateness. Was even the common barley of File and the Lothians to be used, its success would depend entirely on its being early sown. This should be in the season of the oat seed, or immediately after it, that is, between the 10th of March and the 10th of April.

VI. SIX ROWED BARLEY .

The six rowed barley is the principal grain of the barley kind, in some of the most northern countries of Europe. It is the prevailing barley in Ingria, and in other parts of Russia, so far north, as any grain is sown. It is little known in this country, but from small trials that have been made of it, seems to deserve attention.

It forms a beautiful spike with six rows of seeds. A good head of it contains seventy-two grains, which Hordeum *hexastichon*. Linn.

is much more than what is afforded by any other kind of barley. Its reed is stronger, and its quantity of straw larger than that of bear, and of the same quality. It grows and ripens rapidly, which is no small property in a northern country.

Last year it was later than ordinary, the summer being so cold and wet. It was not sown till the 13th of May, and was ripe on the 8th of September.— Though the increase in the ear is large, yet the grain is comparatively small. It does not therefore seem fitted for a soil and climate, capable of producing the two rowed barley in full perfection. But in an inferior soil, and especially in a cold and late climate, it promises to be a valuable crop.

It is the hardiest of all grains. It is sometimes called Hordeum *hybernum* or winter barley, from its withstanding in a remarkable manner the inclemencies of winter. It is of a quicker and more vigorous growth, and has a larger increase than the common bear. It seems therefore a grain that well deserves a serious trial in the Highlands, and especially wherever it may be found proper to sow barley in autumn as a winter grain.

Vol. I.

VII. WHEAT.

There is little or no wheat sown in the Highlands, though it might, no doubt, be produced in many places. From a trial made by the late Shawfield, in the year 17G4, it was evident that wheat may be raised to perfection in Ila. About the 1st of July, there was, near his seat at Killirew, as fine a crop of that grain, horse-hoed, and as far advanced, being then in the ear, as could any where be seen in the south of Scotland.

The dryness of the soil, and the want of intense frost upon the shores and inlets of the sea would be friendly to the production of this grain. A crop also sufficiently.early, might certainly be procured, though not a heavy one. But it is the soil, more than the climate, that is unfavourable to the raising of wheat. In the best soils in the Highlands, the w ant of clay, is the strong objection to the wheat crop. A sandy cr gravelly soil in good heart, may indeed produce

one tolerable crop of wheat; but its effects upon such a soil are most detrimental, more injurious than two or even three crops of oats or barley. For this and other reasons, wheat cannot be recommended at present as a general and profitable crop in the Highlands.

. Triticum *hgbemum*. Linn.

The demand for it is inconsiderable, and confined to the houses of the higher gentry. Was the demand to increase, which will probably be the case, wheat may no doubt be raised to a considerable extent. Where any trial of it is to be made, the red wheat, being the hardiest grain, should be preferred to any of the other varieties at present sown in the. south of Scotland. The crop also should succeed a fallow, as it can then be sown early, and should not be later than the Oth of September.

VIII. SUMMER WHEAT .

The true summer wheat is a grain very little known in this country. When the sowing of the common wheat or Triticum *hybcrnum* is deferred till January, February, or March, it is then termed spring or summer wheat; not from any difference in the grain, but merely from the different season in which it is sown. The real summer wheat, however, is a distinct species of plant, and in its characters and qualities very different from our common wheat. — It is the Triticum *aestivum,* or summer wheat of Linnaeus. By other authors it is termed Triticum *trimestre,* or three-month wheat, because in several parts of the continent, there are only three months between the time it is sown and the time it is reaped.

Triticum *aestivum*. Linn.

Beside other countries, this grain is much cultivated in the northern parts of France, in Guernsey and Jersey, and often in tlie south of England.— During spring, in the year 1766, it was first brought into Ayrshire, from the island of Jersey, by John, Earl of Loudon. It was sown in a heavy clay soil, near the castle of Loudon, on the 7th of April, and was reaped on the 26th of September. Upon a more early soil in the neighbourhood, it was sown on the 4th of April, and reaped on the 4th of Septem-

ber. In both places, it afforded ten Linlithgow bolls of wheat upon the Scots acre. When the grain was weighed, a boll of it was found to be only two pounds less than a boll of winter wheat.

Having remained on the ground only during the same period with oats, it was found not to have been more hurtful to the soil, than a crop of that grain.— It will be allowed, that our common winter wheat could not have afforded such a crop, or indeed any crop, in the same space of time. It appears therefore to be a grain better adapted for a northern than a southern climate: that it might be raised in many parts of the south of Scotland, where winter wheat is not sown; and that of the different sorts of wheat, it is the most promising to be attempted in the Highlands.

When these properties of the true summer wheat are considered, it is surprising that it should be so little known in this country; especially as it may be had in plenty, and at an easy rate, by means of the wine ships trading to Guernsey and the north of France.

From what has now been said on the subject of white crops, it is evident that no improvement in the Highlands, equally considerable, can be executed at so small an expence as what may be done by a total alteration of the different sorts of grain at present in use.

Beside the above, the following kinds of grain deserve at least to be mentioned in this place. Though scarcely known in this country, they are cultivated to great advantage in countries of a similar climate.— They deserve therefore to be enquired after, and made the subject of experiment, as it is highly probable that some of them would form a valuable acquisition to Scotland in general, and others to the Highlands in particular.

1. Avena *inula.* Linn. The naked oat.

This oat is so called, because the grain is not firmly surrounded by the chaffy husk as in other oats, but on the threshing floor, falls naked from the head, like a grain of wheat. It is cultivated on the shores of Cornwall, in dry poor land, exposed to very tem pestuous weather. It is very prolific, but the grain is smaller than that of our white oats. As the head leans all to one side, it is not so easily shaken as mi ht be expected. Sown with us, and in a late situation, on the 29th of April, it was ripe the 15th of September, which shows it to be an early crop, if it was sown on a forward soil, and in proper time. Its meal is very different from that of other oats, and is accounted in countries where it is raised, as equal to that of wheat.

2. Hordeum *nudum*. Linn. Naked barley.

This is a two rowed barley in which the grain separates naturally from the husk, as in the naked oat, and appears on the barn floor in the same form as common barley, after it has been shelled at the mill. There is another sort of barley, having the same property, the Hordeum *cdaeste* of Linnaeus, but approaches nearer to our common bear, as it has four rows of seeds in the spike. These two kinds of grain are cultivated in some of the northern parts of Europe, but have never been made known in this country.

3. Rathripe, or hotspur barley.

This grain is produced on the forward soils in the south of England, and affords, wherever it is sown, the earliest barley crop. It is well known in the neighbourhood of London, especially about Fulham and Putney. In a warm summer it ripens in ten weeks or seventy days; and is, in general, two or three weeks sooner ripe than any other barley. In Cornwall, it has been known to be returned to the barn in eight weeks or fifty-six days. It is not a different species from the Hordeum *distichon,* or our common two-rowed barley: but by being immemorially cultivated in the most early soils, it has become by habit a more early grain; and this early quality appears in whatever soil or situation it is raised. Its crop indeed is light, and not to be coveted where Lincolnshire barley can be raised in perfection: but on a thin soil, or in a late country, where this cannot be done, the Kathripe barley must certainly be valuable.

4. Secale *hybernum*. Linn. Winter rye.

The rye sown in the Highlands, and in most parts of Scotland, is the Secale *vernum*. Linn, or spring rye, and is always sown at that season. It is a weaker plant, a smaller grain, and its crop much inferior to that of winter rye, which should be sown in autumn. They are, indeed, but varieties of the same species of plant; yet, wherever it may be proper to cultivate rye, this winter sort should certainly be chosen. Land of a moderate rent, where the soil is light, in good tilth and clean, but nsufficient to carry wheat, may be profitably occupied with rye. Land of this kind, in some parts of the south of Scotland, affords a crop of rye worth eight or nine pounds the Scots acre, where a crop of oats would not amount to above six pounds. were no less than six inches in length. The ears are remarkably long and heavy, and when it is rank is very liable to lodge. It is the wheat usually imported from Riga, and the adjacent ports in the Baltic, and is a very hardy grain. But it has been found inferior in weight to our best Scots wheat.

5. Triticum *turgidum*. Linn. Grey wheat.

This is a strong bearded wheat, sown in Sussex and other parts of England. It is known in different places by the names of duckbill wheat, grey pollard, and fuller's wheat. It has a strong stem with large heavy ears, and is remarkable for yielding a large proportion of flour. It is believed to have been originally brought from Sicily, and is only a variety of the Triticum *ramosum* cultivated in that island, which has been found to ripen perfectly in Scotland.

6. Triticum *conicum*. Cone wheat.

This is but a variety of the former, and common in the West of England. The spike is of a conical shape and bearded. It is accounted the best for the horse-hoed husbandry.

7. Triticum *polonicum*. Linn. Polish wheat.

This is a bearded wheat esteemed in some parts England. It was in one place successfully raised in this country, and formed a good crop. Its awns 8. Triticum *monococcum,* Linn. One grained wheat. v

This is a species of wheat raised in the poorest and most exposed fields in Germany. Though it does not afford such an ample crop, its flour is equal to that of any other wheat. It was once sown in Scotland, but at a very unfavourable season, not till the 12th of May. It rose on the 27th of that month, flowered on the 15th of August, and was thoroughly ripe on the 1st of October. It will grow well in a soil and climate where our common wheat cannot be raised.

It appeared probable from the above trial, that if this grain were sown early in March, upon land capable of affording five or six bolls of oats on the Scots acre; that it would yield a well ripened crop of much greater value. It seems, therefore, to be a grain that deserves further trial, not only for the Highlands, but for all the higher parts of the South of Scotland.

9. Triticum *Spelta*. Linn. Spelt.

This is another species of wheat which is much cultivated likewise in some of the most sterile parts of Germany. Sown in Scotland in spring, in a field six hundred feet above the sea, it was thoroughly ripe in the beginning of September. This and the former sort of wheat appear to be the best calculated of all others for an inferior soil and a cold climate. They can be sown as spring corn, which is no small advantage, and are capable of being fully ripened even in the higher parts of this country, and in a soil Unfit for our common wheat.

10. Panicum *miliacewn*. Linn. Black millet.

The grain of this kind used in Britain is all brought from abroad. There are two varieties of it, the one having a yellowish, and the other a blackish husk. The black sort was raised at Loudon in Ayrshire. It was sown in the spring, and afforded a very good crop in September. How far it may be renered profitable, must be decided by furthe r experience: but this trial was sufficient to show that it is a crop that can be ripened even in the higher parts of Scotland.

11. Smyrna wheat.

This grain was brought from the east, and immediately from Smyrna, in the year 1757. It was first introduced into Brittany, and has since spread over a great part of the North of Fi ance. It contains one hundred and fifty, and even two hundred grains in a spike; from which superior fertility it is termed in France Bled de Providence. From the accounts given of it, this grain certainly deserves to be enquired after, and tried in Britain.

GENERAL REMARKS.

It may not be improper here, to subjoin a few remarks on the present culture of grain in the Highlands.

r. LATE SOWING.

The whole labour of the country is unreasonably late. The general rule is, not to begin to plough till old Candlemas, nor to sow till after the 20th of March. The month of May is often far advanced before the oat seed is concluded. The inhabitants complain of their late harvest, without once reflecting that they them'selves are chiefly to blame for it.

Their arable lands are in general of a light dry soil, and well adapted for early sowing. It is a common and hurtful mistake, to imagine that oats in the soil can be destroyed by spring frosts. There is no frost in the Highlands that can hurt a grain of oats properly covered, though it remained in the soil the whole winter.

The tillage should commence immediately after the harvest is com pleated. The earliest opportunity of sowing oats should be embraced after the 1st of January. Frequently in that month the soil is sufficiently dry for the purpose. Scarce a year passes in which that grain may not be sown in February; and instead of delaying to sow till after the 20th of March, the oat seed should before that day be fiV nished.

It must be owing to some very uncommon or inexcusable circumstances, if the ten weeks, between the 1st of February and the 15th of April, or between the 15th of February and the 1st of May, are not sufficient for the seed time upon any farm; yet, no bear is sown till May, and much of it not till June is far advanced. Many excuses may be offered for this practice, but none that can reasonably be admitted. Bear in the soil, and while it springs, is as hardy a grain as oats: Its vegetation is compleated in a much shorter space of time. Were bear and oats sown about the same season, early in the spring, the barley harvest

would be finished before that of the oats commenced. This, it is well known, would be a great advantage; but when the sowing of barley is so long delayed after the oats are sown, the two grains come to ripen at the same time. The harvest of both coming all at once, the farmer, with an insufficient number of reapers, which is generally the case, is unable to cut down his crop in due time. Much of it must, therefore, remain long exposed to the dangers of the weather, and especially to shaking winds. The sowing of barley is even sometimes so long and unseasonably postponed, that it is not ripe, nor reaped till after the oats. This practice is unnatural; must always be unprofitable; and b directly contrary to the proper economy of a well regulated farm.

Numerous instances might be given of the good effects of early sowing in a late climate, and in the event of a late harvest. In that of 1787, which was extremely late, a field of common barley, sadly demolished by the weather, was only reaped on the 16th of November; but it had not been sown till the 26th of May. In its immediate neighbourhood, another, and a better farmer had a hearty crop of Lincolnshire barley, a much later grain, in his barnyard on the 25th of October. All this great advantage was obtained, by his having sown his barley on the 8th of March.

Every such instance should be recorded and made known, to eradicate, if possible, the pernicious practice of late sowing, so detrimental, not only to the Highlands, but to Scotland in general.

The crop early sown, and which of course ripens early, always affords grain of a much superior quality, to what is ripened only late in the season. This, no doubt, is a sound argument in favour of early sowing; but farmers in general regard merely the quantity, without paying that attention to the quality of the grain which it deserves. To determine the quality of grain, weight is the only effectual standard. If all grain, instead of being sold by measure, were to be sold by weight, farmers would then be induced to pay more re-

gard to the quality, that is, to the weight of their grain, than they have hitherto done. As the earliest is always the best ripened, and the heaviest grain, the advantage to be obtained in the weight of grain, by early sowing, would then come more into view, and become a powerful argument for promoting the practice.

II. THIN SOWING.

In most parts of the Highlands, the fields are generally under-sown. In spring, the seed corn being usually scarce and dear, it is bestowed on the soil in too sparing a quantity.

In some places, the land lately reclaimed by potatoes, or that which has been long ley, when laboured with the spade, affords a great increase of bear. Such land is sown thin, and very properly; for the crop on a soil in such situations tillers greatly; six, eight, ten, or more stalks arising from each grain.

But the case is quite different with soils kept constantly in tillage, which is the case with much of the arable land in the Highlands. On such soils, especially if they are light, corn does not tiller: each grain produces only a single stem, and seldom more than two or three. A greater proportion of seed corn is therefore requisite upon such lands; but the Highland farmers, not aware of this, sow them thin, and the consequence is a thin crop. The soil is not sufficiently filled; and there is often a deficiency to the amount of two or three seeds, which the land would bear, if it had a larger proportion of seed corn.

III. WEAK SEED CORX.

There is another material error among the Highland farmers, in the management of their white crops. The weakest and worst of their bear and oats, is always made use of for their seed corn. It is true indeed, that very weak corn, which would yield but a small proportion of meal, will grow; but it is equally true, that the plants produced from it, will be weak in proportion: To employ weak grain as seed corn must, therefore, be mistaken economy. The long experience and practice of the most skillful farmers in England and Scotland, is a sufficient warrant for any who are less informed, to employ the grain of the best body they can possibly procure, for their seed corn.

IV. AUTUMNAL TILLAGE.

The proportion of land in crop upon a Highland farm is comparatively small, and the number of horses and servants large. The arable ground should therefore be more thoroughly cultivated than in other places; but this is by no means the case. Fallowing and horse-hoeing are unknown, nor is the plough ever yoked, either during autumn or winter: It is used only in spring, to give a single furrow to the rfmall fields, which are sown with bear and oats. When the seed time is over, the horses are dismissed to the hills, and are never again occupied in turning the soil, till the following spring. The horses upon every farm are surprisingly numerous, and their idleness during the rest of the year, is accompanied with the corresponding idleness of a superfluous number of men servants. In this way, a very great power of labour subsists upon every farm, which is unapplied and lost. In consequence of this, there is no land in the Highlands that is in proper tilth, excepting the spots that have been kept in perpetual tillage. Oats in the most rough and unsubdued land, receive but one imperfect furrow in the spring. It may be some time before fallowing aud horse-hoeing can be established; but, till that is done, and as an introduction to these practices, it would be most useful to introduce autumnal tillage.

The ley ground, not ploughed till March, and sown with oats, produces everywhere a crop of grass, rather than of corn. This and all coarse unbroken land, intended for oats, should certainly be ploughed in autumn, and receive a second furrow in spring. On such land, six seeds might reasonably be expected, which does not afford four by the present practice. This surely would be a great return for the labour bestowed, beside diminishing the weeds, and improving the tilth of the soil.

VOL. I. Q

V. AUTUMNAL SOWING.

The greater part of the Highlands is, no doubt; situated in a later climate than the rest of the kingdom; accordingly, the late harvests, and the severe autumnal rains and winds, are the reigning subjects of complaint. The climate cannot be much altered; but there can be no doubt that, by proper management, the harvests may be rendered more early. There may be local exceptions and accidental cases to the contrary; but, in general, it is unquestionable, that to obtain an early crop, it must be early sown.

Barley being a grain of quick growth, wherever it may be proper to raise it in the Highlands, there is climate sufficient to bring it to perfection, provided it is sown in due time. Oats are a much later grain, and it is in this crop that the Highlands chiefly suffer by the lateness of the harvest.

Well ripened crops of oats may certainly be, raised in most places, if the sowing is not delayed beyond the proper season. But in order to accelerate this important crop, and in place of a late, to procure a very early harvest; it would be a trial highly laudable, to sow them in October, instead of April or May. This, indeed, like every other crop of winter grain, would require either inclosed ground, or winter herding; but in many parts of the Highlands, there are now inclosures fit for such a trial.

Our common wheat is generally about eleven, and even sometimes twelve months in the ground. The natural lateness of the grain requires this period in our climate. Wheat sown about the 1st of October, is usually ripe about the 1st of September; but if this grain be not sown till April or May, the best climate in Scotland will not bring it to perfection. The oat, though a late grain, is not nearly so late.as wheat. In one trial, the Blainslie oat, sown upon the 20th of October, was compleatly ripe on the 20th of July. This suggests a very obvious expedient to remedy the lateness of the climate, and to procure an early crop of oats in the Highlands.

, CHANGE OF SEED CORN.

It is not till agriculture is considerably advanced, that farmers become duely sensible of the advantages that arise from a change of seed-com. The best farmers in the South of Scotland, are not sufficiently attentive to this article, and it is a matter still more overlooked in the Highlands.

There is, in general, a soil and climate that is the fittest for every plant; yet this holds not as a rule quite universal: there are many exceptions from it. Many plants grow prosperously in a soil and climate diametrically opposite to those of another place, where they equally succeed.

There is not in Scotland, any two soils and situations more opposite to one another, than the gravelly sea beach, and a mossy soil on the summits of our highest mountains; yet the Statice *armeria,* the Thrift, or Sea Gilly Flower; and the Cucubalus *ma ritimus,* or Sea Campion, grow naturally and luxuriantly in both places.

It is presumed, in theory, that a plant will always flourish most in its natural soil and climate, or in those to which it has been long habituated; but it is fortunate for our northern climates, that this is often contradicted in practice. When grains have been long accustomed to the same soil and climate, they become less productive, and do in some degree degenerate. Hence arises the necessity, and the advantage of a change of seedcorn in every country. But the difficulty lies in determining the change that is most expedient to be made. Here, the theory of vegetation and of agriculture can avail us little; and all we have to depend upon, is what can be collected from observation and experience.

1. Independent of the soil and climate in which seed-corn may have been produced, it will be always safest to make choice of that which is of the greatest weight. 2. In oats and barley, the grain chosen for seed should be always what has the thinnest husk.

Thickness of husk, in these grains, is an imperfection that arises sometimes from climate, and sometimes from soil. The thinness of husk in the English barley, compared to ours, is probably owing to its being produced in a better climate; but we know, in this country, that the soil also is capable of making a great difference, where the climate is the same. In the heavy carse-lands upon the

Forth, the husk of the two rowed barley is so remarkably thick, in comparison to what it is upon the light dry grounds, not above a mile distant, that the bear or big in this last situation, is judged to be of equal value with the carse barley. In like manner, the barley produced after turnips, in Berwickshire, is of a thinner husk, of a superior quality, and gives a better price at market, than barley from the same ground would give, after any other crop. This difference, therefore, must be owing, not to the climate, but entirely to the state of the soil.

3. All horse-hoed grain should be avoided for seed-corn, as, for obvious reasons, it is never so full bodied as that which is sown broadcast. 4. The best grains imported into the Highlands, from the south of Scotland, from England, or Ireland, by often sowing, will always suffer an alteration for the worse: But this is the very reason why they ought to be frequently renewed. If they succeed, the expence of importation may be greatly overbalanced by a single crop; and by continuing the practice, the grain of the country must become gradually and greatly improved. In Sweden, they import much of their seed-wheat from Podolia, which affords a much better crop than the Swedish wheat; and, though it sutfers a sensible diminution after the second or third year, yet the importation is continued much to the advantage of the country. The easy access to foreign gram, and the frequent use of it for seed-corn, is certainly one reason why the gram and the crops, near the principal ports of Scotland, are superior to those of other places. 5. With respect to the change of grain from one part of the Highlands to another, regard should be had to difference of climate. It will always be safer to transfer grain from a high to a low part of the country, provided it be sufficiently ripe, than to translate it from a low to a high situation.

It is to be regretted that we are not better acquainted with the different sorts of grain in Norway, as it is likely they might be of remarkable use with us. Grain long cultivated in so high a latitude, not only becomes more hardy,

but comes gradually to accelerate its growth. One sort of barley, sown in Lapland, in the parallel of the northern parts of Norway, is compleatly ripe in sjxty-six days. When sown on the 31st pf May it is reaped on the 1st of August. Another sort of barley, raised in the same country, ripens in fifty-eight days; being sown the 31st of May, and reaped the 28th of July. These certainly would be useful kinds of grain in the north of Scotland, if they could be obtained.

It is not even unlikely, that the bear in the Islands of Harris and Lewis, might be translated with advantage, to the Southern parts of Scotland, and to the north of England, where that grain is sown. The habit this grain must have acquired by being sown in a country where there is a short summer, in the course of a thousand years, must be remarkable. In the high parts of the South of Scotland, of Cumberland, and Westmoreland, it is probable that this northern grain would be found more hardy, and ripen more early, than the bear or big that is at present sown in these countries.

6. In the change of seed-corn, however, from one part of the Highlands to another, more depends, certainly, upon the soil than the climate. It is in general the case, and highly remarkable, that a change of seed-corn is most advantageous, when it is brought from a soil quite different from that on which it is to be sown. There is now abundance of experience to convince us that corn-seed for a dry soil, should be chosen from one that is wet; and for a wet soil, from one that is dry; for a light soil, from one that is heavy; and for a heavy soil, from one that is light. These strong transitions, are found to produce the best effects, both upon the crop and the quality of the grain. 7. One thing remains to be urged in favour of grain raised on a dry soil. It is well known in the Highlands, that bear and oats produced on a sandy soil, afford the greatest yield, both of meal and spirits. They are, therefore, more substantial grains, and ought to be chosen in preference to all others, for sowing upon soils of a different quality. SECTION VIII. GREEN

SUMMER CROPS.

The raising of green crops is indispensibly requisite in good husbandry. They are necessary in order to draw from the soil the greatest quantity of sustenance for men and cattle. They do not take place, however, or are but imperfectly cultivated, till agriculture is considerably improved.

The hoeing husbandry was first applied in England to crops of grain. Some accurate and decisive experiments in this way have been made in Scotland. By these it has been proved, that the horse-hoed culture cannot succeed, at least in our climate, in the ,white crops. But it has likewise appeared, that this method of culture is highly beneficial in the green crops, and that without it they cannot be raised to the most advantage.

Wherever the horse-hoeing is practised in the white crops, it must come naturally to be applied to those that are green; and on the other hand, the green crops must come in time to introduce the horse hoed husbandry. The introduction of both, forms one of the greatest improvements that can be established in the Highlands.

The green crops are of two kinds. The one is raised in spring and reaped in autumn. The other is sown or planted in summer and autumn to answer for green food during winter and spring. Of the former kind, or green summer crops, potatoes, beans, and pease, are the best calculated for the Highland countries. After some observations upon these, it will be proper to take notice of the green winter crops which ought to be introduced.

POTATOES.

It would be out of place here to enter into any detail pn the cultivation of potatoes. All that is meant, is to suggest some observations, peculiarly applicable to the Highlands and Islands in the raising of this crop.

The first time potatoes were planted in the Hebrides, or in the Highlands, was in the year 1743, and in the island of South Uist. In the spring of that year, old Clanronald was in Ireland, upon a visit to his relation, Macdonnel of Antrim; he saw with surprise and approbation, the practice of the country, and having a vessel of his own along with him, brought home a large cargo of potatoes. On his arrival, the tenants in the island were convened, and directed how to plant them; but they all refused. On this, they were all committed to prison. After a little confinement, they agreed, at last, to plant these unknown roots, of which they had a very unfavourable opinion. When they were raised in autumn, they were laid down at the chieftain's gate, by some of the tenants, who said, the Laird indeed might order them to plant these foolish roots, but they would not be forced to eat them. In a very little time however, the inhabitants of South Uist came to know better, when every man of them would have gone to prison, rather than not plant potatoes.

In the Island of Barra, though contiguous to South Uist, potatoes were first planted only in the year 1752. Yet in ten years, they came to serve as sustenance to the whole inhabitants, above a fourth part ot the year. They were introduced here, and in other places, very opportunely, where a great deal of the best soil had lately been rendered unserviceable by the progress of the sand drift.

When the horse hoeing husbandry comes to be understood in the Highlands, it will be first and readily applied by all the people to the potatoe crop.— The best arable land, will, therefore be devoted to this purpose, and the present method of raising potatoes in lazy beds, deserted. This, if possible, ought to be prevented. In a cultivated country, it is contrary'to the interest of the tenant, of the landlord, and of the public, to raise potatoes any other way than with the plough. But where there is much wild land that can be profitably reclaimed, by the potatoe crop, and with spade culture, the case is different. In this case, the interest of the landlord, the progressive improvement of the country, and indeed the interest of the tenant, if he has a lease of any considerable length, are all deeply concerned in the efforts of the spade. It is true, indeed, that the horse-hoed potatoe crop, by affording more present profit, and by being ob-

tained with less labour, is more tempting to a tenant. Unless he is restrained, it will therefore occupy the best, perhaps the whole of the infield land upon a farm, and the uncultivated ground will remain neglected. But it should be remembered, that by the lazy-bed culture, much arable ground has already been acquired; and Unit by the same practice, a great addition may be annually made to the cultivated land in the Highlands; and further/that when horse hoeing comes to be practised, though it is certa'nly first to be employed upon the infield land; yet this should not be upon a crop of potatoes, but upon other green crops which cannot be raised on a wild soil. It is for these reasons expedient, that the spade culture of potatoes should continue to be encouraged, and confined as much as possible to uncultivated land.

Sea weeds are much used, but thev are an improper manure for the potatoe crop. They render the potatoes waxy and watery, which are neither so good for present use, nor for long keeping, as the dry and mealy potatoe. It is no small advantage of the lazy-bed culture, that potatoes can be raised in that way, without the aid of dung, or indeed of any other manure. In the lazy bed, the potatoe sets are placed between the herbage and the matted roots of two sods. The roots and the herbage become immediately putrid, and these, upon wild land with a rough surface, will always serve as manure sufficient for a profitable crop.

It is a prevailing and hurtful practice in the Highlands, to cut off the stems and leaves of the potatoes, close by the ground, about the end of August or beginning of September, for green food to the cattle. It can be affirmed from experience, that when the potatoes are thus cut, the growth of the roots is compleatly stopped. The roots of the potatoe, though early formed, make but little progress in point of bulk till towards the end of the season. Like other roots, and like fruits, there is a time in which they swell rapidly, and which is short, compared to the whole period of their growth. In the end of August, the pota-

toe acquires more bulk in a night, than it does in the middle of July, during a week. The potatoe, which at the 1st of August, is but of the size of a walnut, will sometimes be of a pound weight against the end of September. The roots increase both in number and size, as long, but no longer, than the vegetation of the stems and leaves continues.

It must therefore be bad economy to cut away the stems and leaves before their growth is compleated. It is a happy event for the potatoe crop when the autumnal frosts are late of appearing; for till then, the leaves remain green and the roots continue to enlarge. It is in general the most regular and steady crop we have, and liable to less alteration and deficiency than any other. It depends more upon the time, when the freezing degree of cold first takes place in autumn, than upon any other cause. If the growth of potatoes is prolonged till late in autumn the crop is plentiful. If on the other hand their growth is abridged by the early commencement of frost, the crop turns out scanty. The shores of the Highlands and Islands are favoured in this re speck In one of the smallest islands, Inch Marnoch, a very extensive field of potatoes, though fully exposed to the sea, and the south west winds, was not only verdant, but luxuriant, and the roots growing rapidly on the 18th of September. Yet in an inland district in the south of Scotland, remarkable too for raising potatoes, they have been known to be blasted, and their growth finally stopped by a frost on the night of the 16th of August, in consequence of which, the crop was deficient nearly one-half.— The Hebridians, therefore, and their neighbours on the main-land, have no reason *to* complain of their climate in this article. On the contrary, they are more advantageously situated for this and other green crops, than many of the southern and inland parts of Scotland, where these crops are raised with great advantage.

The crops of potatoes in the Highlands raised by the spade with much industry and skill, are every where so abundant, that it is unnecessary here *to* say any thing further on the manner of their cultivation. One article only requires to be particularly noticed, and that is, how to preserve the potatoe crop in the Highland countries from being tainted with the disease of the curl which is now become so prevalent in many parts of the south of Scotland.

THE DISEASE OF THE CURL.

Potatoes are now become the poor man's boll, as pease used formerly to be called; and their cultivation on that account, as well as others, deserves the greatest care.

This valuable crop has of late years been infected with a disease which threatens to increase, and is now but too well known by the name of the curl.

The stems of the curled potatoe are of a gross succulent growth, and decay sooner in the season than those of any other potatoe. The leaves are curled and crisp, and exceed in quantity and weight the foliage of a healthy plant. It is less prolific both in flowers and apples, and is remarkably deficient at the root. The potatoes it produces are few in number, of a small size, and of a bad quality.

The origin, the cause, and the cure of this distemper, form a subject of inquiry which well deserves the attention of the public.

It seems to have taken its rise in Lancashire; but neither the place nor the time of its first appearance are exactly known. It appears, however, to have taken place in that county before the year 176Q, And as Lancashire has always been noted for the best soils of potatoes, the disease has gradually been disseminated through various parts of England and Scotland, by means of seed potatoes brought from that county. Yet it is also probable that the disease may have arisen in other places without any such communication; for it is now well known to prevail in the rich soils of Germany, France, and Italy.

It was first observed in the Lothians, and particularly in the neighbourhood of Edinburgh, about the year J 773, and since that time has made its way into other parts of the country; but the more remote counties, and especially the whole of the Highlands, are happily still free from it.

This new and pernicious appearance in the potatoe crop has attracted very general notice, and many different causes have been assigned for it.

The curling of the leaves resembles in some de-. gree the effect of insects on other plants; and it was therefore naturally enough attributed to this cause. Some have ascribed it to an insect infecting the root, and others to an insect preying on the leaves.

For many years, however, the curled potatoes have been minutely examined with this view, and with magnifying glasses, but no peculiar insect can Vol. i. n be discerned, nor any thing like the work of an insect, can be observed upon them, different from what occurs in healthy potatoes.

The disease has also been supposed by different persons to be owing to one or other of the following, causes.

To the planting of potatoes from very small cuttings.

To the planting of cuttings from very large potatoes.

To the breaking of the sprouts before planting.

To the use of lime as a manure.

To the earthing up of the stems.

To an uncommon dryness in the season.

To the potatoes being kept above ground in win ter.

To planting the potatoes too shallow.

To the seed potatoes being hurt by frost.

To planting the potatoes in old tilled or worn out ground.

To a defect in the seed plant, by taking it from the ground before it is perfectly ripe.

To the seed potatoes having arrived at too great maturity.

All these causes are in themselves unlikely to produce such an effect; and though they have been proposed with much ingenuity, and well intended for the public good, they cannot be admitted as satisfactory. Besides, the various cases here mentioned have occurred times without number, and occur every year in Ireland and Scotland ever since potatoes «ere cultivated in these countries, without the appearance of any

curled plant. The disease, therefore, must in reason proceed from some other cause.

IMMEDIATE CAUSE OF THE CURL.

There is a twofold tendency in every plant; the one is to encrease its bulk, and the other to propagate its species. These two act upon each other as a counterpoise, and where the one is strong, the other is comparatively weak.

Of this principle the following familiar instances may be recollected.

When a tree runs to wood, as it is called, or becomes luxuriant in its stem, branches, and leaves, it is always less prolific in flowers and fruit: and the same thing happens when it sends forth a large growth of suckers from the root. When cabbages are planted in spring, they form during the season a large head composed of foliage; but if any of them shoot into flower, that exuberant growth of leaves is prevented. When turnips are sown in May, such of them as refrain from flowering form large roots, consisting of pulpy, parenchymous, or cellular substance; but if they shoot into flower, the growth of that pulpy substance in the root is checked and diminished.

A similar instance we have in the vegetation of potatoes.

A potatoe consists of two parts; the eyes and the pulp, or cellular substance, which forms the useful part of the root. The eyes are the embryos of so many suckers destined for the propagation of the plant, and where these are prevalent, the growth of the pulpy part of the root is restrained.

Hence in the smallest potatoes the eyes are always most numerous; and the potatoes to be chosen for seed arc those which have the smallest number of eyes compared to their bulk.

Thus we find that luxuriancy in one part of a plant tends to render it less luxuriant in another; which may be further exemplified in the case of the potatoe.

The first cultivation of the potatoe in Britain began in Lancashire, and this county has ever since been the most remarkable for its potatoe crops, and for the best varieties of the root. It has been there planted for above seventy years, on the richest soils, loaded with the greatest quantity of dung.

By this treatment, so long continued, some luxuriancy in such a plant was to be expected: and accordingly, in Lancashire this curled luxuriancy first made its appearance.

It is a luxuriancy, however, exactly similar to what has taken place in other plants that have been long cultivated. In the fertile valleys and favourable climate of Sicily, wheat becomes luxuriant in in the ear, and produces a branched instead of a simple spike. The numerous sorts of cabbages, savoys, cauliflower, and brocoli, are but luxuriant varieties in the foliage, or in the flower, derived by culture from one original plant, which in its natural »tate wears no such appearance. We have also in our gardens plants which have assumed a curled luxuriancy in their leaves, exactly similar to what has taken pi e in the potatoe: such as the curled cress, curled parsley, curled endive, curled tansy, and the curled kail. This appearance in these plants is unknown in their natural state, in which they have all plain leaves. But it has been produced by cultivation and luxuriant nourishment; and when once produced is generally continued.

When a luxuriance of this kind takes place in a plant, it is most effectually perpetuated by evolution; that is, by slips, layers, grafts, or offsets from the roots; but sometimes, also, even from the seeds. Thus the seeds of the curled parsley, cress, endive, and kail, when sown, produce generally curled plants; though along with these, some plants also with plain leaves.

Most of our garden plants are cultivated on account of some luxuriancy in their roots, stems, leaves, flowers, or fruit; for many of them without that luxuriancy would not be worth cultivation. It is to their luxuriancy that we owe our best esculent plants, our finest flowers, and our most choice fruits. These luxuriancies have subsisted for ages; but at what time, where, and in what manner they were at first produced, is unknown. Nor is this surprising, when we find that the cause of the curled luxuriancy in the leaves of the potatoe, which has sprung up in our own country, and even in our time, has escaped observation, and remains a matter of conjecture.

From this detail it appears that the potatoe curl is nothing else but a luxuriant variety in the foliage of the plant, which, as in other cases, restrains and diminishes the growth of the roots: This is evidently.the immediate and general cause of the disease. But as this luxuriance may be produced in different ways, these are to be considered as so many remote causes of the distemper.

THE REMOTE CAUSES OF THE CURL.

Immoderate richness of soil may safely be considered as the most frequent of these remote causes. The rich soils of Lancashire, highly fed with dung, would be naturally productive of such a luxuriancy; and the same probably has happened in other places. Great fertility of soil is well known to be the parent of many such luxuriancies in other plants.

Of the common parsley we have two remarkable varieties: the one with plain leaves, but with large esculent roots, approaching to the size of a parsnip, that first sprung from the rich soils of Holland; the other with curled leaves, exactly similar to those of the curled potatoe, which originated in the same country and from the same cause, being also exactly similar to thc curled potatoe, in having roots so.lender, as to be of no use.

On the contrary, poor soils, or those of moderate fertility, are never productive of such a luxuriancy in the leaves of plants; and accordingly it has never been known to take place where potatoes arc cultivated on such soils.

A wet soil and a wet season, if they do not produce, they at least tend to promote this disease. It is most remarkable in wet soils, and never makes such progress in those that are dry. The curl is also most prevalent in the seasons most favourable to the luxuriancy of the stems and leaves of potatoes, and is less frequent in seasons of an opposite nature.

The summer of the year 1800 was the hottest and driest that has occurred in this country since the year 1723. The effects were but too well known in the shortness of every crop. During the whole summer, the potatoes were of a sparing and stinted growth, and had no luxurance; but the curl scarce anywhere appeared; a circumstance which has not been known for many years. In many fields, not a diseased plant was to be seen, where, in an ordinary-rason, many were to have been expected.

The raising of very early potatoes has been long practised in Lancashire, and in a very peculiar way. The sprouts of the seed potatoes, with their young leaves, are made to spring to a considerable length in the air, before they are planted in the ground, and are then committed to the richest soil.

It is most probable that this may have given rise to the distemper. That by this forcing practice the form of the leaves should come to be altered, is not surprising. It is well known, also, that the curl first appeared, and has ever since most prevailed, among the early potatoes in Lancashire, and also in distant places into which the early potatoes of that county have been imported.

There is sometimes a crowth of knots on the stems of potatoes, immediately above ground, and of the size of the smaller roots. They are called oukles by the common people. These knots, by exposure to the air, are of a different colour from that of the roots below ground, but they are very full of eyes, which grow freely.

, They have been long propagated in Lancashire,. and there is reason to think that it is from these that the early Lancashire potatoes have derived their origin. Being themselves a sort of monstrous production, it is not unlikely, that they may have occasioned

Such an unnatural luxuriancy as the curl in the leaves.

From entire potatoes there proceeds always a more rampant growth of stems and foliage, than from cuttings which contain one, two, or three eyes. From this luxuriant growth of stems and leaves, afforded by entire potatoes, it is probable that the disease does sometimes also arise.

REMEDIES FOR THE CURL.

To one or other, or perhaps all of these

causes, the potatoe curl is evidently to be ascribed, each of them having a strong tendency to create or increase this diseased luxuriancy. Its pernicious effects, when they have taken place, may no doubt be gradually removed by reversing these causes; but to prevent them is certainly a far more easy and effectual remedy.

Where potatoes have been infected with this disease by excessive fertility of soil, it is pretty certain that they can be recovered, and brought again into a healthy state, by being repeatedly planted in a soil of an opposite nature.

In the year 1765, I received from an ingenious friend (Mr Kendal) a parcel of the early Lancashire potatoes, which were planted that season at Moffat. Many oi rhem had curled tops; and this, it is probable, was the first appearance of the disease in Scotland. The roots of these plants were insignificant; but the whole being again planted for three or tour years in lazy beds, and in a lean gravelly soil, the curl disappeared, and the roots became larger and more numerous.

But to recover potatoes from the disease in this way, is tedious and unnecessary. To refrain from setting potatoes in a wet soil; to avoid all the early sorts tor a common crop; and to abstain from using entire potatoes as seed;—these are means not only well adapted to obviate the disease, but expedient for the right cultivation of the potatoe crop.

In whichsoever of the above ways this disease may have been introduced, it is clearly nothing more than a luxuriant variety in the foliage of Uie plant, occasioned by culture.

Was the potatoe cultivated for its leaves, this luxuriancy would deserve to be encouraged, as in the case of the garden plants with curled leaves above mentioned. But as the root is the valuable part, upon which the luxuriancy of the leaves has a most hurtful effect, it must therefore be restrained, and if possible removed.

Like luxuriancies in other plants acquired by culture and exuberant nourishment, this disease may probably be done away by planting the curled pota-

toes again and again in a poor soil. The plant, as in other cases, might then return to its natural state. But there is no necessity to be at such pains in pursuing a tedious and precarious remedy. For if potatoes have once acquired this luxuriancy, though it may be removed by planting them in a poor soil, it will probably again recur whenever they are planted in one that is rich. We should not attempt, therefore, to cure the diseased plants, but to get rid of them. To prevent this distemper is of more consequence than to cure it. It is the extirpation, not the cure of this disease, that ought to be the object with the public and every farmer. It is not a contagious, but a hereditary disease. It is confined to the potatoes of one race; and where that race can be exterminated, the disease would be extinguished.

For this purpose, the most effectual measure that can be proposed, is to dig up the curled potatoes in every field as soon as they appear, and ot throw them away root and branch. By throwing them away, there is in fact but little lost; and the labour of the operation is nothing compared to the advantage of it. Was this done universally, the disease would soon be eradicated. But many are unwilling to lose even the scanty produce from these diseased roots, and suffer them to grow till they are ripe. They are then raised and mixed with the healthy roots; and along with them serve as seed potatoes for the ensuing season. By the cottagers, and many others who raise potatoes, the smaller roots, from an ill-judged economy, are allotted for seed; and among these, the curled potatoes, of course, must always make the largest proportion. In this way the disease is disseminated through the country, and there is no coercive method to obstruct its progress. But, in imitation of an old Scots statute, it would be no arbitrary or severe law, but one salutary both for individuals and the public, to fine the person in every parish, who had the greatest proportion of curled potatoes in the field!

The extirpation of the curled potatoes by this method, is not, perhaps, soon to be expected: but, while the disease

continues in the country, the following means to avoid it may be suggested.

1. Never to use seed potatoes from a field in which the curl has in any degree appeared. 2. To bring seed potatoes from those parts of the country where the disease is yet unknown.

In the year 1754, there was no potatoe in MidLothian but the round smooth red. and the long white kidnev. A few vcars before this the Irish swatterock had been brought into Galloway and Lancashire; a smooth white potatoe of an ova! and flat snape. It was then accounted the best potatoe, and is perhaps the best still. A dozen of that sort were first planted in this county, at Newhall, in spring 1754. Soon after this, it was brought in abundance from the south of Scotland and west of England. It quickly superseded the culture both of th, round red and kidney potatoe; and has been ever since, as it is at present, the prevailing potatoe planted, not only in this country, but over the most of Scotland.

It was this potatoe that was chosen in Lancashire for their early crops. By the peculiar mode of managemement in producing these crops, the plant, in a course of years, has acquired some peculiar properties; among these, it would appear, the disease of the curl. Even in this diseased state, however, it is still a smooth white potatoe of an oval and flat shape. By these means, its roots are not easily distinguished from those which were originally of the same kind, but which still remain in a sound state. The two are now mixed together in almost every field, and it is become a matter of difficulty to have the diseased separated from the healthy plants.

The safe expedient, therefore, is to dismiss all the potatoes from a farm in which the curl has once appeared, and to bring seed potatoes from a distance where the distemper is unknown. The same potatoe. deservedly preferred in the Lothians, and originally called the swatterock, is still to be had sound and of an excellent quality in Galloway, and in the higher parts of Nithsdale, Clydesdale, Annandale, and Tweedale. It may also be obtained from the countries beyond the Forth, where the curl has never yet appeared.

3. To avoid raising the early Lancashire potatoe.—These are not only most liable to the curl, but even when free from it, they afford such a diminutive crop, and of such an inferior quality as to be improper for general use. They are fit only to be raised where they can bring a high price, merely on account of their coming early in the season. The encouragement thrown out for their culture during the scarcity of the years 1800 and 1801, has even had a detrimental effect in spreading them too much through the country.

Those potatoes should rather be cultivated, in which the disease has never occurred. Such is the smooth round red, which affords a valuable crop, though not in all things equal to the smooth white flat potatoe at present in use.

BEANS.

There can be no doubt, that many parts of the Highlands would reap much advantage from the introduction of beans. Where they are sown broadcast in the Lowlands, if the soil is fit for them, they always produce a more beneficial crop than pease, and much more friendly to the white crop that succeeds. But every well informed farmer knows, that to reap the full advantage of beans, it must be by means of a horse-hoed crop; and in this way only, they should be raised in the Highlands.

They would there serve to introduce the horsehoeing husbandry, which is much wanted. In a proper rotation, they would afford a meliorating crop, and increase the quantity of grain.—They would yield a bulky crop of dry provender for the cattle.—They would likewise add much to the sustenance of the inhabitants. In the carses, bread made of bean meal is now the staple food of some of the strongest and most laborious people in Scotland.

It is true, indeed, that beans make little figure on a light and dry soil; and that they succeed best upon one that is heavy and adhesive, which is not frequent in the Highlands. Yet the black soil, as it is called, though it contains but little clay, is, in many places, deep,

moist, and fertile, and would, undoubtedly, answer well for horse-hoed beans.

A stronger objection against the sowing of beans in the Highlands, is the lateness of their growth. The bean, though hardy, is a very late plant: It does not, like the white crops, close its vegetation within the season: It continues to spread its branches; to spring from the root; and to vegetate vigorously till it is cut off by the frost. The great benefit it communicates to the soil, probably arises, indeed, from this manner of growth; but when sown in March, even in the early parts of Scotland, it is frequently not in the barn-yard till November.

If beans are to be sown at all in the Highlands, the very earliest season must therefore be adopted. In many places, and in most years, they might be sown in January; but where there is inclosed ground for them, October would probably be the most proper season. Plants of the same natural order, such as the Sweet scented pea, the Winged peaf, the Tangier peu'j;, the (Jhihcling vetch , and the different Lathyrus *odoratus,* Linn. Sweet scented pea.

+ Lotus *lelragonolobuSf* Linn. Winged pea.

J Lathyrus *lingitanus,* Linn. Tangier pea.

U *sativus,* Linn. Chichling vetch.

VOL. I. *S* species of lupine when sown in the spring, continue verdant, and vegetate briskly like the bean, till they are demolished by autumnal frost; but when these plants are sown in October, though much more tender than the field bean, they come forward early in spring, finish their growth, produce a profusion of well ripened seeds, and pass into an arid state before the approach of the frosts in autumn. There can be little doubt that the same would be the case with our beans, were they sown in autumn; and, that instead of being the latest and most imperfectly ripened, they might be one of our earliest and best ripened crops.

This, we are entitled to think, from the most reasonable analogy, would be the case; but to be ascertained and established, experiments are requisite. Trials

for this purpose should first be made in the Lowlands, where beans are already cultivated. Were these trials to succeed, as is here supposed they would everywhere introduce a great improvement in the bean crop; but especially in the Highlands, where the lateness of the climate is rather adverse to the raising of beans in the spring.

Lupinus *altnis,* Linn. White lupine. *hirsutus,* Linn. Great blue lupine. *variut,* Linn. Small blue lupine. *luteus,* Linn. Yellow lupine. III a late country, or in the case of a late crop, beans should not be cut till their vegetation is entirely stopt, either by frost, or the advanced season. A slight frost in September or October, though sufficient to prevent any further growth of the plant, will not injure the grain. Alter this, beans dry more in one day, standing on the ground, than they would during a week in the sheaf. If late in the season, they never, therefore, should be cut green and succulent. If allowed to stand, and to dry to a certain degree, they will be sooner in the barn-yard, and in better order. PEASE.

The soil, in general, in the Highlands, is much better adapted for the pease crop than that of beans. Broadcast pease is a crop seldom to be recommended; and ought, indeed, to be laid aside in most places where it is used: but there is a more favourable opportunity of raising this crop in the islands, and on the west coasts, than perhaps anywhere else in Scotland.—This arises from the nature and cleanness of the infield land, and the mildness of the winter.

On the farms in these parts, the infield land is not only light, dry, and fertile, but the cleannest of any that can be seen. This is owing to perpetual tillage, without any manure but sea weeds. It receives no annual supply of the seeds of grass and other weeds, from the dung of animals and their litter, like the infield of other countries. This renders it peculiarly suitable lor a broadcast crop of pease, which never succeeds except where the land is perfectly clean.

The mildness of the winter is likewise a favourable circumstance for the introduction of the pease crop. It is a crop that requires a great deal of season, even more than we can afford it in the south of Scotland, when only sown in the spring; for sometimes, not one half of the blossoms produce ripe pease; but in the islands, and on the Udjacent coasts, the pease ought to be sown in October. In these parts, there are no frosts in winter that will destroy or hurt them. If sown at this time, they will have season enough to afford a well ripened crop. Sow n at this time, we raise the White garden pea, a more tender plant, which never fails, unless the winter is uncommonly severe, and is compleatly ripened before the 20th of July. Even in the Lowlands, where pease are sown broadcast, were they sown in autumn, they would undoubtedly afford a more advantageous crop; but green crops of every kind are so necessary for improving the husbandry of the Highlands, that the raising of pease in this way, and for these reasons, ought certainly to be attempted. The infield lands in the islands, and on the coasts. from Clvde to Sutherland, are generally of a drier and more forward soil; nor is the climate more wet than those places, among the high mountains of Tweeddale, where the Magbiehill pea is raised with so much advantage. This sort of pea is the hardiest, the earliest, and the most prolific of any we have; and should, therefore, be preferred for cultivation in the Highlands.

GREEN WINTER CROPS.

The want of winter and spring food for cattle, ie the great want over all the Highlands, and product.tive of much calamity. It frequently ruins the tenants, and impoverishes the landlords. The remedy for this evil, is a proper provision of green food and dry provender, both which, with skill and industry, the country is well able to supply. Of green winter crops for cattle, the Highlands are as yet entirely destitute; though these crops may undoubtedly be raised everywhere to advantage. They are elsewhere cultivated, indeed, for the fattening of cattle, which is not the chief object in the Highlands; but they are also of the greatest moment in a breeding country, especially where numbers of cattle are apt to fall in winter and spring, merely for want of food. As the introduction of these green winter crops must therefore be a matter of the utmost consequence to the Highlands, they deserve here to be particularly considered.

TURNIPS.

Most parts of the Highlands, and all the Islands, afford favourable situations for the culture of turnips. 1 hey may be there raised with more advanvantage than perhaps anywhere else. The soil is dry, fertile, and low rented. The wetness of the autumn may be hurtful to grain, but it greatly favours the turnip crop. The winter is open, and free from the intense and long continued frosts which so frequently destroy the turnips in other places, if allowed to remain in the ground till late in winter. In all the low parts of the Highlands, they might be preserved through the whole winter, and the great losses prevented, which are so frequently incurred by the death of cattle, from the want of sufficient provender.

The soil first to be employed for turnips, is the infield land which has been immemorially in tillage. It is light, dry, free from weeds, and in good tilth. A piece of land of this kind, is to be found almost upon every Highland farm. That it should be inclosed, is indeed necessary; but many fields proper for raising turnips upon Highland farms, are already inclosed with dry-stone dykes. Wherever a sufficient inclosure is wanting, it must, no doubt, be made before the cultivation of turnips can be attempted.

The horse-hoed crop of turnips is everywhere the largest,'and the most profitable. They should be, therefore, raised in the Highlands only in this way; especially as it is the means of introducing the horse-hoeing husbandry, so beneficial in other crops, and in every country. The horse-hoed, excells the the broadcast crop of turnips; because it is less expensive, affords a greater increase, cleans the land more effectually, and is much superior as a preparatory fallow for a white crop. No reason can be discerned why the broadcast crop of turnips should be so prevalent in England, but the being wedded to an old practice. The whole value of the drilled turnip crop, however, depends on its being frequently and seasonably hoed.

In the turnip crop, much depends on the season of sowing. It requires, in this article, to be more nicely regulated, according to the climate and situation of the place, than almost any other crop. If the field turnip is sown at the proper season, it affords a great increase; if it is sown too early, it shoots, atid turns to no account; if it is sown too J ate, the turnips never arrive at a proper size, nor afforda sufficient crop. These are great differences, and yet they will all arise from the difference of about a month or six w eeks in the time of sowing.

The best time for sowing turnips in the south of England, is the 10th of June; yet, it is often delayed till the end of the month, and even till July is advanced, which is certainly too late, even in that favourable climate. As we have borrowed the turnip culture from England, the same time of sowing has been injudiciously observed in some of the higher parts of Scotland. Proper allowance is not made for the difference of climate: for in such a situation with us, turnips sown after the 10th of June, have not season to produce a full crop: for this purpose, they require to be sown more early in the south of Scotland than in the south of England; and more early in the north, than in the south of Scotland.

The turnip, like all other plants, vegetates more quickly, in an early, than in a late climate. Were turnips sown in Norfolk, before the 1st of June, many of them, especially in a dry season, would go into flower; but the same turnips sown in the Highlands, or in the south of Scotland, five hundred feet above the sea, on the 20th of May, would never aim at flowering. A winter crop of turnips can now here be sown too early, provided none of them.shoot. The early sowing gives full time for the growth of the root, and for a large crop. In two situations in the south of Scotland, very similar to a great part of the Highlands in soil and climate, it has been found, that the sowing of turnips on the 20th of

May, and on the 20th of June, made all the difference between a plentiful and a scanty crop.

In a northern and backward climate, if turnips are not sown more early than in the south of England, they have not season to arrive at their full size or to form a beneficial crop. There are indeed some varieties of turnip which compleat their growth in a shorter space of time than others. These, for a winter crop, ought to be sown late. But such as arc of a later growth, and which generally afford the weightiest crop, should be sown more early.— Though the earliest sorts of grain, are indeed the most eligible, it is the latest turnip that is tl»e most proper for the Highlands. The red topt is the hardiest, the latest, and the most reluctant to shoot. It therefore admits of earlier sowing, and is the variety to be chosen.

It would be unnecessary here to touch upon the common culture of the tumip crop, as it is now understood by every ordinary ploughman in Berwickshire, the Lothians and other places. But it may not be improxr, in a few words, to enumerate the advantages that accrue to a country by the cultivation of turnips.

. They are the best means of converting dry, moorish wild land and sandy downs, or links, as they are called, into arable. 0. In a cultivated soil, they afford what is equal to a fallow, while they yield a profitable crop. y. They clean the ground, both of root and annual weeds.

X. They feed a large quantity of cattle, when the green pasture is gone, and when the dry provender requires to be spared.

t. They raise the size and improve the breed both of black cattle and sheep. ?. They afford a great supply of dung. n. They are the best preparative for a white crop. 8. They increase the quantity, not only of cattle but of corn.

They promote a progressive improvement of the soil.

x. They serve to introduce a polished and accurate plan of husbandry. K. Wherever they have been extensively cultivated, their advantageous effects have been experienced by enriching the farmer, and by increasing the value and the rent of land.

In all these articles, the turnip crop is excellently adapted, and must be highly beneficial to every country that is at present in the state ot the Highlands.

TURNIP ROOTED CABBAGE.

This is the Brassica *napobrassica* of Linnaeus. It was introduced from Germany into England, about forty years ago, where it has ever since been in some degree cultivated. It was hi st brought into Scotland in spring 1766. About the same time, it was translated from England to Sweden, and from thence the seeds have of late years been sent back to this country, as the seeds of a new and useful plant, and with the Swedish name of *Rula baga*. It is a plant, indeed, whose properties render it much more useful in a northern climate, than in that of England.

It is a biennial plant, with a root of the shape and nearly of the size of a turnip; but being of the colewort kind, its foliage is smooth, and affords greens for the table, from its early state, till the time of its flowering the second year. Even after the stem is 6hot, the root continues solid and fit for use; a presumption that it would remain fresh in the ground and spring after the second year.

It is one of the hardiest roots that is kno%vn. It subsists not only during the whole winter, but during the whole spring, long after the turnips are gone. — Though by horse-hoeing it does not arrive at so large a size; yet in a garden, it is usually larger than our turnips. For family use, it is as agreeable, and much more nutrimental than the turnip, so that no garden of a farmer or a cottager should be without it.

When the turnip shoots in spring, the root becomes exhausted and decays. But this is not the case with the turnip cabbage; for though it shoots into stem and flower, the root still remains firm and solid. Both the root and the foliage are in perfection, as food both for men and cattle, in the end of April, and even during May, when the usefulness of this plant becomes very remarkable,

When a two inch cube of the white field turnip and one of the yellow garden turnip were weighed. The yellow was found to be one eight part heavier than the white. The yellow turnip is therefore a root of more substance, and would be more valuable in feeding cattle than the white, if k could be obtained of equal bulk. Any person may observe at table, that it is of a firmer and less watery texture than the white turnip. It might, no doubt, be raised to a larger size, by field culture, than what it arrives at in a garden.

Another cube of the turnip cabbage, or *rut a baga,* of the same size, was found again to be of greater weight than that of the yellow turnip, and above one fifth part heavier than the white. This renders it bulk for bulk, of much more avail in the feeding of cattle, being a more nourishing root than the field turnip. It is this compactness and solidity of substance which makes both the yellow turnip and *ruta baga,* resist degrees of frost, which destroy the common turnip, and renders the *ruta baga* such a valuable food late in the spring.

When raised in the field, it should always be horse-hoed. Its culture is in general the same with that of the turnip, and it is a plant that deserves more attention than has been paid to it, wherever turnips are cultivated. It is of a much slower growth than the turnip, and does not flower the same year in which it is sown. To have it in perfection, it is therefore requisite to sow it, not when turnips are sown, which is commonly the case, but much more early in the season. It ought to be sown by the 1st of May, for though sown at that time, it is in no danger'of shooting before autumn. If it is to be transplanted, it should be sown about the 1st of April.

The crop of *ruta baga* is indeed inferior in quantity to what a crop of turnips would be on the same ground; but this deficiency is fully compensated by its other qualities. Beside its being a more substantial food for cattle, it withstands the utmost rigour of our winters unimpaired, and can be had in perfection in February, March, and April, when the turnips fail, and when hay and straw become scarce. It has generally been used for the fattening of cattle, and for that purpose succeeds the turnips; but in. the Highlands it would answer a different, and more important end, to support the stock during the scarcity of the spring, and especially to preserve the lives of the young cattle.

BRASSICA CAPITATA, LINN. WHITE CABBAGE.

The field cabbage is another green crop that may with advantage be introduced into several parts of the Highlands. The plant to be chosen is the cabbage most commonly raised in this country, and cultivated in Kngland, by the name of the Scots, the Flat, or Drum-headed cabbage. It is now become a profitable crop in many parts of the south. The crops of cabbage, turnip, and turnip-cabbage, in succession, are now found capable of feeding and fattening cattle, from the 1st of October to the 1st of April and even later.

The greatest disadvantage of the cabbage crop, is its short duration; and that, while there is yet green food in the fields lor a breeding stock. No sooner do the cabbages arise to their full size and perfection in October, than they are liable to be demolished by the early frosts of winter. Yet in the low and maritime parts of the Highlands, they would be less liable to this misfortune than in many places in the south.

To remedy this defect, it is surprising that the Dutch red cabbage is nowhere cultivated in the field. It is a much more hardy plant than any sort of white cabbage, and is capable of remaining till late in the spring unhurt. 1 hough its size is sometimes large, even in the garden, there is no doubt but by horse-hoeing, it would be greatly increased.

BRASS1CA SABELLICA, LINN. BORECOLE.

Several different sorts of colewort are now raised in the fields by the horse-hoeing husbandry. The common open colewort, the green and yellow savoy, the green curled kail, and the parsley colewort have all been tried. These are all proper for the garden, and useful at the table. But the brown, or rather the red German borecole, deserves a preference for field culture, as it not only affords a weightier crop, but stands the

winter better than any of the others.

It has been called in England the Siberian borecole. But many plants have got names from Siberia and Lapland, which never grew in these countries. It came to Scotland from Germany, which its name indeed intimates, as the English word cole, and the Scots word kail are evidently derived from the German. It approaches nearest to the red curled colewort of Ayrshire, known in the west by the name of Kilmaurs kail, but it is still more hardy, and of a stronger grow th. Where the seeds of it cannot be procured, the Kilmaurs kail is certainly the best of all our coleworts for field culture.

The borecole, and likewise cabbage, are of great use in supplying the cattle, when early frosts prevent turnips from being dug out of the ground. Eor this and other purposes, they well deserve to be raised in a certain proportion, wherever turnips are cultivated.

WIXTER VETCHES.

The summer and the winter vetch are the same plant, and are only distinguished by these names, from the season in which they are sown, and the purpose for which they are designed.

The summer vetch is sown in spring in the Lothians and many other places. It is designed to afford a crop of green forage, to horses and cows, for about two months, between the first and second cutting of clover. This end it compleatiy answers, and forms a most convenient crop; but green food at that season is so abundant in the Highlands that it is not consumed. The sowing of summer vetches is therefore unnecessary.

The winter vetch again, is sown in England during autumn, with a view to provide green food in spring. This is the purpose for which it ought to be cultivated in the Highlands. Like every other winter crop, it requires, indeed, inclosed ground, but that is now to be had in many places. It should be sown with a very slight furrow and rolled, upon barley or oat stubble, in the end of August or before the 20th of September. On the shores of the Highlands, it would afford a plentiful crop of green herbage in April and May, and prove the best

preparation for a turnip crop.

There is a plant of this kind, was it sufficiently known, that would repay the attention of British agriculturists; the Narbonne vttch, or Vicia *narbonnensis* of Linnaeus. It is a plant of a much more VOL. I. T vigorous and rampant growth than the common vetch. When both were sown in a garden together in Scotland, and in but a poor soil, it afforded more than double the crop.

MANGEL WUBZEL. ROOT OF SCARCITY.

This plant was introduced a few years ago from German', but we have scarcely had sufficient experience to ascertain its precise value. Mangel wurzel signifies the scarcity root, but the real German name of the plant is Mangold wurzel, or beet root. It is indeed but a variety of beet, yet differs greatly from the green, white, and red beets raised in our gardens; and still more, from the Beta *maritime,* Linn, or sea beet, which grows upon our shores, and is the parent plant of all these varieties.

From a few years observation, it appears, that both the foliage and the root of this plant, are much more luxuriant than those of any other beet. When sown, even early in the spring, it does not shoot like other beets, but, without attempting to flower, holds on its growth till winter, when the root arrives indeed at a very considerable size.

Its foliage, at every period of its growth affords excellent greens, and they are still more tender and sweeter when frequently cut; but the cutting of the the leaves impedes considerably the growth of the root.

The root is sometimes white, sometimes red, and frequently partakes of both colours. In its other qualities, it is scarcely to be di..ting iibhcd from the root of the beetrave or red beet.

It is unquestionably a wholesome food both for man and cattle; and as a vegetable aliment, one of the most substantial and nourishing. For, excenung the parsnip and skinet, it contains more saccharine matter than any other of our culinary roots. But it is doubtful, whether the quantity of crop would be sufficient for the expence of field culture, and profitable for the feeding of cattle. It is certainly capable, however, of affording a greater quantity of sustenance than either the carrot or the parsnip, which in many places are cultivated in the lield for that purpose.

The plant is at any rate, a considerable acquisition to our gardens. Both the greens and the root are capable of being dressed in a variety of ways, and of being rendered very useful and agreeable as an article of diet. It affords so large a quantity of wdiolesome vegetable food, upon so little ground, and with so little trouble, that it certainly ought to have a place in the garden of every farmer, and of every cottager in Scotland. In this view, the cultivation of the plant over the Highlands in general, might certainly be useful. It would be a great and additional point gained if, upon further experience it should be there found profitable in field culture.

There are still two other plants to be mentioned, which are fit to supply the cattle in the Highlands with green food in winter. These, though extremely common in the south, and easily propagated, would probably turn out as generally useful as any of the former. They are whins and broom.

WHINS.

The whin bush , though now spread over many tracts of the South of Scotland, scarcely appears to be an original native of the country. It is known at least, within a century past, to have been introduced into several parts, by seeds brought from England and Ireland. Even at present, it exists not in Cantire, nor upon any of the western coasts and islands of Scotland north of that promontory.

In arable and fertile grounds, whins ought to be completely extirpated as a nuisance. But the case is quite different in a wild and pasture country.— There, they deserve to be encouraged and propagated; for they afford to all sorts of cattle, a large Ulex *curopaeuS)* Linn. quantity of green and wholesome food in winter and spring, when there is but little or nothing to be had in the fields. Their usefulness in feeding both black cattle and horses is well known. Where

they grow on a sheep pasture, every person may have observed, how greedily and accurately the whin-bush is cropped by the sheep, so far as they can reach. — In short, no black cattle, horses, or sheep will starve in winter or spring, if they have abundance of whins to eat.

The superiority of the Galloway cattle is acknowledged. But no part of Scotland abounds so much in a luxuriant growth of whins as Galloway, and their good effects, in affording both winter food and shelter to the cattle of that country, are well known.

Whins ought therefore to be extensively propagated in the Highlands. This may be easily done, by sowing the seeds, which will rise and prosper, almost upon every soil, except peat moss. They may be sown at any height, to the extent of about one thousand feet above the level of the sea, for higher than this, indeed, they will not grow. But beyond this height, the grasing grounds in the Highlands are seldom occupied by cattle in winter. It may be further noticed, that when the poorest arable land has been overgrown for some years with whins; if they are then burnt, and ploughed or grubbed up, the soil is always found in the highest state of fertility.

BROOM.

Broom , though an indigenous plant, is confined to particular districts of Scotland. It subsists chiefly in the lower parts of the country, and seldom grows at more than six hundred feet above the level of the sea.

The usefulness of this shrub, in some of our grasin'4 countries, where it abounds, is well known. In the south, the sheep feed much upon it in w inter, where it is reckoned a food so salutary, as to keep them free from several diseases.

A broom park, as it is called, in the shires of Angus and Mearns, is reckoned a necessary article upon every farm. This is a field of broom, allowed to grow up till it is six or seven feet high. This field is the resort of all the black cattle upon the farm in winter. It supplies them, when pressed by ivant in the scarce season, with a great quantity

of wholesome food. It affords them compleat shelter during the night; and when this field comes to be broken up, at the end of seven or eight years, it not only yields tbe best crop of corn, of any field on Spartium *scoparium,* Linn. the farm, but likewise a great quantity of fuel, which is a scarce article in these countries.

These are advantages exactly adapted to the state of the Highlands, which have hitherto been neglected. From the Clyde, to the north extremity of Scotland, there is little broom to be seen upon any of the western coasts or islands, and still less in the more inland places. Yet in these countries there can be no doubt, that it would grow luxuriantly, and prove equally advantageous as in other parts. The plantation of broom, ought therefore, to be every where immediately attempted, and may be easily accomplished by seeds brought from the South.

GENERAL REMARKS. . We are not to expect a plant fit for green forage, that is capable of growing during the frosts of winter, as has been imagined by some. For the growth of every plant is brought to a full stop, whenever the freezing degree of cold takes place. But the plants we want for this purpose, are such as can withstand the frosts of our climate, and can grow in some measure, when Fahrenheit's thermometer stands between the thirty-sixth and forty-eighth degree, which is the most frequent temperature in the Islands and low parts of the Highlands, during five months of the year, that is, from the 1st of November to the 1st of April.

Such are the six plants above described, under the head of green winter crops. Others may, and probably will be discovered, more valuable for the purpose, but these are the best we know at present. They all produce a great quantity of sustenance, and would be of much service in the Highlands, for the support of the people as well as of the cattle. Their cultivation in the field, employs much labour within a narrow compass, which is a fortunate circumstance in a country where the proportion of cultivated land is comparatively small. The

Highland practice ot working the soil with the cascrome or crooked spade, would also be friendly to the introduction of these crops. In this way, the garden culture might be gradually transferred to the field, which is the perfection of husbandry in every country.

2. The dry provender at present in the Highlands, goes but a little way in the sustenance of the cattle; and, though it may, and should be greatly enlargedi yet it never can be had in such quantity as to support them sufficiently. Hence the necessity of green winter crops, which, fortunately, the country is well able to supply.

In Norway and Sweden, the cattle must be housed, and are entirely excluded from the fields, for three or four months with frost and deep snow. The climate also renders every green winter crop impracticable. The cattle have nothing to depend on but dry provender, and that even is so scarce, that the leaves or trees are employed for the purpose. The extensive summer pastures of these countries, can only be consumed in part; because it Is only a certain number 01 cattle that can be sustained in winter. The case, happily, is quite different with our Highlands. The cattle, if it is necessary, can keep the field the whole winter. The dry provender may be easily augmented, and, with the addition of green winter food, the stock of cattle may be greatly enlarged. The summer pasturage is plentiful and excellent, but much of it is lost for the saute reason as in Norway and Sweden. Let sufficient winter provision be secured, and then every pile of grass may be turned to account. If the winter food for cattle in the Highlands could be rendered adequate to the summer pasture, the produce of the country might at least be doubled:—This, however, must be the work of time. In the mean while, it is the interest, and ought to be the endeavour of every proprietor and farmer to keep the maxim here inculcated constantly in view.

Cabbage, turnip, and turnip-cabbage, afford crops in succession, by which cattle may be compleatly made up for the butcher, between the decay and the return of the grass. Such management. however, is more the object of a fattening than of & breeding country. These, and other green crops in the Highlands, assisted by the dry forage, ought to be applied merely for the maintenance of the cattle during winter and spring. The lives of many of them might thus be saved, their numbers increased, and the breed also gradually improved.

3. By the methods here proposed for augmenting the quantity, both of green and dry forage to serve during winter, it maybe safely presumed, that the following ends would be obtained, much to the advantage of the Highland countries. *a.* That the heavy losses sustained by the death of cattle would be effectually prevented.

It is by the loss of cattle that the Highland farmers are generally either hurt, or ruined in their circumstances, and the revenue of the proprietors impaired. This is a calamity which must frequently happen in the present state of the country. The cattle having no food in winter, but what they can find in the open fields, are, before spring, reduced to an impoverished state. They can subsist for the most part, till about Candlemas, upon the decayed herbage of the former summer; but from thence, till the return of the grass, they,are always, even in the best seasons, in great necessity. If the winter is severe, or the spring backward and inclement, a third, an halt, and sometimes a larger proportion of the cattle upon a farm, perishes for want of food.

At no very distant period, many tracts in the South of Scotland were in the same situation, and liable to the same disaster. They have been happily relieved from it, merely by providing abundance of winter provender. There can be no doubt, that the like method may be pursued in the Highlands with similar advantage. If, upon any Highland farm, ten weeks either of dry or green forage can i)C secured for the cattle, between the 15th of February, and the 1st of May, which may unquestionably be done, they would then be as safe from the spring mortality, as any cattle that are kept abroad all the year in the south.

p. That the number of cattle might be greatly enlarged.

The Highlands have always depended chiefly, and should at all times chiefly depend, on the production of cattle: Almost every agricultural improvement ought, therefore, to be subservient and conducive to this end. The increase of winter food is certainly the most obvious and important expedient to increase the number of cattle; for the summer food is in such abundance, that it is not consumed. 3

The summer pasture that is lost upon the Highland hills, is a vast quantity; the' cattle during summer, not being able to overtake it. When autumn approaches, they naturally desert it, to get down to the more sheltered places; hence, in September and October, a luxuriant and excellent herbage is everywhere to be observed at the greatest heights, almost untouched, and which remains useless.

All the high pastures, more than a thousand feet above the sea, should be compleately eaten up between the 20th of June and the 20th of September; but this indeed, would require a greater number of cattle than what occupy these pastures at present. From that time till the 1st of December, the lower fields are capable to afford sufficient pasturage; but from thence till the 1st of May, if the cattle are to be properly supported, or their numbers increased, it must be with provender provided for them by art. Were this done, their number, great as it is at present, might undoubtedly be doubled; for all that the summer pasture is able to sustain, might then be preserved through the winter.

By the deplorable defect of winter provision, many cattle are cut *off,* not only by mere want, but a still greater number perishes by diseases incident to a state of poverty. All cattle, when allowed to fall down in the body, and to become lean, are liable to numerous discases, which would not take place were they kept in good condition. Poverty is the parent ofdiseases in ail animals. Neither man nor beast are so liable to disease, while in a fattening state, or while their frame is fully supported, as when it happens to diminish by want of food. A sufficient supply of winter provision, and especially of green forage, must therefore prevent diseases and death, and increase the number of saleable cattle annually upon every farm, even as they stand at present.

7. That the breed of cattle would be improved.

It is pretty certain, that cattle will always enlarge or diminish in size, according to their pasture; and, that their bulk will always be in proportion to their sustenance. The Highland cattle are at present as small as the country at any time can produce. The soil and climate, without any interposition of art, affords the present size. But are the Highlands of Scotland the only country in Europe where the breed of cattle cannot be improved and enlarged by the exertions of art? As in other countries, the cattle of the Highlands must increase in size, as the quantity of their food is augmented. The winter and spring feeding here proposed, must necessarily have this effect. Time, no doubt, is required to make any considerable alteration in the breed of cattle. If an increase of their size is the alteration wished for, it will be attempted in vain, merely by the introduction of a larger breed; and can only be attained by additional sustenance. It is not unreasonable to suppose, that in the course of but a few years, the Highland cattle, by this single expedient, might so far increase in size, as to exceed by a sixth, or even by a fifth their present value.

SECTION IX. GRASS. INTRODUCTION.

' There is no part of husbandry," says Miller, "of '" which our farmers are, in general, more ignorant, "than that of pasture ." But, if there is ground for this complaint in England, there is certainly much more room for it in Scotland. Our improvements in tillage have been considerable; but our improvements in the management of grass grounds have not advanced in proportion. This is the more to be regretted, as a great part of Scotland, and especially all the Highland countries, must depend chiefly on Miller's Dictionary.—Pasture.

pasture. In England, and everywhere else, tillage has been more particularly the object of experiment and improvement; but pasturage is likewise susceptible of many beneficial alterations, and of great advancement.

In a pastoral country, such as the Highlands, the proper management of the natural grass, the preservation of hay, and.the increase of food for cattle, by means of artificial pasture and provender, ought to be leading objects in the eye of the farmer. The observations to be made on this subject, may, therefore, be referred to the three articles of Pasture, Natural Hay, and Artificial Grasses.

That tribe of plants, called by botanists, the "Gramina," contains all the gramineous plants or grasses, strictly so called, and also the culmiferous pidnls, which comprehend all the various sorts of grain.

There is no tribe of plants so useful and important; none so universally disseminated over the face of the earth; none that so highly deserves our care and attention, nor any that is capable of regarding our researches with equal emolument. There is, indeed, no class of herbs or trees equally numerous with that of the gramina, whose roots, leaves, or fruit, afford so little either of food or physic to mankind; but this is amply compensated by the support which the gramineous foliage affords to the domestic animals, and by the seeds of this tribe of plants, which serve as the staff of life to the whole human species. These two considerations render them the most invaluable of all the vegetable tribes, with which our great Creator hath been pleased to bless and beautify this lower world. The late progress of Natural History has been attended with this happy consequence, of making the philosophers in several parts of Europe apply their speculations in science to the purposes of life. The botanists in their enquiries concerning the gramineous plants, have not stopt at the scientifical determinaton of their species, but have proceeded to consider them as the objects of cultivation, and, particularly, how far they are capable of being ren-

dered serviceable as artificial pasture. It is obvious to every person who views these plants, that they are the most natural food of cattle; it is known also that they are capable of giving a more plentiful crop by culture, than is afforded by nature. To endeavour, therefore, to discover which of them, by cultivation, is capable of yielding the best produce and the greatest quantity, is a very palpable enquiry; and yet, obvious and useful as it is, it has, till of late, been unattended to and neglected.

PASTURE. PASTURAGE IN GENERAL.

The increasing exportation of corn and cattle, is usually supposed a certain sign of prosperity; and it may be so, under particular circumstances; but, in others, it seems rather a proof of the defective state, or of the decay of a country. The exportation of corn is a security against famine; it improves the soil, and promotes agrestic industry; it is a neat profit to the kingdom, and a great advantage to the landed interest. To preserve, at all times, a certain overplus quantity of corn in a kingdom, is undoubtedly a wise regulation; but it is not clear, that this overplus should be so large as to furnish a very extensive and increasing exportation trade. The exportation of corn since the Revolution, though a high national expence, has been of great national advantage. The advantage is great indeed, if the increase of this export, during a hundred years, has been entirely owing to extended cultivation; but if it has arisen, in any considerable degree, from a diminished or restrained population, it is a symptom rather of the decay, than of the advancement of the kingdom. It must be owing to some defect, if the number of inhabitants does not nearly keep pace with the quantity of corn which a country affords.

But, at any rate, the exportation of corn from a Country is far more eligible than that of cattle. The pastoral life is unfriendly both to industry and population. It cannot, therefore, be the interest of the public to pursue it in preference to cultivation. The exportation of cattle implies a bad commercial habit in any state. It arises from the want of encouragement to cultivators, or from the want of manufacturers, who are every whore the great consumers of meat The chief produce of Scotland, from the union of the crowns to that of the king, doms, was cattle. The country, then, uas little else than a mere grasing field to England. But as Scotland has advanced in agriculture and arts, though the quantity of cattle has been much enlarged, yet their exportation has diminished. This diminution appears not to have been sensibly felt till after the year 1720. But it has since gone on, and we may safely judge, in time to come, of the prosperity or decay of the country, by the decrease or increase of this export. The population of Scotland, since the year 1720, has been greatly augmented by very natural causes,—extended cultivation and the introduction of manufactures, and accompanied with a diminution in the quantity of exported cattle. About the time of the Union, the cattle sold to England amounted annually to tw hundred thousand pounds sterling. When the Valuer of money, at that period, is considered, one may easily perceive how much that article of exportation must now be abridged. Latterly, too, it has diminished more rapidly than in times not far distant. Even so late as the year 1750, cattle formed the most considerable export from Scotland; but they are now become not above the fifth or sixth article the soil as would have supported his grandfather several days. The quantity of grain, therefore, exr ported from England, and the quantity of cattle consumed, more than in former times, are not arguments to persuade that the kingdom has increased in population during the present century. Even England has fallen under the disadvantage of becoming a grasing country for other nations by the exportation of horses. In this, as in many other cases, the gain of individuals is accompanied with loss to the public. It is indeed but a late trade, and not at present, perhaps, so considerable as to be highly detrimental; but bein gainful, it may go to a hurtful extent, and call upon the legislature to prevent its progress.

Peter Ileroir, Esq. of Heron, faid out his own estates *ivt* Galloway, with those he held of other proprietors, Hi grass farms, and commenced the greatest cattle dealer to England, in the year 1697. A few years before 1707, the English parliament, in order to promote the Union, passed an act prohibiting the importation of cattle and linen cloth from Scotland. In the autumn of the year 1706, Heron was informed at London by his friend Lord Townshcnd, the secretary of state, that England had begun to feel so much inconreniency from this act, that ministry had resolved to repeal it upon the meeting of parliament. This intelligence communicated from friendship, Heron was well qualified to turn to advantage/ He hastened down to Edinburgh, and carried out with him a large sum of money to Criell' fair. The sale of the Highland cattle having been stopt for more than two years, their price had fallen almost to nothing. He purchased a great part of the numerous droves at the market, and had them taken into Galloway, where he waited the repeal of the English act, which accordingly happened in November. He had them then driven into England, where they were sold to singular advantage. Some of them which he purchased at Criell' for four pounds Scots, were sold in Norfolk at the price of Jour pounds sterling. of exportation. If the country continues to thrive, the time may not be far off, when few or no cattle will be exported from it at all.

But, as the quantity of cattle which Scotland can spare diminishes, we find the demand from England increases. For a few years past Scotland has therefore been more drained of cattle, and at higher prices, than at any former period. This may be thought to arise from an increased population in England. But it is doubtful whether or not this is the case; and it seems rather indeed to be occasion ed by a different cause. Manufactures and trade, by creating wealth, increase the demand for cattle. In a state of opulent prosperity, mankind consume a greater proportion of animal food, than in a less advanced stage of society, when they live more upon vegetable produce. The labourers of the soil live chiefly on grain and the productions of the dairy j but all manufacturers and people employed in trade live more upon meat. In the flesh of cattle, the vegetable produce of the soil is concentrated, as if were, and comprised within narrow bounds. The extent of land, necessary to add ten or fifteen stone weight to an ox, would produce many times his weight in grain. But the grain goes so much farther in the sustenance of the people, that the manufacturer who uses a pound of meat and a bottle of porter at a meal, consumes as much fronj

But, though it may be contrary to the interest of the public to encourage pasturage in preference to tillage, yet, in every country, there are lands which cannot be so beneficially applied to any purpose as that of pasture. A great extent of Scotland, and especially in the Highlands, remains either uncultivated, or is incapable of culture. Beside the quantity of pasture that must necessarily accompany cultivation, these unreclaimed and irreclaimable parts of the country must always render the pasturage of Scotland very considerable in the eye both of proprietors and of the public. It is, therefore, to both a material object, to have that pasturage managed in the most profitable manner.

There is much improvement still required in the management of the pasture in the Highlands. It is composed of such a variety of plants, and situated in such a variety of climate, that much knowledge and art are necessary to turn it to the best account. The pastures at the bottom, and towards the summit of a Highland mountain, are so different, both with respect to their herbage and climate, that to use them indiscriminately, is to lose, in a great part, the profit of both.

HIGH AND LOW PASTURES.

There are some pastures that yield only early grasses, which rise and decay during the summer, and which afford little or no supply in winter and spring. But there are others which afford effectual support, during these seasons, both to black cattle and sheep. These two different sorts of pasture are to be found in most parts of the Highlands, on the same farm, and even on the same hill.

The art of the grasier is to convert each of these to its proper use; to consume compleatly all the summer pasture in the summer season; and to reserve the more late and hardy pasturage for winter. Though this is an obvious and reasonable piece of economy, it is far from being sufficiently observed in the Highlands; it is even overlooked and neglected. The cows, merely on account of their milk, are tended with some degree of care, but the barren cattle are allowed to traverse every part of the farm at will, instead of being restrained, by skillful herding, to the spots and tracts most proper for them at each season.

In many places, the calves are suffered to range, during the whole summer, through the fields of corn. This liberty is granted to them from an anxiety to have them well fed, and not starved, as it is said, in the calfs skin. That the people should be anxious to have their young cattle well reared, is most adviseable. But to attain this end, can there be a more preposterous and pernicious method devised? The corn, while yet young in the ear, is cropt by the calves; and to this loss must be added, what they tear up by the roots and trample under foot. To those who have not seen this custom, it may seem scarcely credible that such an inconsiderate practice should prevail, in a country liable to scarcity of corn and scarcity of bread. It is the more inexcusable, as, by keeping the calves in a small inclosure, or by herding them upon a piece of good summer grass, they would be better fed and reared than in this wasteful manner.

SUMMER SHIELINGS AND GRASIXG.

In most Highland farms there is a small portion of arable ground, and a large extent of mountain pasture, considerably distant. The homestead is on the arable land, and generally situated on the sea shore, by the side of a lake or river, or low in a valley. Here the farmer, with his cottagers, live in what are called their winter houses. Soon after the middle of June, when the arable land is sown, they emigrate from these dwellings, with their cattle, to a mountainous place belonging to the farm. Here they quickly erect, or repair, their summer houses or shielings, which are composed chiefly of sods and the branches of trees. In these dwellings they live during the summer. Their only occupation is tending the cattle on the heights, and the manufacture of the butter and cheese. Their chief sustenance is oat or barley meal, with milk in its different forms. In this way they pass the fine season, in a pastoral and cheerful manner of life, of which the people are extremely fond. When the corns begin to ripen, about the middle of August, they leave their pleasant summer residence, and return to their winter houses. This method of management is natural to the situation of the country, and is not peculiar to the Highlands. The same prevails in other parts of the world, and especially in Swisserland. There the inhabitants live and labour in the vallevs for the greatest part of the year, among their corn fields and vineyards; but during the height of summer they enjoy what is called the Alpinage. They ascend the Alps to considerable heights, and live, with their flocks, in the same manner, though in a preferable situation, with the inhabitants of the Highlands.

By far the greatest part of the pasture in the Highlands is situated at great heights; and much of it in places inaccessible to cattle from October till May. Yet upon these heights, and even about the summits of very high mountains, there is, in the summer time, a profusion of excellent herbage. To these places the cattle do not willingly repair but in the finest season; and will even desert them in summer on the approach of wind and rain. For in rigorous weather they are at all times more covetous of shelter than pasture. These high pastures, therefore, never can be fully applied to use, or be consumed, but by means of diligent herding. By the neglect of this, the greatest part of them goes to waste. They are not sufficiently eaten up during summer, and no cattle are kept upon them after the end of August. In consequence of this, a rank and excellent foggage is everywhere to be seen at these great heights in September and October, which is entirely lost. All this might be avoided, and much gained, if the cattle were confined to these high pastures, by careful herding, which they might very well be, till the end of October. The foggage in the low grounds would then be spared during the whole autumn, and become highly serviceable in winter, when it is most required.

HERDING.

The above art is well understood, and carefully practised, hv the storemasters of the south, in the pasturage of sheep. The flocks are attentively herded from morning till evening. They are not suffered to stray at large; but are directed by the shepherd in their walk during the day, and to their resting phice at night. They are conducted to the pasture proper for them at the different seasons, and in such a manner, that the whole herbage upon the farm is rendered useful. This practice of the south country herds is now known to many people in the Highlands, and they ought to observe it carefully in the management of their sheep. But to observe it in the management of their black cattle, is a matter of $ till greater moment. Yet in this article they are in most places inexcusably inattentive. The cattle are not properly herded, nor directed to their pasture with sufficient care; they are allowed to roam at large over the whole farm; they are suffered to pick and chuse their own pasture; which can never turn out either to the advantage of the farmer, or to the benefit of the stock at large. The grass at great heights is neglected, and left to decay and w ithcr in the winds. The coarser grasses in the lower parts, to which the cattle ought to be confined during summer, are avoided, and in a great measure lost. The spots of fine grass, which should be their relief early in spring and late in autumn, are perpetually eaten to the ground. In this matter, there is no dependance to be had on the instinct of cattle; for they woulil rather have a mouthful of such fine grass, than a bellyful of grasses Df a coarser kind. To consume the coarse pasture upon a farm at the proper season, they must be compelled by careful herding. It is only in this way that the whole pasture upon a Highland farm can be turned to its full account.

The farm servants in the Highlands are not accustomed to that regular and assiduous herding of cattle that is necessary in a pastoral country. They look after them only by fits and starts, and without a due regard either to the nature of their food, or of the grounds which they ought to occupy. The servants employed are not even cloathed for the purpose. Hardy as they are, a tartan jacket, a kilt and brogues, that take in and give out the water as it comes, cannot afford sufficient shelter to a man who is to remain the whole day abroad, in cold winds, rains, and snow. In the mountainous parts of the South of Scotland, and in as severe situations as any in the Highlands, the herds are cloathed in a different manner. Beside an under waistcoat, they have cloathes of warm coarse cloth, warm stockings, of a double thread, strong thick shoes, and a large thick plaid, to cover them entirely upon every emergency. Thus cloathed, they can continue all day in the most boisterous weather, and remain abroad, as they often do, in the most tempestuous nights. But without such raiment they could neither pursue their business, nor do justice to their masters.

THE DIFFERENT SORTS OF PASTURE.

All the grass grounds in the Highlands, and in Scotland at large, may be considered as belonging to one or other of the four following kinds.

1. The first comprehends all that are commonly and strictly termed with us meadows. These are lands too wet for tillage, or that are liable at all times to be overflowed. Such, likewise, are the sea inks, or salt marshes, on the shores. These lands have never been opened by the plough; they are kept perpetually in pasture, or saved for the production of natural hay. They are generally situated by the sides of brooks, rivers, and lakes, or on the sea shore. Such meadows are frequently the richest pastures we have; and, when properly water fed, throw up a greater weight of hay than any other land whatever. 2. The second sort of pasture is that produced on infield, or croft land, which has been immemorially dunged and tillaged. This land is generally dry; it naturally throws up the best pasture jrases; and is preferable to any other for the fattening of cattle. In the South of Scotland, where the quantity of this sort of soil is considerable, it is often allotted to pasture with great profit. But in the Highlands its proportion to the rest of the country is so small, that it never can be advisable to convert it into pasture. It should always be inclosed, and devoted entirely to the production of grain and winter provender. 3. The third kind of pasture is afforded by outfield land, or that which has at intervals been in tillage, but without receiving any manure. To this also may be referred the tracts of natural grass, which are often of an excellent quality, at the bottom and about the skirts of hills; but so encumbered with hillocks and rocks, as to be mcapable of culture. 4. The fourth consists of mountain pastures, comprehending those which are situated from about eight hundred to three thousand feet above the sea. These, from the poverty of their soil, the roughness of their climate, or the declivity of their situation, are generally incapable of culture. Of the same kind are all the moors and commons covered with heath and aquatic grasses, though in low parts of the country, which, from the above or from other causes, have never been in tillage. OLD GRASS.

It is commonly considered as a maxim, " That "pasture grass improves by age; and that the old"est is always the best. " An idea certainly entertained by many to their own prejudice. The maxim is only true with respect to those soils which are so rich and dry, that the growth of mosses never takes place upon them. This is the case with but a very small part of the pastures of Scotland. Nine, at least, out of ten parts of all our pastures, are liable, upon resting but a few years, to be over-run with mosses. These gradually overspread the surface, and occupy the soil to such a degree, that the grass not only becomes thin, but less luxuriant in the blade. The pasture is thereby so much diminished, as to render it very unprofitable to retain such lands in grass beyond five or six years. For during such a period, though the pasture decreases, it i3 well known that the soil improves.

It is imagined by some, and maintained by a late writer, that as the fertility of a soil.is advanced, Brugmaas, De Plant is inutijibus. p. 59. the plants which form the best herbage are naturally increased both in size and number; and on the other hand, that useless weeds are enlarged both in size and number by poverty of soil. This, however, Is far from being invariably the case; nor is it a rule on which any person should depend. The most luxuriant weeds are as fond of a rich soil as any of our cultivated plants. Without skill and care, the richest soil, when suffered to rest from tillage, will not of itself produce the most valuable herbage. The lands in Galloway were long enriched with shell marle before the introduction of sown grass. When they were left ley, after some crops of corn, they were covered with such a load of useless plants, as had never been seen in that country,—with such a rampant growth of mugwort, dock, ragweed, burdock, and the different thistles, that the pasture was rendered entirely useless; but when sown grass came to be used, and the land was carefully weeded, the nop of clover and rye grass became equally luxuriant OLD HAY GROUNDS.

It is held by Mr Miller, " That where grass "ground is every year mown for hay, it must be fre"quently dressed with manure; otherwise the soil "will be soon exhausted." It is certain, that every grass crop may be improved by manure; but it i& likewise certain, that a hay crop taken off land for a great number of years, and without any manure, does by no means impoverish the soil. Numberless instances might be given, in which many successive hay crops have been taken without manure, and the land always found richer than it was at the beginning. Natural hay is always to be considered, therefore, as a meliorating, not as a deteriorating crop. Unless the ground is of the richest kind, the hay crop will certainly diminish, indeed, in a course of years; but not by impoverishing the soil. The grass, by being repeatedly and closely cut, like all other plants, comes to be of a stunted growth. From year to year it is also rendered thinner and thinner by the prevalence of mosses. The dwindling of the hay crop is thus presumed to proceed from a decay in tlie soil, when in fact it is owing to these other causes. When a field of natural hay comes thus to degenerate, the remedies are, tillage, the covering of the surface with manure, or grasing it every third, or even every second year. Where these methods are inconvenient, it is of great use to go over such a field, early in the spring, with a short-toothed harrow, so as to raise and eradicate the mosses, and make way for the tillering and growth of the grass.

NEGLECTED SPOTS OF GRASS.

In every field grased by cattle in summer, there are certain spots which are neglected, on which the grass grows rank, and at length withers without being touched. All cattle avoid the spikes and panicles of grasses, and the flowers of plants. When the herbage in any place has accidentally got a-head of the rest of the field, and has shot forth its flowering stems, such a spot is shunned by the cattle; as they prefer the places where the grass has been kept short, and where there is nothing but foliage. They nauseate for a long time the spots where fresh dung has been dropped. Some parts are occupied by a growth of plants which are refused by cattle; and they have generally a predilection for particular places, where the pasture is sweetest. For these, or for other reasons, it often happens, that, towards the close of summer, these neglected spots form a very considerable portion of a field.

If it is designed to grase such a field compleatly during autumn, these spots should be all gone over with the scythe in the end of summer. This is to convert ground, that would be otherwise waste, into good after-grass; for the soiled and withered herbage will cause the young grass mixed with it to be still neglected by the cattle, till urged by necessity. But if the field is intended for winter pasturage, then all such spots of rank decayed 'grass should be permitted to remain: they will be eaten down in winter by the same cattle that would not touch

them in summer. But if they are not thus either cut or eaten down, the ground should be effectually cleared of them early in spring, before the new grass appears. It may be noticed here, that if a due regard is paid to good after-grass, no cattle should be permitted to pass the night upon it: such grass is always of a soft sloamy substance, soon spoiled by the lying of cattle upon it, and appears at the season when ground is usually wet and easily poached.

i WOODLAND PASTURE.

Wherever there is wood or grown up coppice on a farm, there the herbage should be carefully preserved for winter. The numerous tribe of wood plants is refused by cattle in summer, and some they will not touch even at any season. The best grass under trees they neglect, for the same reason that a gooseberry in the sun is preferred to one in the shade. During summer, indeed, they often crowd into woody places, for shelter from the sun; but not for the pasture, which they tread under foot and abuse with their dung. From all such places they should therefore be excluded during summer. But when winter is advanced, the wood not only affords them the most comfortable shelter, but abundant pasturage, of which they would not have tasted one mouthful in summer.

WEEDING.

The advantage of weeding our corn crops *is* generally acknowledged, and in some degree practised. They are every where observed to be the best farmers, who are most sensible of the advantages of having clean land. But much of this necessary labour would be superseded, were there some pains taken in weeding our pastures. In most of the corn fields in Scotland, a third, a half, or two-thirds of the soil are occupied by weeds. Even our poorest arable lands, were they but clean, would produce double the crop they do at present. To weed the soil while in tillage, though highly necessary and useful, will not completely answer the end proposed, unless due attention is paid to the extirpation of weeds, in the pasture grounds and other parts of the farm. The scythe is the instrument

that must be chiefly depended on for this purpose. Not only every grass field on a farm, but the barnyard, all the waste places about the farm-stead or elsewhere, and all the spaces by the sides of roads or inclosures, should be so cleared of stones, hillocks, and shrubs, that the scythe may go easily over them. It is not so much the fields, as these waste and vacant spots, that are the great nursery of weeds upon every farm. Were these places gone over with the scythe, even but once every season, at the proper period, the annual weeds would be removed and their propagation prevented for that year. In a couple of years, the strength of the biennial weeds would be overcome. Even the strong rooted perennials would not only be kept from propagating any further, but in a short term of years would be destroyed. The good effects of this practice would soon be seen on any single farm of a considerable size. Was it to take place on a number of adjacent farms, it would have yet greater influence; and would prove still more effectual, if it was extended to any large tract of the country. It must be noticed, however, that this practice, though highly expedient, would be but of little avail if not continued from year to year. It is only by length of time that the weeds on any farm can be extirpated. It is a labour that lessens indeed every year, but only when it is continued without intermission. The labour of weeding, during one or a few seasons, is thrown away, if, in a single year, the weeds are allowed to come to maturity, and and spread abroad their seeds. So true is the maxim, generally known, but little attended to by our fanners: " That one year's seeding costs seven years weeding." Rosa *canina*, Linn. Red dog rose.

The general negligence in suppressing weeds, and preventing their increase, is indeed deplorahle. When a held or corn is cut, the rank mugworts, docks, ragworts, and thistles, are suffered to remain on the stubble. The com is cut from about them with some trouble; but they are left untouched, and, to appearance, even caretfully preserved, though loaded with ripe seeds to poison the soil. It is sufficiently negligent not to have them pulled by the hand between the middle of June and the middle of July, but altogether inexcusable to allow them to remain after harvest. A boy or a girl, as a gleaner, might clear as much ground of these weeds, as a large band of reapers would go over in a day. — Many rich grass fields are quite encumbered, and rendered in a great measure useless by the same weeds, during August and September, when they are suffered to go to seed; whereas, if they were cut with the scythe about the middle of July, which is but a slight piece of work, their propagation would not only be prevented, but the pasture would be enlarged.

Such weeds as those now mentioned, and indeed all others, when cut at the proper season, that is, before the seeds are formed, may be made to add greatly to the stock of manure. They may be considerable in quantity, and their quality makes them a valuable addition to a compost dunghill. By a slight fermentation, they are totally convertible into vegetable mucilage, the most beneficial of all manures. But if they are not thrown to the dunghill till after the seeds are ripe, which is often the case, this is only to propagate the evil, as from thence they will be spread over all the farm. It is not by lying a few months in a dunghill, that the seeds of these plants will be deprived of their vegetating power.

The methods of extirpating weeds now suggested, with the other remedies of summer fallow, horse and hand-hoed crops, would soon and greatly enlarge he produce of the kingdom, both in com and grass.

After these general remarks on our pastures, and especially those of the Highlands, it may not be improper to take notice of those particular plants that are remarkably prejudicial in the grass grounds allotted to black cattle, and which every careful grasier ought to restrain and extirpate as far as possible.
SHRUBS.
Prunus *spinosa,* Linn. Sloe thorn.
Rubus jruticesus, Linn. Common bramble. *idaeus,* Linn. Raspberry.

Rosa *arvensis,* Linn. White dog rose. *villosa,* Linn. Apple rose. *spinosissima,* Linn. The cat hep.
Crataegus *oxyacantha,* Linn. White thorn.

These thorns, brambles, and briars, occupy considerable spaces in many pastures, They form sometimes numerous and large clumps, and generally on good soil. They afford to cattle neither food nor shelter, but, being strongly armed, exclude them from a great deal of the best grass. By burning, or by being cut over, they are only strengthened at the root, but cannot be destroyed. The only remedy is to grub them up; a piece of labour that will generally be well bestowed. They are particularly hurtful in a sheep pasture, by tearing off the wool before it comes to maturity, and thereby exposing the sheep to cold, wetness, and diseases. On a sheep walk especially, not one of these shrubs should therefore be permitted to remain.
Ononis *inermis,* Linn. Smooth restharrow.
spinosa, Linn. Prickly restharrow.
Genista *tinctoria,* Linn. Woodwaxen.

The plants with a pea blossom generally afford an agreeable and wholesome forage. But, though these three shrubby plants have a flower of this kind, they are nauseated by all cattle. Having strong creeping roots, they overspread large spots, and sometimes even considerable tracts of grass grounds, &nd to the entire exclusion of every sort of grass. Many grasing fields in the Western Islands are rendered good for little by the prevalence of the two first of these plants; and some of the best pastures in Galloway are greatly impaired by the prevalence of the last. Where land is to lie long in pasture, their progress can only be prevented by rooting them up on their first appearance.

Myrica *Gale,* Linn. Gale.

This shrub is an inhabitant only of a mossy soil, and engrosses a great part of the surface in many of our moors and mountain pastures. In summer, it perfumes the air for miles together, with its aromatic smell, which to many is very agreeable, and from which it has the

name of sweet gale. By its sensible qualities, it might be presumed to be a plant of considerable powers as a medicine. But these it may possess, and yet be disagreeable and even noxious to the domestic animals, which it certainly is. None of them, not even the goat, ever touch it from choice; and it is pernicious to sheep, when, from necessity, they are forced to browse upon it. It is avoided even by insects, and bunches pf it are laid up by our country housewives, among their woollen cloaths, to preserve them from the moth. A shrub so copious, of no known use, so detrimental, and of such suspicious qualities, dcserves certainly to be discouraged. As it grows only in the coarsest and least valuable pastures, the labour of rooting it up would scarcely, perhaps, be recompensed; but it usually occupies those tracts of moorish soil that are the fittest for paring and burning. In this way it might be completely demolished: and, indeed, this practice of burn baiting should certainly be followed, for the improvement of our moorish pastures, as well as for the purposes of tillage.

The annual weeds, though baneful to our tillaged crops, are, comparatively, so little detrimental to our pastures, that they scarcely deserve notice in this place. It is by means of tillage, and the right management of tillaged land, that they are to be overcome. But the biennial and perennial weeds that annoy our pastures, are indeed numerous and formidable. To extirpate them requires particular attention and particular methods; and, for this purpose, the nature of the plants themselves, and their manner of vegetation, wherever it is known, must be consulted.
BIENNIAL WEEDS
Echium *vulgare,* Linn. Vipers bugloss.
Digitalis *purpurea,* Linn. Foxglove.
Verbascum *Thapsus,* Linn. Shepherds club.
Daucus *Carota,* Linn. Birds nest.
Heracleum *SphondylUum,* Linn. Cow parsnip.
Chaerophyllum *sylvestre,* Linn. Cow weed.
temulum, Linn. Wild chervil.
Erysimum *officinale,* Linn. Hedge

mustard.

Anthemis *arvensis,* Linn. Wild camomile.

Arctium *Lappa,* Linn. Burdock.

Senecio *Jacobaea,* Linn. Ragwort.

Carduus *lanceolatus,* Linn. Spear thistle.

. *crispits,* Linn. Welted thistle.

acanthoides, Linn. Curled thistle.

The foxglove is a plant of a highly deleterious nature, which is probably the case also with the shepherds club. Though they abound and throw out a luxuriant and succulent foliage, they are never tasted by cattle, even though urged by necessity, and are avoided even by insects.

The Daucus *Carota,* Linn, is our common birds nest, frequently called wild carrot, and is, by Linnaeus and most botanists, considered as the plant from which all our garden carrots arc derived. It is one of the most copious and hurtful of all our biennial weeds. Many arable fields of a light soil, on the shores of the West Highlands and Islands, when left out in grass, are entirely covered with it. They are, therefore, almost utterly lost, as it is not eaten by any quadruped, and yet every field overrun with this useless plant, is capable to afford a good crop of turnips or of clover and ryegrass. It appears in general that all the umbelliferous aquatic plants, are in some degree poisonous to men, and likewise to cattle. On the other hand, those which grow on a dry soil, are aromatic, carminative and wholesome to us, and yet we find many of them avoided by cattle, such as the birds nest, the cow-parsnip and others.

The birds nest is very properly considered by Miller as a different plant from the Garden Carrot, and he terms it Daucus *sylvestris* though it rather should be *campestris,* as it grows not in woods but always in dry and open fields. This plant differs greatly from the garden carrot, in the form of its foliage and roots and especially in their properties.— Those of the garden carrot are greedily eaten by horses, cows, sheep, and hogs, but those of the birds nest are untouched, and rejected by all these animals; so that, beyond doubt,

they are to be accounted as two different species.

This was further confirmed by the cultivation of the Daucus *Visnaga* of Linnaeus. The seeds of this plant sent me by Signior Ortega, botanist to the King of Spain at Madrid, were raised for several years, and are still preserved in my garden. This is evidently the parent plant of all our garden carrots.— Miller. Diet. v. Daucus.

The roots indeed are white, and not so large as those of the cultivated carrot, but of the same quality.— The colour of the root, however, makes no essential difference, as in different countries the garden carrot is found to be purple, red, orange, yellow or white; the same being the case with the common garden radish, which is in different places found to be of a purple, red, yellow, or white colour.

The ragwort grows only in a dry and rich soil, and for nothing else should the farmer wish to see it in his fields. Its seeds, like those of the thistles, are winged with down, and are thereby adapted to fly abroad far and wide. Though a biennial, if interrupted in its growth, it will last three or four years. The best pastures in Scotland are not so much molested by any other weed, as they are by this. It is of a nauseous smell, and is never eaten either by black cattle or horses; yet it often covers a great part, and sometimes the most considerable part of an excellent grass field. When it first shoots, sheep will crop it a little, but this is of no use in destroying it. It seldom appears, and that but accidentally, in land under crop. We are not therefore to expect from tillage, the extirpation of this very hurtful weed. It is only to be diminished or exterminated, by proper care bestowed upon the pasture fields, and vacant places, where it abounds.

The biennial weeds of the above list, are the most frequent and hurtful in our dry pastures, and none of them are eaten by cattle. They are all bulky, of a luxuriant growth, occupy much of the soil, and greatly diminish the quantity of food, which many of the best pastures should produce. Like all other hiennials,

they do not propagate by the root, but depend entirely for the preservation of their species, upon the seeds, in which they are very prolific. It is needless, therefore, to attack them at the root. The obvious and only method to prevent their progress, is to prevent their seeding. This is to be done by cutting them over with the scythe while in flower, but before any seeds are formed.. If a second growth appears, which promises to seed, it should also be removed in the same manner.

PERENNIAL WEEDS,

That propagate chiefly by the root, in dry pastures.

Aegopodium *Podagraria,* Linn. Ashweed.

Urtica *dioica,* Linn. Nettle.

Tussilago *Farfara,* Linn. Tussilago.

Potentilla *anserina,* Linn. Mascorn.

Triticum *repens.* Linn. Dogs Grass.

Pteris *aquilina,* Linn. Braken.

Polypodium *Filiv mas,* Linn. Fern.

Mercurialis *perennis,* Linn. Dogs Mercury.

These, like many other plants, which shoot with vigorous creeping roots, produce comparatively but few seeds, or at least few that are fertile. They depend not so much upon the seeds, for the preservation of their species, as upon the roots. These arc renewed and enlarged from time to time, and by means of these, the plants maintain their ground for many years, nay even for ages, in the same spot.— On the other hand, the plants that do not propagate by the root, are always remarkably productive of prolific seeds. In general, as the power of reproduction in the one way increases, it usually diminishes in the other.

The ashweed and the nettle are commonly to be found in gardens, or in the neighbourhood of houses and dunghills. For the same reason, that they are attached to these places, they always possess themselves of the richest soil, when they get into the field. Wherever they prevail, therefore, some of the best pasture must always be lost. When land is subjected to tillage, they may be easily destroyed; but if they subsist in a field that is to be long preserved for pasture, they should be rooted up with the spade. Nor is this a very difficult or tedious operation; for, having close.matted roots, these plants are more easily eradicated, than would at first be imagined. Though cows are never known to touch nettles in the field, yet they eat them freely when c,ut and presented to them in the stall.

The tussilago and mascorn are extremely hurtful both to grass and corn. They are avoided by all our quadrupeds, though the flower of the tussilago is an innocent medicine, and the farinaceous root of the mascorn, is not only esculent but agreeable.— To free a pasture of them would be a vain attemptThe soil is only to be delivered from them while it is in tillage, when it can be effectually cleared. The roots of these weeds when thrown up by the plough, are eagerly fed upon by sheep, who are useful and excellent weeders on ploughed land, in the winter season.

The dogs grass, or couch grass, is a weed universally known and reprobated. It is the most hurtful of all others, to the corn crops of Scotland, and very pernicious to many of the best pastures. It is of a rough harsh substance and taste. It is an emetic to dogs, and is disagreeable to cattle. They will indeed eat it from constraint, but they avoid it whereever they can. It grows in the best soils, and though it sends forth but few flower spikes, wherever its roots get a footing, they spread and predominate, and get the better of almost all other herbaceous plants. In some old pastures, this plant forms a green but unprofitable sward, and wears out all the finer grasses that are natural to a good soil. Yet, while it occupies pasture land, there is no obvious method to destroy it. Nothing shews more the imperfection of our tillage, than the prevalence of this pernicious weed. Large quantities of its roots, or quickens, as they are called, are, and must be hauled out by every harrow; but as every chip of them grows, a sufficient quantity is always left to fill the soil and suffocate the crop. Yet, till the lands in tillage are freed from it, the loss which it occasions in the pastures, must be endured.

Not only the braken, but the whole tribe of ferns, is cautiously avoided by cattle, and almost all other animals . Even insects, which prey on many poisonous plants, are scarcely ever seen to eat any of the fern kind. This would insinuate, that there is something in them, noxious to animal life; though from their sensible qualities, no degree of virulence or poison could be presumed. On one occasion, a field which had anciently been in tillage, but which had become overgrown with luxuriant brakens, was ploughed up in winter. A herd of black cattle having access to the field, eat the roots of the braken, which were gross and succulent. The cattle were in consequence all disordered, and four of the numVol. i. y The stomach of the Tetrao *Tetrix,* Linn, or Black cock, after the bird had Ifved in woods during winter, was several times found stuffed with the foliage of the Poly podium *vulgare,* Linn, or Common polypody. This is the only certain instance that has occurred, of any animal liriag upon a plant of the fern kind in this country.
ber died. The braken never grows but where there is a tolerable soil and good pasture. It rises early in summer with the grass, and being of a quick luxuriant growth, overshades it during the whole season. No cattle ever feed beneath its shade. The grass that rises under it, is weak, soft, and sloamy, of little use to black cattle, after the fall of the braken in autumn, and at that time, very detrimental to sheep. Many of our best mountain and moorland pastures, arc in this way greatly injured by the braken. It may indeed be compleatly eradicated by tillage; but it is hurtful in many places where the plough cannot be used. Neither can it be rooted up by the spade, in such a situation, as it consists of distant straggling stems, that are all connected below at the root. In this case, the only remedy is to cut them with the scythe, when they are at the height of their growth, about the end of July. Where they are very plentiful, this is done with profit for obtaining fern ashes. But it is well known to the persons employed in this business, that when the brakens are cut two or three years suc-

cessively in the same place, they become so diminished, as to be no longer profitable, in the way of that manufacture. If the cutting of them is prolonged for a few years more, they come to be entirely worn out m the soil; and it would certainly be advantageous to have many pastures freed from them in this way.

The fern also pesters many grasing fields, but is more easily got rid of than the braken. It grows usually in large tufts, proceeding from one root, which is easily thrown out by the spade. The Dogs mercury also frequently occupies considerable spots in the best pastures, where it is not only useless but poisonous. As it grows always in clumps, with matted roots, it may likewise be easily eradicated with the spade.

PERENNIAL WEEDS,

That propagate both by roots and seeds in dry pastures.

Rumex *Acetosella,* Linn. Sheeps sorrel. Chrysanthemum *Leucanthemum,* Linn. Ox-eye daisy.

Geranium *cicutarium,* Linn. Hemlock cranesbill.

Galium *varum,* Linn. Cheese-renning.

These plants are the stationary inhabitants of a poor gravelly or sandy pasture. Labour would be ill bestowed, either to prevent the progress of their roots or the falling of their seeds, while the ground remains in grass. They are easily destroyed by tillage, but arc more effectually banished by rendering the soil richer; for it is only on a poor neglected soil that they can prosper and propagate.

The Sheeps sorrel and the Hemlock cranesbill, are of no use to any sort of cattle. The Ox-eye daisy is in some degree eaten by sheep early in the season; but this is of no avail to diminish it in the soil.

The Cheese-renning is not a plant of a simple herbaceous substance, which, indeed, may be presumed from its quality of curdling milk, and is also refused by cattle. It is known in the Gaelic language by the name of *Ruagh,* and overruns many extensive sandy fields on the shores of the Highlands and Hebrides.

The root, which is of the nature of madder, affords to the inhabitants their best red dye. They are therefore eager to procure it; but in some places are very properly prohibited from digging it up. This happens where the plant grows, as it frequently does, in a sandy soil that is apt to blow; and where the breaking of the surface is capable to give the beginning to a sandy deluge.

Galeopsis *Ladanum,* Linn. Allheal.

, *Tetrahit,* Linn. Nettle hemp.

Achillaea *Ptarmica,* Linn. Sneezewort.

Rumex *acetosa,* Linn. Sorrel.

Stachys *pa/ustris,* Linn. Clowns allheal.

Stachys *sylvatica,* Linn. Hedge nettle.

Geranium *pratense,* Linn. Meadow cranesbill.

sylvaticum, Linn. Wood cranesbill.

The plants here enumerated are all nauseous to cattle of every kind. They inhabit only a strong and rich soil. They are luxuriant and very bulkv, and occupy much space that ought to be better employed. They require, however, a moist and weeping soil. It is in spots of this kind that they chiefly prosper, and from which they may be effectually dislodged by draining. Where this cannot be executed, and where the land is to remain long in pasture, it will generally be found beneficial to root them out.

Rumex *obtusifolius,* Linn. Common dock.

crispus, Linn. Curled dock. *acutus,* Linn. Sharp pointed dock.

Scabiosa *arvensis,* Linn. Field scabious.

Antirrhinum *Linaria,* Linn. Toad flax.

Lamium *album,* Linn. White dead nettle.

Galeopsis *Gakobdolon,* Linn. Yellow nettle
hemp.

Malva *sylvestris,* Linn. Common Mallow.

Artemisia *vulgaris,* Linn. Mugwort.

Matricaria *itwdora,* Linn. Corn feverfew.

Centaurea *nigra,* Linn. Knapweed.

Scabiosa, Linn. Greater knapweed.

These are some of the worst perennial weeds that annoy our driest and best pastures. They are the more difficult also to overcome, because they propagate vigorously by the root as well as by the seeds. The docks are particularly prevalent, and a spade of a peculiar construction has been contrived to eradicate them. Any labour exerted in rooting them up will always be well bestowed. But a constant attention to prevent this set of plants from propagating their seeds is no less necessary, by cutting them with the scythe at the proper season, which is neither a difficult nor expensive piece of work.

\# \# \#

Serratula *arcensis,* Linn. Corn thistle.

This, upon the whole, may be reckoned the most hurtful weed over all Britain, both in arable and pasture ground; being the most frequent and copious of all the thistle kind. It has been called the Carduus *viarum,* or Way thistle, from its abounding so much by the side of high roads; but it prevails, also, so much in corn fields, that with us it is peculiarly termed the Corn thistle. All arable and all pasture lands are liable to be infested with it; from those of the highest value, down to such as are not rented at above a crown an acre.

Though it will grow almost anywhere, it is peculiarly attached to a soil that is of a calcareous nature. It is most vigorous, therefore, in the neighbourhood of limestone quarries; by the sides of roads that have been covered with limestone; and in all land that has been limed or marled. It is an ir tolerable and increasing evil in the marled and limed lands of Berwickshire, Galloway, Forfarshire, and many other countries where there are no effectual efforts used to suppress and destroy it.

To pull it up by the hand from among the corn in summer, used to be a very general practice. The thistles were suffered to lie in the sun during the day; by which means they were much softened, and served as supper to the horses at night, though they will not touch them in the field. This laudable piece of carefulness has rather been neglected of late, where there is a command of clover and rye grass in summer. But its usefulness is manifest; and it is a practice that should by no means be laid aside.

The corn thistle has not merely a perennial, but a strong creeping root: so that wherever a plant of it takes place in a pasture, it continues to spread from year to year. At its first appearance it is easily checked; but if it is allowed to propagate its roots for two or three seasons, it becomes scarcely practicable to expel them from the soil by digging; for the roots are easily broken, and every fragment of them will grow. The thistles of this sort in the corn fields are usually but seedlings, or of the former year's growth: these have not as yet spread in the ground; so that on pulling, the whole root is brought up: this is one of the most favourable opportunities, therefore, of resisting the progress of this pernicious weed. Its roots are succulent, and fed upon by sheep. Wherever it prevails in land that is broken up by the plough, sheep may therefore be rendered very useful in destroying it.

The seeds of the Corn thistle, being copiously winged with down, fly far and wide. They are, indeed, disabled from flying by rain; but the plant well knows how to obviate this difficulty, and never spreads its down but when the weather is dry. It then removes with the least breath of wind; so that a farm happily free from this plant may be poisoned with it in a day from lands at a great distance. It is necessary, therefore, by means of the scythe, to prevent its coming to seed in every pasture. But to clear the tillaged and pasture fields of it will not be sufficient, if, by the same means, it is not restrained and extirpated by the road-sides, and other waste places upon every farm.

PERENNIAL WEEDS,

Which prevail in the wettest meadows.

Iris *Pseudacorus,* Linn. Bog lily.

Menyanthes *trifoliata,* Linn. Marsh trefoil.

Comarum *palustre,* Linn. Marsh cinquefoil.

Rumex *aquaticus,* Linn. Water dock.

Polygonum *amphibium,* Linn. Willow-leaved knotgrass.

Persicaria, Linn. Spotted knotgrass.

Hydropiper, Linn. Pepper knotgrass.

Alisma Plantago *aquatica,* Linn. Greater water plantain.

. *ranunculoides,* Linn. Lesser water plantain.

Ranunculus *Lingua,* Linn. Great spean-vort.

—— *fiammuia,* Linn. Procumbent spear-wort.

Sysimbrium *amphibium,* Linn. Water radish.

Bidens *tripartita,* Linn. Marsh hemp agrimony.

Typha *latifolia,* Linn. Reed mace.

Sparganium *erectum,* Linn. Burr reed.

Equisetum *palustre,* Linn. Marsh horsetail.

fiuviatik, Linn. River horsetail. *limosum,* Linn. Smooth horsetail.

These plants grow chiefly in our most watery meadows, or such as are always overflowed in winter, and that are so wet and soft, even in summer, that they can scarcely bear the tread of cattle. All these plants, without exception, are not only rejected as food, but there is never any pasture for cattle in the places where they grow; yet, there can be little doubt, that those places might be made productive of useful provender. No attempt, indeed, has ever been made to render such meadows useful. It is true, that they are frequently incapable of being drained; but even where this is the case, these plants might undoubtedly be removed, and others that are useful, and which grow in a similar situation, substituted in their place. Such meadows, wet as they are, might all be replenished with plants capable of affording either green or dry forage; and of this number, and for these purposes, the following species may be suggested.

Scirpus *palustris,* Linn. Marsh club-rush.

sylvaticus, Linn. Marsh cyperus-grass. Poa *aquatka.* Linn. Water meadow grass. Phalaris *arundinacea,* Linn. Common reed grass.

Arundo *Calamagrosiis,* Linn. Branched reed grass.

epigejos, Linn. Small reed grass.

Carex *gigantea.* Giant carex.

—— *trigona.* Bog pointed grass.

These are all gramineous plants, and though of the coarsest kind, they are wholesome, and eaten by cattle when destitute of more agreeable food. The Common reed grass, the coarsest of the w hole, when it first springs, and is yet tender, in the end of May, is eagerly fed upon by the Highland cattle, and affords great relief to them at that season. These gramineous plants, that may in some degree be useful, grow naturally in the same wet situation as the useless and pernicious plants of the former list, and may, with a little care, be substituted in their room. Their chief use would be to serve as bog hay. They are all plants of a tall vigorous growth, and when suffered to arrive at maturity, become too hard and harsh for this purpose; but were they cut early in the season, while yet tender and succulent, they would afford a heavy crop of coarse but useful hay, in many tracts of marshy meadow ground, that are at present useless, and inaccessible to cattle even in summer.

There are other grasses, however, of the aquatic kind, which grow in a similar situation, and that are more palatable to cattle. These would not afford an equal weight of hay, but they would yield an excellent pasture, in meadows sufficiently dry to admit of cattle in summer, in place of the hurtful weeds with which they are occupied at present:—Such are the following plants.

Alopecurus *geniculatus,* Linn. Flote foxtail grass.

Agrostis *stolonifera,* Linn. Creeping bent grass.

alba, Linn. Marsh bent grass.

Aira *aquatica,* Linn. Water hair grass.

Poa *palustris,* Linn. Marsh meadow grass.

Festuca *Jluitans,* Linn. Flote fescue grass.

Holcus *mollis,* Linn. Creeping soft grass.

Some of the grasses of this list, though aquatic plants, are the most coveted by cattle of all others. In deep miry and watery places, cows, in the summer time, often endanger, and sometimes lose their lives, to get at the Water hair grass, the Marsh meadow grass, and the Flote fescue.

From this account of these plants, and those of the former list, it appears that, by their means, many of our most watery meadows may be changed from a state of utter sterility, to become essentially beneficial. Nor is any high degree of labour or expence requisite for this purpose. It is only necessary to collect the seeds of the above gramineous plants, which may be done in most parts of the country. All these plants, or the greatest part of them, are to be found in almost every district. They usually form, indeed, but detached spots; yet from these, a sufficient quantity of seeds may be obtained to cover a considerable extent of wet meadow land. The seeds ought to be sown about the beginning of May, partly on land, and partly perhaps in water, and left to their fate. Being sown in the situation in which they naturally grow, they would certainly prosper. It is the property of these, and of all perennial grasses, that wherever they get possession in a soil, they propagate by the root, to the exclusion of almost all other plants: They would in time wear out all the useless aquatic plants of the above list, and form an herbage that would answer both for hay and pasture.

PERENNIAL WEEDS,

That predominate in meadows moderately wet.

Aira *caespitosa,* Linn. Turfy hair grass.

Veronica *Anagallis oquatica,* Linn. Water speedwell.

Myosotis *scorpioides,* Linn. Marsh Scorpion grass. Angelica *sylvestris,* Linn. Wild angelica. Juncus *conglomerates,* Linn. Common rush.

effusus, Linn. Hard rush.

Anthericum *ossi/'ragttm,* Linn. Lancashire as podel. Epilobium *hirsutum,* Linn. Codlings and cream. Lythrum *salicaria,* Linn. Purple loosestrife. Spiraea *ulmaria,* Linn. Meadowsweet.

Ranunculus *acris,* Linn. Upright crowfoot Ficaria, Linn. Pilewort.

Caltha *palustris,* Linn. Marsh mary-gold.

Trollius *curu/peus,* Linn. Lucken gowan.

Erysimum *barbarea,* Linn. Winter

cress.

Pedicularis *palustris,* Linn. Marsh lousewort. *sylvatica,* Linn. Common lousewort.

Mentha *aquatica,* Linn. Water mint.

Scrophularia *nodosa,* Linn. Figwort.

Carduus *palustris,* Linn. Marsh thistle. *helenoides,* Linn. Deers ear.

Senecio *aquaticus,* Linn. Marsh ragwort.

Tussilago *Petasites,* Linn. Butter bur.

Equisetum *arvense,* Linn. Padock pipe. *sylvaticum,* Linn. Wood padock pipe.

Polytrichum *commune,* Linn. Goldenlocks.

Sphagnum *palustre,* Linn. Bog moss.

All these weeds are the inhabitants of a wet soil. They are either of a hard harsh substance, or of an unwholesome nature; and are therefore repudiated by cattle, unless forced to eat them from necessity. Though not directly poisonous, it is certain that some of them, and probable that many of them, are the cause of diseases in our domestic animals. They abound in all our wet meadows, from which, if possible, they ought to be expelled.

Many of them are usually to be found in the same meadow; in other places, only a few of them are prevalent. Sometimes a large space of ground is entirely covered with one of these plants; and as they are in general very bulky, they frequently compose almost the whole herbage of extensive meadows.

Such a number of plants on the same ground, so copious, and of such a rank growth, yet all distasteful to cattle, certainly deserve the notice of the grasier; as they often fill our wet meadows to such a degree, that the real pasture obtained from them is very inconsiderable.

It is to be regretted, that the precise nature and effects of the plants that are disagreeable or hurtful to cattle are so little known. The Marsh marygold, the Lucken gowan, and the whole tribe of Ranunculus, excepting the Common butter cup, are plants so acrid, as to blister the skin. It is not surprising, therefore, that they are avoided by cattle, and they are known to render sheep hydropic. They are cropt indeed a little in spring, when perhaps they are less virulent; but they become more acrid and venemous as they advance in their growth. It is remarkable also in these plants, that though they are Ranunculus *repens,* Linn.

noxious when green, they are harmless when made into hay:—Their venom is volatile, and flies off in drying:—It is lodged in the sap, and not in the fibrous or solid substance, which is the case in many other plants.

The Butter-bur covers the whole surface of the ground with its expansive leaves, which are soft fresh and succulent, yet they are neglected by all animals. The roots, however, are the favourite food of hogs, and by their means, this rampant weed may be easily extirpated.

The different sorts of Horse tail or Padock pipe, are not only useless, but noxious. They are supposed, indeed, not to hurt horses, but they occasion bloody urine in cattle, and abortion in sheep.

Such meadows as are here described, and filled with the useless and baneful weeds now enumerated, stand certainly in need of being altered and reformed: Wherever they are capable of tillage, that may be made an effectual remedy; but where the plough cannot be used, which is often the case, another method of improvement must be adopted. The soil of such meadows having never been moved, but immemorially possessed by these strong perennial weeds; it is usually to the depth of a spade or more, of the nature of turf, from the successive decay of their roots. The surface, which is very inflammable, when irtoderately dried, ought therefore to be pared with the flaughter,spade, to the depth of four or five inches, and burnt. This will not only clear the soil of its former unprofitable inhabitants, but the ashes will prepare it for the production of a more beneficial herbage. The new herbage to be introduced, should chiefly consist of the best grasses that are natural to a wet soil. Their seeds should be collected in autumn, and sown in the beginning of May. If the ground is so dry as to admit of a harrow going over it after they are sown, it will be much in their favour. The grasses to be chosen for this pur-

pose, are the seven species of the above list, which are calculated for watery places; but there are others which, though not so directly aquatics, naturally grow in a very moist soil:—Such are the following species.

Phleum *pratense,* Linn. Timothy grass.

Briza *media,* Linn. Quacking grass.

Poa *pratensis,* Linn. Great meadow grass.

Festuca *tlatior,* Linn. Tall fescue grass.

Avena *pratensis,* Linn. Meadow oat grass.

Holcus *lanatus.* Linn. Soft grass.

These are all excellent grasses, both for pasture and hay, in a moist soil. With these, and the other seven species mentioned above, our wet meadow grounds in Scotland should be made chiefly to abound. Rye grass, White and Yellow clover, are fit only for dry and rich soils. How often do we see Vol. i. z them sown for pasture, in a soil not natural to them, and in which they were entirely out after the second or third year? but the above thirteen species of grass, which are equally, if not more valuable, will flourish in a wet and poor soil, where these cultivated plants cannot succeed. This shows the propriety of attending to the propagation of the native and valuable grasses of the country, which, in many situations, may be rendered more advantageous, than those that are already cultivated.

SOWING OF PASTURE GRASSES.

Little attention has hitherto been paid to the sowing of grasses or other plants that are the fittest for pasture. In the most improved parts of the country, where ground is designed to remain long in grass, it is sown with rye-grass, red, white, or yellow clover, or ribwort : These are the only plants, that are as yet used for this purpose. The rye-grass, the red, and yellow clovers, are fitter for the scythe than for pasture. The white clover is, no doubt, one of the most valuable pasture plants; but it is of no avail to sow it, unless the soil is precisely suited to its nature, and upon such a soil it always comes of itself. The ribwort is indeed grased by cattle, but they Plantago *lanceolata,* Linn. Ribwort planlaiu.

prefer to it those gramineous plants that are always to he found wherever it grows.

It is well known, that when any or all these five plants are sown, they generally wear out soon. They answer not the purpose of establishing a durable pasture:—They disappear in the course of three or four years, and the soil is left to be replenished with such grasses as accidentally spring up. Some of these afford but a poor pasture; others of them are quite improper for it; and yet we frequently find fields of excellent soil entirely engrossed by them. Such are the following grasses, which are either altogether useless, or of a very inferior quality; yet they are often seen to fill the soil that has been sown with the above five plants, commonly called grass seeds, in order to procure a permanent pasture.

Aira *caryopkyllea,* Linn. Silver hffSr grass.

caespitosa, Linn.

Phleum *nodosum,* jLinn. Bulbous cat-stail grass.

Festuca *bromoides,* Linn. Barren fescue.

myuros, Linn. Wall fescue.

Bromus *secalinus,* Linn. Goose grass.
sterilis, Linn. Barren brome grass.

Dactyli3 *glomerutus,* Linn. Orchard grass.

Avena *elatior,* Linn. Tall oat grass.

Lolium *tcnntkntum,* Linn. Darnel.

Triticum *repem,* Linn. Dogs grass.

Hordeum *murinum,* Linn. Way bennet.

Juncus *pilosus,* Linn. Hairy wood rush.
campestris, Linn. Small hairy wood rush.

Instead of these unprofitable grasses on a good soil; and instead of the common sown grasses, which remain but for three or four years, it would certainly be better to have the ground filled with the seeds of those grasses that constitute the best pasture, and which are capable to continue in every good soil for a great length of time without diminution. Such arc the grasses contained in the following list.

Anthoxanthum *odoratum,* Linn. Vernal grass. Alopecurus *pratensis,* Linn. Foxtail grass. Agrostis *capillaris,* Linn. Fine bent grass. Poa *trivialis,* Linn. Common meadow grass. *pratensis,* Linn. Great meadow grass. *angustifolia,* Linn. Narrow leaved me dow grass. *annua,* Linn. Suffolk grass.

Festuca *duriuscula,* Linn. Hard fescue.

Avena *jlavescens,* Linn. Yellow oat grass.

Cynosurus *cristatus,Uxm.* Crested dog-tail grass.

Holcus *lanatus,* Linn. Soft grass.

These are the grasses which constitute our best pastures, and are the inhabitants of our richest and driest fields. They are also capable of yielding a full crop of hay, which, in quality, is preferable to every other kind. Wherever a field chiefly consists of any, or all *of* these grasses, especially those marked with an asterisk, their seeds should be carefully preserved. If the field, or a part of it, is kept for natural hay till the seeds are ripe, they can then be easily collected, and with these seeds, the land should be replenished that is intended to remain in pasture, in preference to rye-grass, or the other sown grasses at present in use. Wherever natural grasses are thus sown for pasture, it is requisite, however, that the soil in which they are lodged, should approach as near as possible, in its qualities, to that on which they grew; for the duration of the pasture is not to depend on the plants raised from the seeds sown; but upon the progress of their roots, and upon the seeds sown spontaneously, neither of which will prosper, unless the plants are in their natural soil. Jt would be a still greater improvement, if the seeds.of some of the best of these pasture grasses were collected separately, and sold pure and unmixed, as,the rye-grass and other sown grasses are at present.

POISONOUS PLANTS.

All animals have a surprising power in distinguishing the salutary plants, from those which are poisonous, or that are hurtful to their frame. Birds distinguish chiefly by the eye, and the herbivorous quadrupeds by the smell. Horses and cows distinguish also by the taste. For, when in a mouthful of herbage, they take up any plant that is disagreeable to their taste, they separate it from the rest and drop it out, at the side of the mouth.

It is alleged, that man is remarkably deficient in this talent. He is not destitute of it, however, by nature; though he may become defective in it, by want of exercise. The American savage, possesses it in a higher degree, than the civilised European; because the talent is improved in him, by his manner of life, which remains, as it were, dormant in the other. By experience, skillful men come to have a nice knowledge of the qualities of plants, from the smell and taste. Yet it is not unlikely, that in men, as in animals, there may be an instinctive discernment, of what is salutary or noxious, exclusive of experience. There is, for example, a natural and general disinclination to the taste of cellery, parsnips, and parsley, which seems rather founded on instinct than experience. These culinary plants are perfectly wholesome; but they have been rendered so, only by cultivation. The wild cellery and parsnip in our swamps, and the parsley as it grows in the springs of Sardinia, are known to be noxious. They are among the umbelliferous plants growing in water, which are almost all of them endowed with virulent. and poisonous qualities. There is a peculiar taste which prevails in them all; nor is it quite eradicated, even in these cultivated garden plants. It is this probably, that occasions a natural aversion to them, which is only to be overcome by habit.

Cattle which are housed and hand-fed, lose much o/ their power, in distinguishing between wholesome and hurtful plants; but those which live constantly in the fields, do still retain it in some degree. Yet, urged by necessity, they frequently devour noxious plants, which occasion diseases and death. As it is a matter of moment to the grazier, to be well acquainted with these plants, that they may be either avoided or extirpated, such of them as are most common, and most frequently injurious, may here be noticed.

Hyoscyamus *niger,* Linn. Black henbane.

Conium *maculatum,* Hemlock.

Oenanthe *crocata,* Linn. Hemlock drop-wort.

Sium *aquaticum,* Linn. Water parsnip.

Phellandrium *aquaticum,* Linn. Water hemlock.

Cicuta *virosa,* Linn. Long leaved water hemlock.

Ranunculus *sceleratus,* Linn. Marsh crowfoot.

Taxus *baccata,* Linn. Yew.

All the vegetable poisons, may be consideied as being of an acrid, or of a narcotic quality. This indeed is only a very general division, but it is un, necessary to be more particular, in considering their Jethal effects upon cattle. Most of the plants in this list, appear from their effects, tQ belong to the last class; a? they affect cattle with stupor, delirium, and convulsions which terminate in death. The Marsh crowfoot, is the only plant among them that is remarkable for its, ac rid substance.

The Black henbane is generally detested by all cattle. Exclusive of its smell and taste, it might even be suspected from its lugubrious aspect. Its very vapour is noxious to man, and its external application produces delirium. It infests the pastures in Holland and in some parts of England. With us, it seldom makes its way into the field, but is happily confined to ruins, rubbish, and the neighbourhood of dunghills. Yet even in these places, cattle have been known sometimes to suffer, by eating its seeds.

The hemlock is an inhabitant of a damp cadavprous soil, and grows chiefly about towns and houses. It seldom takes place in pastures, which is fortunate, for cows have been often disordered and sometimes killed by it. It is of a smell nauseous, and of a substance poisonous both to man and beast. It is said, that horses labouring under the fiercy will eat of it; but not as a food, only as a medicine prescribed by nature; as it is prescribed by art, to a man labouring under the cancer.

4

The Hemlock dropwort is a certain poison to cattle, as well as to man. It appears not only where water stagnates, hut in springs, and by the sides of clear running brooks and rivers. It grows generally in large patches, and rises in summer with a luxuriant growth, three or four feet high. During that season, cattle never approach it. In the spring, its large white succulent roots appear above the earth pr the water, with the young green leaves at top.— They are then preyed upon by cattle, which happen to be in a starving state, and prove very soon mortal. They immediately affect the cattle with delirium, which quickly terminates in convulsions and death. Some cattle in Annandale, are poisoned almost every spring by this plant. Mr Macdonnel of Boisdale was sensible, that he lost at least three or four cows by it every year, on his farm in South Uist; but a considerable number of cattle are certainly killed by this plant in the Islands, and along the west coast, where it is not known nor suspected to be the cause of their death. As it is usually confined to spots, as it does not spread to any great extent in a particular place, and grows from bulky perennial roots, with a little care, and at a very trifling expence, it may be extirpated from any farm .

A Painter in drawing a figure of this plant, was seized with a degree of meagrim and sickishnesss, from the effluvia of a parrel of it on his table. The same effects were felt by a botanist, while he was preparing some specimens of the plant.

The foliage and roots of the water parsnip, are similar in quality to those of the water dropwort, but not quite pf such a virulent nature.

The Water hemlock is poisonous to all cattle, and more destructive to horses, when it is dry, than when it is green.

The long leaved Water hemlock, is immediate death to oxen and swine; but as it is alleged, can be browsed upon by goats with impunity.

Of the whole baneful tribe of Ranunculus, the Marsh crowfoot, frequent in our wet meadows, seems to be the most acute and penetrating poison. It cannot be tasted, or applied to the skin, without danger, and its vapour even is noxious. Among the old officinal simples, it used to be termed the Apium *risus,* because persons poisoned with it, die in fits of convulsive laughter. Its venomous part, being very volatile, it is, likely that by distillation, there might be obtained from it, a more violent poison than what is yielded by the laurel bay , or any other plant of the European climates. It is a plant probably more detrimental to cattle, than is commonly known, and ought to be carefully exterminated wherever it appears.

» Prunus *laurocerasus.* Linn.

The yew tree now grows in a wild state, only in a few parts of Scotland, but it is frequent in plantations and other places to which cattle have access. There are several instances recorded of horses being killed by it. Some cows having broke into a plantation, during the night, where there was a good deal of yew, at Arbigland in Galloway, two of them were found dead in the morning. They were immediately opened, and their stomachs were found full of yew twigs, which were but slightly chewed, and not in the least digested. The poison of the yew, had, therefore, in this case proved mortal, without entering into the circulation. An ass, having browsed on the yew hedge of the bowling green at Moffat, became delirious, convulsed, and dropped down dead, within three or four hours. It is certain that several plants, which are poisonous to some animals, do not affect others. It is said, that the yew produces no bad effect upon deer. In the natural yew wood, upon the island of Inch Lonach in Loch Lomond, each tree is cropt as far up, as the deer can reach. By the report of the forrester, the deer are there seen daily to browse upon the yew, without any bad consequence.

There are, no doubt, other plants, beside those of the above list, to which cattle owe many of their diseases, and oftimes their death; but for want of due observation, they are not known to be the cause of these bad effects, w hich are often very sensibly felt by the husbandman. Whenever any cattle happen to die suddenly, the contents and state of their stomach, ought to be immediately and narrowly inspected. This would probably give some useful iaformation upon the subject.

FLOODING OF PASTURES.

Wherever dry pastures upon declivities can be watered, by means of rills drawn by the plough; the quantity of grass will be greatly enlarged, and its quality improved. Its growth also in the spring, will be much more early, than in the places that are not watered. The early grass, obtained in this way, affords a most seasonable relief to cattle, but being of a very succulent substance is improper for sheep.— When hanging grass grounds, though of the poorest kind, are thus traversed with furrows, for two or three years, to humour the slow overflowing of the surface water; the pasture is not only much increased, but the soil is so fertilised, as to afford a luxuriant crop of corn, whenever it is broken up.

There are some meadows, called water meadows, which are liable to remain covered with water, during the greater part, or the whole of winter. These meadows in summer, are sometimes used for pasture, and sometimes for hay. When water every year continues stagnant on grass ground for such a length of time, it does indeed enrich the soil, but it extirpates all the finer sorts of grass. The coarsest aquatic grasses spring up, and take full possession of the soil, which afford the very worst pasture, and the worst hay. Such are those in the following list:—

Schoenus *mariscus,* Linn. Thatch rush.

Scirpus *palustris,* Linn. Marsh club rush.

sylvaticus, Linn. Water cyperus grass.

Aira *coespitosa,* Linn. Turfy hair grass.

Phalaris *arundinacca,* Linn. Reed grass.

Poa *aquatica,* Linn. Water poa.

Arundo *Phragmites,* Linn. Common reed.

Juncus *effusus,* Linn. Common rush.

conglomeratic, Linn. Round headed rush.

articulatus, Linn. Spret. *bufonius,* Linn. Toad rush.

Triglochin *palustre,* Linn. Arrow-headed grass. 'Typha *latifolia,* Linn. Reed mace. Sparganium *erectum,* Linn. Bur reed.

Likewise those which follow, which are known among our country people by the general name of one pointed grasses.

Carex *polygamia. leporina,* Linn. *vulpina,* Linn. *attenuata. ballonetisis.* Carex *brizoides,* Linn.

jftava, Linn. *limosa,* Linn. . *turgida.* . *coespitosa,* Linn. *acuta,* Linn. *trigona. vesicaria,* Linn. *hirta,* Linn.

Though the soil of these water meadows, naturally produces only such coarse and unprofitable grasses; yet, being constantly water-fed, it is extremely rich, and capable to afford grasses of the best kind, was it but freed from excess of water. It is not to the soil, but merely to the watery situation, that these plants are attached. The stagnation of water upon such meadows, for so long a time, ought, therefore, if possible, to be prevented, which in many places may certainly be done. Water should never be permitted to remain upon grass ground above forty-eight hours, in a stagnant state, if it can be avoided. A transient flooding of such duration, enriches the soil, without impairing the more valuable grasses, or introducing those of the aquatic kind.

SAND DKIFT.

The sand formed by the triture of the stones rolled in the ocean, is thrown in upon the shores, and by the sea blasts, often makes its way gradually into the country. This has long been a calamity on the shores of Holland, on the eastern coast of England, and in many parts of the north of Scotland. As the sand consists of very minute sharp particles, it is kept in motion by every gale; and varies the direction of its course, according to the prevailing winds. In our stormy climate, it is never suffered to rest so long, as to acquire herbage on the surface sufficient to arrest its progress, without the assistance of art.

These moving sands have long made considerable havoc in some fertile tracts in Aberdeenshire. In the county of Nairn, they have also occasioned such devastation, that the Scots Parliament, in the year 695, passed a law for the preservation and propagation of the sea bent . This was done in imitation of a

similar law in Holland, and'upon the presumption, that this plant was the only effectual remedy, against the encroachments of blowing sand.

Arundo *arenaria.* Linn.

This evil likewise prevails on many estates in the West Highlands. The grounds overblown with sand in the Island of Coll, may amount to above three thousand acres. In one place, there is near five hundred acres of excellent land, which have of late years, been laid entirely desolate. The sand being now several yards deep, where some people yet alive, have reaped the best grain in the island.— The crops in the island of Barra, are every year greatly hurt, by the fields of blowing sand, which turn and wheel and spread over the country, often in an unexpected direction, and in a very destructive manner. This sand drift, against which the inhabitants have no defence, has obliged them to remove houses, and even entire villages, in several parts of the Island, and to resign some of their best lands to the sandy deluge. There is a great extent of flat country, in the Islands of South and North Uist and Benbecula, which affords excellent pasturage in summer, though in whiter it appears but like a sandy plain. The blowing of the sand renders the inclosure of this valuable tract impracticable. The surface could not be broken by ditches, without endangering the whole country. Neither is there any rock near the surface for building walls; and though there was, they would soon be blown up and rendered unserviceable. Many of the houses in these Islands are heaped up to the roof, on one or more sides, by the sand. On the shore of South Uist, about the present flood-mark, the accidental removal 6f the sand, sometimes discovers the walls of a village, and of an ancient chapel. On this low sandy coast of the Long Island, for about fifty or sixty miles, the sea has evidently made, and continues to make great encroachments. Similar devastations are made by blowing sands, in the Islands of Tirey, Harris, Lewes, and many other places.

To remedy this calamity, is an article, in which many proprietors and many farmers are deeply interested. Its bad consequences may undoubtedly be obviated in most places, but not without considerable attention and labour.

The growth of the sea bent, has long been considered both in Holland and in this country, as the chief means of checking the progress of blowing sand, but it is very insufficient for the purpose. This plant forms strong deep matted roots, and when the sand is blown down to these roots, its further motion *is* in some degree stopt; but it is a plant that forms no sward on the surface. It grows usually but in thin detached patches, and even where it is thick, the sand continues to blow without opposition, through its long hard slender leaves and stems. Though it is serviceable in fixing the sand at a considerable depth, it is not adapted to fix it at the surface, which is the great object required. Accordingly, the sea bent is found growing in most places, even where the blowing sand is most destructive. Vol. 1. A a

There is a tribe of plants which grow naturally *in* the sand on the sea shore, as well as the Sea bent; and many of these are much better calculated to stop the blowing of the sand at the surface. It may be proper, therefore, to insert a list of such plants in this place, and the uses to which they may be applied. They may be arranged under the three following divisions.
1. The perennial plants, which, though unfit for pasture, may serve to cover the surface of blowing sand with herbage.
2. The grasses and other perennial plants which may not only answer the same purpose, but which likewise serve for pasture. 3. The annual plants to be used. PERENNIAL PLANTS UNFIT FOR PASTURE.

Galium *verum,* Linn. Cheese-renning.
Pulmonaria *maritima,* Linn. Sea bugloss.
Convolvulus *soldanella,* Linn. Scottish sea
bindweed.
Glaux *maritima,* Linn. Saltwort.
Eryngium *maritimum,* Linn. Sea eringo.
Ligusticum *Scoticum,* Linn. Scottish sea parsley.

Statice *armeria,* Linn. Thrift.
Rumex *maritimus,* Linn. Golden dock.
Polygonum *maritimum,* Linn. Sea knotgrass.
Arenaria *peploides,* Linn. Sea chick weed.
Chelidonium *glaucium,* Linn. Yellow horned poppy.
Cochlearia *officinalis,* Linn. Scurvy-grass.
Sisymbrium *Monetise,* Linn. Manks rocket;
— *arenosum,* Linn. Sand rocket.
Geranium *cicutarium,* Linn. Hemlock-leaved cranesbill.
. *sanguineum,* Linn. Bloody cranesbill.
Ononis *repens,* Linn. Creeping restharrow.
Artemisia *maritima,* Linn. Sea wormwood.
Anthemis *maritima,* Linn. Sea Camomile.

None of the plants of the above list are much coveted by cattle; yet none of them are known to be hurtful, or poisonous, except the Yellow horned poppy. Like those of the two following divisions, they all grow naturally in blowing sand; and it is upon plants of this kind that we are chiefly to depend in order to stop its progress; first by raising a thick herbage, and then by forming a sward or turf upon its surface. For this purpose, the seeds of all these plants should be collected in the end of summer and in autumn, and they are to be had in abundance everywhere on the sea-shore. This mixed mass of seeds must be preserved till spring is far advanced, that they mav be sown when their vegetation will be most rapid. The field of blowing sand being then passed over, in the time of rain, with a light harrow, wattled with thorns, the seeds should be sown and rolled. A thick growth of these various plants would immediately take place, and, being in their natural soil, they would, in the course of the summer, cover the sandy surface entirely with herbage. It would be proper, also, to begin with sowing the windward side of the field, or that side which lies next the prevailing winds.

PERENNIAL GRASSES AND PASTURE PLANTS.

Aira *aquatica,* Linn. Water hair grass.
Poa *Jlagellijera,* Linn. Sea meadow grass.
Festuca *GaUovidiensis.* Galloway fescue
Elymus *arenarius,* Linn. Sea lime grass.
Triticum *caninum,* Linn. Dogs grass.
junceum, Linn. Sea wheat grass.
maritimum, Linn. Sea spiked grass.
Carex *arenaria,* Linn. Sea carex.
Oscar is. Oscar's carex. *maritima.* Maritime carex.
Plantago *maritima,* Linn. Sea plantain.
carnosa. Succulent plantain.
Triglochin *maritimum,* Linn. Sea spiked grass.
Beta *vulgaris,* Linn. Sea beet.
Cucubalus *maritimus.* Sea campion.
Raphanus *maritimus.* Sea radish.
Crambe *marit'vma,* Linn. Sea colewort.
fiunias *caJcile,* Linn. Sea rocket.
Vicia *cracca,* Linn. Tufted vetch.
Astragalus *araiarius,* Linn. Sand vetch.
Tragopogon *pratense,* Linn. Yellow goats beard.

These, likewise, are all inhabitants of blowing sand. The plants of the former division may serve to cover the surface with herbage; but these are to be preferred, as they not only answer this purpose, but also serve for pasture. The particular properties of such of them as promise to be most useful may be here noticed.

It is remarkable, that some plants which elsewhere grow in water, are found also to grow in blowing sand. This is owing, perhaps, to the ease with which they can spread their roots in both situations. The Water hair grass has been so called from its being observed to grow usually in watery places; but it grows still more vigorously in the blowing sand immediately above flood mark. It is a perennial grass that remains verdant in winter, and may be easily propagate'd by seeds. Its vegetation is so quick and vigorous, that the creeping suckers which it sends out on all hands grow sometimes above a yard long in a season. They take root at every joint, and come to form a large turf around the original plant. At each of these joints a new / plant is formed, which, next season, shoots forth suckers in like manner, till the whole surface is matted over, like a plot of strawberries suffered to run wild in a garden. It is a plant of too low a growth to give grass for the scythe, but is capable of affording the sweetest pasture. It is more naturally allied to the Poas than to any other kind of grass, and cattle have been observed to prefer it even to the annual Poa, which, of all the grasses common in our pastures, is their principal favourite. From these properties of the plant, it seems, therefore, better adapted for covering a surface of loose sand than any other that has yet been tried.

The sea meadow grass emits runners sometimes three or four feet long, which spread on the ground and take root at the joints; it therefore soon forms a close and thick turf on the surface. It grows on sand, between the lowest flood-mark and the boundary of the highest spring tides; but beyond this it is not to be seen. AH cattle feed upon it with great avidity, and especially sheep, for whom it is reckoned extremely wholesome. It affords a thick and low sward, and is better adapted as a pasture for sheep, from the shortness of its growth, and the fineness of its foliage, than for larger cattle. Wherever it is pastured by sheep, the flower-stems are so eaten up, that few of them are to be found; which is the case with few other grasses, 4

The Galloway fescue is a maritime grass first discovered at Arbigland in Galloway; but is to be found plentifully on the shores of the Western Islands and Argyleshire. It grows vigorously in sand, and affords a crop of grass very agreeable to cattle.

The Sea lime grass is a beautiful plant; and, though not frequent, is to be found in several parts of the North of Scotland, where the seeds ought to be collected and the plant propagated. It is the principal plant used in Sweden for checking the sand drift, and is in all respects preferable to the Sea bent. In the Island of Pabbay,, where it abounds most, its foliage, when young, is eaten down to the very sand by the cattle.

The other grasses of the above list are more remarkable for their spreading roots, and for their usefulness in fixing the surface of the blowing sand, than for their goodness as pasture plants. Oscar's carex is, however, an exception. This plant This plant was first discovered on Elian Oscar, a small island near Lismore, from which the trivial name was adopted. The island has upon it a spring of fine water, and was by tra. dition a favourite retreat of Oscar, whose name is so much celebrated in the antient Gaelic poetry. This fine plant has since been observed in several other places, both on the West and East coasts of Scotland.

. throws up a tall crop of smooth, soft, light, green foliage, which is more coveted by cattle than any other plant of the numerous tribe of carex. It certainly might be cultivated to advantage in a sandy soil, both as a hay and as a pasture grass.

The Sea plantain forms a good pasture for cattle and might be sown in maritime places, as the Ribwort f, a plant nearly allied to it, is sown in our inland fields. The Succulent plantain, however, is still more valuable. This plant grows on our shores both within and without the highest flood-mark. The leaves arc fleshy, or succulent, brittle, and of a glaucous colour. Wherever cattle have access to it, they eat it down to the ground, in preference almost to every other plant. It is known to be a salutary and fattening pasture both for black cattle and sheep; and in some places makes a considerable part of the herbage on the sea inks, where it will rise above a foot high. Were these grounds to be anywhere cultivated for pasture, this seems to be the most proper crop to be sown upon them. Like other succulent plants in the maritime station, the leaves of the succulent plantain are salt to the taste. It is doubtful whether these plants receive the sea salt by their roots, or imbibe it by their leaves from the sea spray; but it is certain that this quality renders them pe . Plantago ianceolata, Linn.
culiarly agreeable, and peculiarly wholesome to cattle.

The Sea radish grows oo the West coasts and in the Western Islands, in gravel and blowing sand on the sea shore. Its large leaves are spread like a star on the surface; and it shoots up gross succulent stems two or three feet high. It vegetates and remains fresh and green all the winter, being much more hardy than the turnip or any colewort. It is eagerly sought after by black cattle, who not only eat the leaves, but the very stems of the plant down to the ground. It is excellently adapted for covering a surface of blowing sand; and, as no frost can impair it, it might, probably, on cultivation, afford a valuable pasture in the early spring, before the fields yield any thing of new growth. This plant has been kept many years in a garden, where it grows luxuriantly. The root has become larger and more succulent. It is sometimes two feet long, and of the size and shape of a parsnip. It is white, and resembles in taste that of the Spanish radish. When scraped down, it is preferred by some people both to that root and the root of the Horse radish.

The Sea campion prevails everywhere on our shores. Its crisp succulent foliage, having exactly the smell and taste of the pods of the Garden pea, is cropt by cattle with great avidity, and is well known to be a very wholesome pasture. Its strong perennial roots form a thick and firm turf on the surface of sand. It is extremely prolific in seeds, of which a quantity sufficient to sow a considerable extent of sand, might be collected in a small space. It is remarkable, that this plant, so abundant on the sand of the sea shore, grows also near the summits of some of our highest mountains, along with the alpine plants.

During the height of summer, the sandy pasture fields in the Hebrides are diversified with a great variety of flowery plants. They are in some places almost entirely filled with the white, red, and yellow clovers; the Sea campion, Sea gillyflower, Sea rocket, Sandy vetch, Bloody cranesbill, and a variety of ranunculuses, forming altogether a most beautiful embroidered carpet. The Tufted vetch covers entire fields with its rich and copious purple flowers, and affords a thick weighty crop, of which the farmers make the best hay that these islands produce. They esteem it likewise highly as a pasture. It has the remarkable property of making the cows which feed plentifully upon it to take the bull readily and early in the season; which is a matter of great consequence where they have such difficulty to support and preserve their calves in winter. They consider this vetch to be the true lucerne; but though it is widely different from that plant, it is of great value as a natural grass, and might still be of greater consequence if it was raised by art. From the places in which this plant appears in the south, one would not suspect it to be an inhabitant of blowing sand, which it really is in the north. In this situation, which it naturally occupies, it ought, therefore to be cultivated with the greatest care, ANNUAL PLANTS.

Phalaris *arenaria,* Linn. Sea canary grass.

Chenopodium *maritimum,* Linn. White glasswort.

Salsola *Kali,* Linn. Prickly glasswort.

Atriplex *laciniata,* Linn. Sea orache.

hastata, Linn. Spear-leaved orache.

Spergula *arvensis,* Linn. Spurrey.

These and other annual maritime plants may be used with those above in covering the surface of blowing sand; though the perennial plants with strong creeping roots are certainly fitter for the purpose. Of all the annual plants, spurrey is the most valuable; and has been long used with advantage in Holland. It is of such a quick growth, as to be capable of covering a field of blowing sand with verdure in a few weeks. It is fed upon by cattle; but if intended to fix blowing sand, it should rather be. suffered to ripen and shed its numerous seeds on the ground. Of the annual seeds sown in our fields, the common tare and buckwheat are the most promising to be sown on a surface of moving sand.

Blowing sand is always most dangerous when it comes to form eminences, or sand hills, which it frequently does. These being most easily set in motion by the wind, it is more difficult to get their surface covered with herbage. It is a great point gained, however, if they

can be kept from blowing to any considerable depth. This can only be done by deep rooted plants. The Sea bent, and the Sea lime grass are of this kind; but there are different sorts of willows that would be much more effectual; and two, especially, which grow naturally in blowing sand. The one the Silver willow , whieh inhabits the east coast of Scotland. The other the Hebridian willow f, which abounds on the shores of many of the Western Islands. These not only prosper in blowing sand, but they spread and take root on its surface. Cuttings of these willows plunged in the spring from one to three feet deep in a sand hill, would be the most effectual means to prevent the Salix *argenlea.* On the sandy shores of East Lothian and Forfarshire.

+ Salix *Hebridianu.* This was supposed by Dr Afzelius, Adjunct.Professor of Botany at Upsal, to be the willow dis. covered by Linnaeus on the sandy shores of Scania, and men. tioned in his Iter Scanicum, but by some omission not inserted in his Species Plantarum. sand being carried off to any considerable *depth.* Where these shrubs cannot be obtained, there are other willows which grow in watery places, and which take root on the surface, that might be successfully used. Wherever blowing sand lies deep, it is a soil fit almost for every willow. For, although it is dry and loose for a few inches next the surface, at a greater depth it is always compact and wet, and that not so much from the rains, as from the percolation of the water upwards through the sandy soil. STATE OF THE CATTLE ITT WINTER.

Though cattle have always been, and must be, the staple produce of the Highland countries; yet the great losses that are sustained by their death in the spring season, from poverty and the consequent diseases, are but too well known. They are indeed sufficiently fed in summer, but they are starved in winter. They are never housed, but kept abroad the whole year rourtd. During winter and spring they receive no dry or artificial provender, and have nothing to support them but the decayed gleanings of the herbage of the former summer.

During the summer season, the grasing fields are greatly understocked. The summer pasturage far exceeds the winter provision; yet no more cattle can be kept and preserved, than what the winter forage in the field or in the house can support. Hence there is a great loss in the summer produce of the country. The summer grass is not sufficiently pastured, in order that some remains of it may be left on the ground for the cattle in winter. In this way, a great part of the produce of summer runs to decay and is lost, without affording any sufficient supply for the exi! gencies of winter.

In all the Islands the cattle are in general better fed in summer than upon the main land, as their pasture is more upon the sea-shore, or near its level, and consists of the finest grass; but they are subject to a still greater scarcity of winter food, as that pasture is less able to withstand the rigours of the winter season. The hay that is made, is every where inconsiderable. In many places there is none provided; and the straw of the grain does little more than serve as thatch to the houses. The sea weeds afford a principal article of sustenance to the cattle. These they prey upon daily, and, though at the distance of a mile or two from the sea, they know exactly when to repair to the shore at the time of the ebb. They are forced also to have recourse to the sea bent; a plant scarcely fed upon by cattle elsewhere. This, however, they eat down to the sand on which it grows, and devour it still more greedily when it shoots in the spring. Its young leaves have then a degree of sweetness in them, on which account it is called sweet grass by the inhabitants.

It is thus the great disadvantage of the country, that the winter is altogether inadequate to the summer feeding. To procure sufficient sustenance for the cattle in winter, is therefore to be considered as the great object of agriculture in the Highlands. The first thing to be suggested for their support, is the food which the country does already afford. The improvements in tillage and the cultivation of green crops, are, no doubt, effectual means for this purpose, and may be introduced with a prospect of success. But the introduction of these will always have difficulties to encounter, and can, at best, be only gradual, perhaps slow in their progress. If any method of supporting the cattle in winter can be fallen upon, from what the country already produces, and with which the people are already in some degree acquainted, it would certainly be the most eligible. Before considering the introduction of new crops, it may therefore be proper to take notice of one great source of winter food for the cattle in the Highlands that has hitherto been neglected,—that is, to provide large quantities of natural hay. This is the most immediate remedy for the great defect in question, and the most obvious and easy to the common people.

NATURAi HAT.

It is not a very remote period since the making of hay was first introduced into the Highlands. No hay was made in the Hebrides or on the opposite coasts, till about the year 1756; and all that is yet made is still inconsiderable, and sufficient only in some places to fodder their stirks in winter. It is every where made, too, only of the finest grass, produced upon the best soils; but there are extensive tracts capable of yielding a large stock of natural hay, which, for that purpose, are entirely neglected.

In every part of the country there is an opportunity of making great quantities of hay, which, though coarse in its quality, would afford sufficient sustenance to prevent that great mortality of cattle in the spring, which frequently happens from mere want of food.

The plants from which this hay is to be made, are chiefly the following:

Scirpus *palustris*, Linn. Club-rush.
caespitosus, Linn. Deers hair.
Nardus *striata*, Linn. Bent.
Eriophorum *polystachion*, Linn. Cotton grass.
Eriophorum *vaginatum*, Linn. Moss crops.
Agrostis *alba*, Linn. Marsh bent grass.
Aira *coeruka*, Linn. Fly bent.
Juncus *articulatus*, Linn. Spret.
squarrosus, Linn. Wire bent.
Jlesuosus, Bog wire.
Triglochin *palustre*, Linn. Arrow head-

ed grass.

And the numerous sorts of Carex or one pointed grass.

These plants form the general bulk of the herbage, in the boggy places and in the mossy soils, upon the sides, and towards the summits, of all the Highland mountains. Yet, from these plants, and in these places, no hay has hitherto been made; though, in the height of summer, they afford a thick and sufficient crop of grass for the scythe. One cannot, however, traverse any Highland farm of considerable extent, upon which it may not be undertaken, from these plants and in these places, to form such a quantity of hay, as would be sufficient to prevent the cattle upon the farm from perishing by want during the winter and spring seasons.

These plants are fed upon by the cattle early in summer, but they are neglected by them as the season advances, and affords finer sorts of grass. In the height of summer, when at their full growth, they are neglected by the cattle; and are therefore Vol. i. B b neglected by the inhabitants for the purposes of hay. But these plants, like many others, though postponed by cattle for more agreeable pasture when green, are very acceptable to them in winter when dry. In July, these plants, upon almost every Highland farm, come to form extensive tracts, and a thick sward fit for the scythe; but at this season they are untouched by cattle, and, before winter, fall into straw and litter upon the ground. In such tracts, and from these plants, there might undoubtedly be reaped such a quantity of coarse hay as might obviate the calamity to which the Highlands are subjected in the death of cattle.

A most favourable opportunity of making such hay occurs to the Highland farmer when he resides at his shealings in the summer season. These are generally erected, where the tracts of coarse grass, fit for making this hay, do most abound. At these dwellings, all the people on the farm are collected, from about the middle of June till near the end of August. They experience, there, a season rather of relaxation than of

labour. They are only employed in tending their cattle, and in the management of the dairy—occupations that need not interfere with hay-making to a considerable extent. During their residence for about eight or ten weeks at these summer shielings, they might every where make such a quantity of hay as would save the lives of many of their cattle in winter. 3

It is true indeed, that the hay here meant, is of the coarsest quality, but it is wholesome, and what cattle will not refuse when urged by want. It would be insufficient either to fatten them, or to support them well in milk; but these are not the objects of a breeding country. The plants of which this hay would be formed, even when they are decayed, blasted by the weather, and in the most sapless state, arc fed upon by the Highland cattle . It cannot, therefore, be doubted, that were they made into hay, during July and August, when they are fresh and succulent, that they would afford a most useful provender in winter.

This hay should be reserved for use, till past the middle of winter. The Highland cattle never suffer greatly for want of food, till after the 1st of February.

It was with great difficulty that the farmers in many parts of the south could be prevailed on to fodder their sheep with hay in winter. It was even strongly asserted, and believed by them, that their sheep would not eat hay. This was the persuasion of a considerable storemaster, who, in a long con. vernation over night, could not be convinced of the contrary. Next day, in passing over one of his farms, when the snow lay deep and glazed on the surface, a great number of his sheep were pointed out *to* him who were eating voraciouly the withered aud bleached tops of the rushes which appeared above the frozen snow. Though all other reasons had failed, this ocular argument made him renounce his opinion, and resolve to feed his sheep with hay, which afterwards he always did much to bis advantage.

From that time, till the end of April, they are often in great distress, when this hay would afford a most seasonable and effectual relief.

The Highland cattle are not, and indeed cannot be housed; but the same is the case with the extensive herds of cattle in Galloway. The practice in Galloway, ought to be the practice in the Highlands: There, though the cattle are kept abroad all winter, they are regularly supplied with dry forage; they are brought down every evening, to a sheltered grass field; the farmer and his servants carry out on horses, trusses of straw or hay, which they spread about among them; the cattle feed upon these all night, and manure the soil almost equally to a fold; they are at first driven to the place, but after a few days, they of themselves repair regularly in the evening, and sometimes from a great distance, to the spot where they are to be foddered.

PROVENDER FROM LEAVES OF TREES.

In several countries of the North of Europe, particularly in Sweden and Norway, the peasants gather and preserve the leaves of trees, as winter provision for their cattle. The leaves of most of our forest trees and shrubs are applied to this purpose; such as those of the ash, oak, elm, birch, alder and hazel, and especially those of the different willows, which are found to be the most agreeable of any to the cattle. Though this may not be a very nourishing or eligible provender, yet, from long experience, it is found to be wholesome, and sufficient to preserve cattle from perishing by want. Wherever that calamity takes place, and it certainly often does in the Highlands, if no better remedy to prevent it can be found, this expedient should not be despised or neglected. Upon many Highland farms, where there is plenty of wood, a favourable opportunity occurs to make trial of this practice. In October, during the fall of the leaves, after one or two days of wind, they are rendered sufficiently dry, and whirled into heaps where they can be easily collected. They require then only to be formed into cocks, and afterwards into stacks. In woody places, a great quantity of this sort of provender may certainly be soon and easily preserved.

END OF VOL. I.

Lightning Source UK Ltd.
Milton Keynes UK
UKOW05f1506050915

258083UK00014B/1613/P